TRIUMPH
TR5-PI
WORKSHOP MANUAL SUPPLEMENT

PUBLICATION PART NUMBER 545053
1st Edition

Issued by the

SERVICE DIVISION

STANDARD-TRIUMPH SALES LIMITED

A member of the Leyland Motor Corporation

COVENTRY ENGLAND

INTRODUCTION

The information contained in this supplement applies specifically to the TR5-PI models and in intended for use in conjunction with the Triumph TR4 and TR4A Workshop Manual.

Triumph TR4 and TR4A Workshop Manual . . . . ISBN: 9780948207952

© Copyright Standard-Triumph Sales Limited 1967
and Brooklands Books Limited 1996 and 2016

This book is published by Brooklands Books Limited and based upon text and illustrations protected by copyright and first published in 1967 by Standard-Triumph Sales Limited and may not be reproduced transmitted or copied by any means without the prior written permission of Rover Group Limited and Brooklands Books Limited.

Whilst every effort is made to ensure the accuracy of the particulars contained in this book the Manufacturing Companies will not, in any circumstances, be held liable for any inaccuracies or the consequences thereof.

Brooklands Books Ltd., P.O. Box 146, Cobham, Surrey KT11 1LG, England
E-mail: sales@brooklands-books.com   www.brooklands-books.com

ISBN 9781869826024   Part No. 545053   Ref: T152WH   11T6/2469

CONTENTS

		Page
GROUP 0 —	General specification, Lubrication charts and Nut tightening torques	4
GROUP 1 —	Engine, Cooling, Petrol injection and Exhaust system	19
GROUP 2 —	Clutch and Gearbox	73
GROUP 3 —	Brakes	79
GROUP 4 —	Steering	91
GROUP 5 —	Body	94
GROUP 6 —	Electrical	105

TRIUMPH
TR5-PI
WORKSHOP MANUAL SUPPLEMENT

GROUP 0

Comprising:

General specification, Lubrication charts, Maintenance schedules and Nut tightening torques

0·101

TRIUMPH TR5

WORKSHOP MANUAL

SUPPLEMENT TO GROUP 0

CONTENTS

	Section
General specification	**0·102**
Lubrication summary	**0·105**
Maintenance schedules	**0·106**
Recommended lubricants (British Isles)	**0·108**
Recommended lubricants (Overseas)	**0·109**
Tightening torques	**0·110**

GENERAL SPECIFICATION

ENGINE

Number of cylinders	6
Bore of cylinders	74·7 mm.　2·94 in.
Stroke of crankshaft	95 mm.　3·74 in.
Cubic capacity	2498 c.c.　152 in.^{3}
Piston area	263 cm.^{2}　40·7 in.^{2}
Compression ratio	9·5 : 1
Valve rocker clearance (cold)	0·25 mm.　0·010 in.
Valve timing. Inlet	opens 35° B.T.D.C.　closes 65° A.B.D.C.
Exhaust	opens 65° B.B.D.C.　closes 35° A.T.D.C.
Valve position	Overhead
Lubrication (Engine)	
Pump	High capacity eccentric lobe type.
Filter	Full flow replaceable element type.
Cooling system	Pressurized "no loss" system incorporating a translucent overflow bottle.
Circulation	Impeller type pump driven by 'Vee' belt. Thermostat controlled.
Fan	8 blades, 12·5 in. dia. (31·6 cm.).
Fuel system	Lucas Mk. II petrol injection.
Metering unit	Vacuum controlled shuttle type metering.
Fuel pump pressure	106 - 110 lb/in.^{2} (7·452 - 7·733 kg/cm.^{2}).
Injectors open	40 - 50 lb/in.^{2} (2·812 - 3·515 kg/cm.^{2}).

BREATHING

Air cleaner	Replaceable paper element type.
Crankcase breathing	Close circuit breathing through filter from rocker cover to air intake manifold.

TRANSMISSION

Propeller shaft	All metal shaft with needle roller bearings.
Clutch	Diaphragm type 8¼″ dia. (21·5 cm.).
Gearbox	Four forward gears, all synchromesh, one reverse.
Overdrive (Optional)	Laycock de Normanville. Ratio ·82.

	Top	3rd	2nd	1st	Rev.
Gearbox ratios	1·00	1·33	2·01	3·14	3·22
Overall ratios	3·45	4·59	6·94	10·83	11·11

Rear axle	Semi-floating half shafts, three-piece casing. Hypoid bevel gear 3·45 : 1 ratio.
Wheels	Steel disc type 4½J, simulated magnesium wheel trims. Centre nut locking wire wheels, optional.
Tyres	Dunlop SP41 165 HR — 15 or Michelin 165 HR — 15 'XAS'.
Pressures — front	22 lb/in.^{2} (1·547 kg/cm.^{2}).
rear	26 lb/in.^{2} (1·828 kg/cm.^{2}).

BRAKES — Girling Dual HYDRAULIC TANDEM MASTER CYLINDER.

Handbrake	Centrally mounted, mechanically coupled to rear wheels only by twin cables.
Front	Caliper disc 10⅞″ (27·62 cm.) dia.
Rear	Drum 9″ dia. × 1¾ in. (22·9 cm. × 4·45 cm.).
Front lining area	20·7 in.^{2}　174·2 cm.^{2}
Front swept area	233 in.^{2}　1483·8 cm.^{2}
Rear lining area	60·5 in.^{2}　419·3 cm.^{2}
Rear swept area	99 in.^{2}　638·7 cm.^{2}
Total lining area	81·2 in.^{2}　522·8 cm.^{2}
Total swept area	332 in.^{2}　2130·0 cm.^{2}
Maximum retardation	·98 G.

GENERAL SPECIFICATION

0·103

CHASSIS DATA
Frame .. .. Channel steel pressing of box section side members braced by a cruciform member.

STEERING
Steering unit .. .. Rack and pinion — 3¼ turns lock to lock.
Steering wheel .. .. 15 in. 3-spoke leather covered steering wheel.
The following dimensions apply to the vehicle only when it is static laden; the condition is obtained by placing a 150 lb. (68 kg.) weight on each front seat.

Wheelbase	7′ 4″	2240 mm.
Front track — Disc wheels	4′ 1¼″	1251 mm.
Wire wheels	4′ 1¾″	1263 mm.
Rear track — Disc wheels	4′ 0¾″	1239 mm.
Wire wheels	4′ 1¼″	1251 mm.
Toe-in (front and rear)	0″ to 1/16″	1·6 mm.
Ground clearance	6″	152 mm.
Turning circle (between kerbs) ..	33′	10·1 m.
Front wheel camber	0° ± ½°	
Rear wheel camber	1° negative ± ½°	
K.P.I.	9° ± ¾°	
Castor angle	2¾° ± ½°	
Maximum back lock	30°.	
Maximum front lock	31½°.	

20° front lock gives 19¾° back lock.

SUSPENSION
Front .. .. Low periodicity independent system. Patented bottom bush and top ball joint wheel swivels. Coil springs controlled by telescopic dampers. Taper roller hub bearings.

Front road spring
  Number of coils 6
  Rate .. .. 312 lb/in. (3·595 kg/m.).
  Free length .. .. 10·28″.

Rear .. .. Semi-trailing arm independent suspension with coil springs controlled by piston dampers. Mounted on frame through rubber bushed pivots and with rubber insulation of the spring.

Rear road spring
  Number of coils .. .. 6¾.
  Free length .. .. 10·92″.

CAPACITIES
	Imperial	Metric
Fuel tank	11¼ galls.	51 litres.
Engine sump	8 pints	4·52 litres.
Gearbox	2 pints	1·13 litres.
Gearbox and overdrive (where fitted) ..	3½ pints	2·0 litres.
Rear axle	2½ pints	1·42 litres.
Cooling system including heater and water bottle	11 pints	6·2 litres.

EXTERIOR DIMENSIONS
Overall length	12 ft. 9⅝ in.	3902 mm.
Width	4 ft. 10 in.	1470 mm.
Height — hood up (unladen)	4 ft. 2 in.	1270 mm.
hood down (unladen) ..	3 ft. 10 in.	1170 mm.

WEIGHT (approx.)
Dry (excluding extra equipment)	19¼ cwt.	938 kg.
Complete (including fuel, oil, water and tools) ..	20¼ cwt.	1034 kg.
Maximum gross vehicle weight	24 cwt.	1226 kg.

ELECTRICAL SYSTEM

Voltage	12
Polarity	Negative earth.
Fuses — fuse box	35 amp.
Alternator — type	Lucas 15AC.
maximum output	28 amp.
Alternate control unit	Lucas 4TR.
Battery — type	Lucas BT9A.
capacity @ 20 hrs. rate	57 amp. hour.
plates per cell	9
normal charge rate	5 amp.
Starter motor	Lucas M418G.
Flasher unit	Lucas 8FL 4·1A.
Brake pressure differential switch (L.H.D.)	Lockheed.
Hazard flasher unit (L.H.D.)	Signal — Stat 180 (Made in U.S.A.).
Hazard relay (L.H.D.)	Lucas 6RA.
Fuel and temperature indication	Smiths bi-metal resistance — 10 volt system.
Oil pressure indication — switch operating pressure	4·7 - 7·5 p.s.i.

IGNITION SYSTEM

Coil	Lucas HA12.
Distributor — type	Lucas 22D6.
contact gap	0·014 - 0·016 in.
rotation — viewed on rotor	Anti-clockwise.
Firing order	1 - 5 - 3 - 6 - 2 - 4.
Sparking plugs — type	Champion N-9Y.
gap	0·025 in.
Ignition timing (static)	11 degrees B.T.D.C.

ROAD SPEED DATA

ENGINE speed at road speed of:

	O/D Top	Top	O/D 3rd	3rd	O/D 2nd	2nd	1st
10 m.p.h.	386	471	514	626	777	947	1479
10 k.p.h.	240	296	319	393	482	585	940

Road speed at 1,000 r.p.m.	21·21 m.p.h.	33·93 k.p.h.
Road speed at 2,500 ft/min. (762 m/min.) piston speed in top gear	85 m.p.h.	136 k.p.h.

LUBRICATION SUMMARY

0·105

Chart Ref.	Items	Details		Intervals × 1000			
				Miles	Kms.	Miles	Kms.
A	Air cleaner	Clean	—	6	10		
		Renew	—			12	20
B	Radiator	Top-up	Weekly				
C	Water pump	Grease	—			12	20
D	Lower steering swivels	Grease	—	6	10		
E	Front hubs	Re-pack	—			12	20
F	Upper ball joints	Grease	—	6	10		
G	Breather — Filter	Wash in clean fuel—dry and replace	—	6	10		
H	Propeller shaft	Grease	—	6	10		
J	Rear axle	Top-up	—	6	10		
K	Fuel filter	Change element	—			12	20
L	Drive shafts	Grease	—	6	10		
M	Transmission	Top-up	—	6	10		
N	Battery	Top-up	Monthly				
P	Oil filter	Renew element	—			12	20
R	Master cylinder — Clutch	Top-up	Monthly				
	Master cylinder — Brake	Check	Weekly				
S	Engine oil sump	Top-up	Daily				
		Drain and refill	—	6	10		
T	Steering unit	Grease	—			12	20

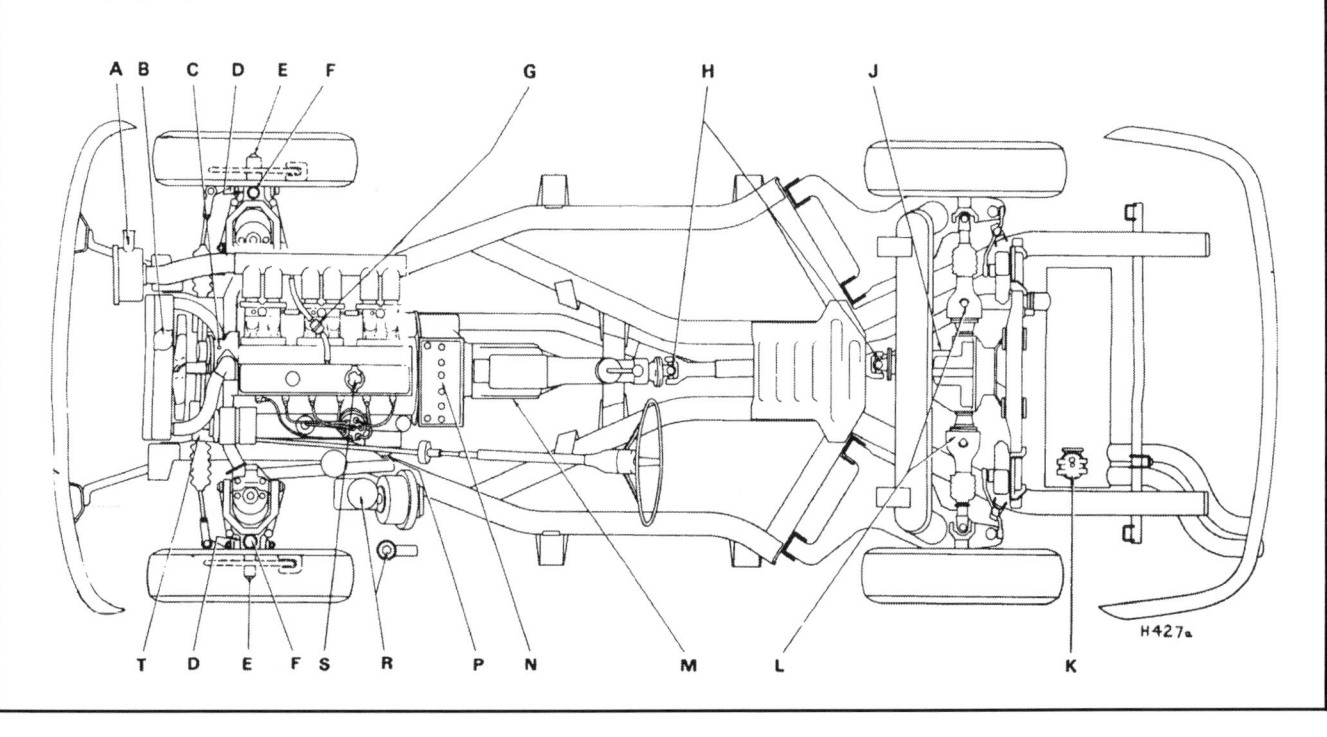

H427a

MAINTENANCE SCHEDULES

SCHEDULE OF OPERATIONS RELATING TO
1000 MILES (1600 KM.) "FREE SERVICE"

ENGINE
Coolant—Check level
Oil sump—Drain and refill
Accelerator control linkage and pedal fulcrum—Oil
Mounting bolts—Check tightness
Cylinder head—Check tightness
Manifold—Check tightness
Valves—Adjust rocker clearances
Fan belt—Adjust tension
Oil filter—Check for oil leaks
Distributor—Lubricate and adjust points

TRANSMISSION
Transmission/Overdrive—Check level and top-up
Rear axle—Check level and top-up
Universal joint coupling bolts—Check tightness
Rear drive shafts—Grease
Propeller shaft—Grease

STEERING AND SUSPENSION
Front wheel alignment—Check with aid of tracking equipment
Rear wheel alignment—Check by condition of tyre tread
Steering unit attachments and "U" bolts—Check for tightness
Tie rods and levers—Check for tightness
Lower steering swivels—Oil
Upper ball joints—Grease

BRAKES AND CONTROLS
Handbrake cable and linkage—Lubricate
Hydraulic pipes—Check for leaks, chafing and for hose clearance
Master cylinder—Check level and top-up
Brake shoes and handbrake cable—Adjust as necessary

WHEELS
Wheel nuts or wire wheel adaptor nuts—Check tightness
Tyres—Check and adjust pressures

ELECTRICAL EQUIPMENT
Battery—Check and adjust electrolite level. Check charging rate
Alternator and starter motor—Check fixing bolts for tightness
Headlights—Check alignment and adjust if required
Lights, heater, windscreen washer, wipers and warning equipment—Check operation

BODY
Door strikers, locks and hinges—Oil and check operation
Body mounting bolts—Check tightness
Door handles, controls and windscreen—Wipe clean

SCHEDULE OF OPERATIONS RELATING TO
"A" SERVICE — 6,000 MILES INTERVALS

ENGINE
Oil sump—Drain and refill
Air cleaner—Clean element
Distributor—Lubricate and adjust points
Sparking plugs—Clean and adjust
Accelerator linkage—Lubricate
Petrol injection—Check for leakage. If required—adjust slow running.
Engine breather filter—Wash in clean fuel, dry and replace

TRANSMISSION
Transmission/Overdrive—Top up
Rear axle—Top up
Rear drive shafts—Grease

Propeller shaft—Grease
Clutch—Top up master cylinder, check for leakage

SUSPENSION AND STEERING
Wheel alignment—Check by tyre wear
Lower steering swivels—Oil
Upper ball joints—Grease

BRAKES
Front brake pads—Examine
Rear brakes—Adjust
Hydraulic pipes and hoses—Check for leakage and chafing
Master cylinder—Check fluid level

ELECTRICAL
Check operation of all electrical equipment

WHEELS AND TYRES
Wheel nuts or wire wheel adaptor nuts—Check tightness
Tyre pressures—Check and adjust

BODY
Door locks, strikers and hinges—Lubricate
Wipe clean controls, handles and windscreen
Road test car and report any defects

SCHEDULE OF OPERATIONS RELATING TO "B" SERVICE — 12,000 MILES INTERVALS

ENGINE
Oil sump—Drain and refill
Oil filter—Renew element
Valves—Adjust clearances
Sparking plugs—Renew
Distributor — Lubricate. Adjust points and check ignition timing
Accelerator linkage—Lubricate
Crankcase emission valve—Clean
Air cleaner—Renew element
Fan belt—Adjust tension
Exhaust system — Examine condition
Water pump—Grease
Fuel filter—Renew element

TRANSMISSION
Transmission/Overdrive—Top up
Rear axle—Top up
Rear drive shafts—Grease

Propeller shaft—Grease
Clutch—Top up master cylinder, check for leakage
Universal joint coupling bolts—Check tightness

STEERING AND SUSPENSION
Wheel alignment—Check by tyre wear
Lower steering swivels—Oil
Upper ball joints—Grease
Steering unit—Grease
Steering unit attachments, tie rods and levers—Check tightness
Front hubs—Adjust

BRAKES
Front brake pads—Examine
Hydraulic pipes and hoses—Check for leakage and chafing

Master cylinder—Check fluid level
Handbrake cable and linkage—Lubricate and adjust
Rear brakes—De-dust, examine and adjust

ELECTRICAL
Check operation of all electrical equipment

WHEELS AND TYRES
Wheel nuts or wire wheel adaptor nuts—Check tightness
Tyre pressures—Check and adjust

BODY
Door locks, strikers and hinges—Lubricate
Wipe clean controls, handles and windscreen
Road test and report any defects

RECOMMENDED LUBRICANTS (BRITISH ISLES) — ANTI-FREEZE SOLUTIONS

(The products recommended are not listed in order of preference)

COMPONENT	BP	CASTROL	DUCKHAM'S	ESSO	MOBIL	PETROFINA	REGENT	SHELL
ENGINE AND OIL CAN	Super Visco-Static 20W/50	Castrol GTX	Duckham's Q20-50	Esso Extra Motor Oil 20W/50	Mobiloil Super 10W/40 or Mobiloil Special 20W/50	Fina Multigrade Motor Oil SAE 20W/50	Havoline Motor Oil 20W/50	Shell Super Motor Oil 100
GEARBOX AND OVERDRIVE, LOWER STEERING SWIVELS, REAR AXLE	BP Gear Oil SAE 90 EP	Castrol Hypoy	Hypoid 90	Esso Gear Oil GP 90/140	Mobilube GX 90	Fina Pontonic MP SAE 90	Multigear Lubricant EP90	Shell Spirax 90EP
FRONT AND REAR HUBS REAR CABLES GREASE GUN	Energrease L2	Castrolease LM	LB 10	Esso Multigear Grease H	Mobilgrease MP	Fina Marson HLT2	Marfak All-Purpose	Shell Retinax A
CLUTCH AND BRAKE RESERVOIRS	CASTROL GIRLING BRAKE AND CLUTCH FLUID, CRIMSON. WHERE THIS PROPRIETARY BRAND IS NOT AVAILABLE OTHER FLUIDS WHICH MEET SAE 70R3 SPECIFICATION MAY BE USED							
APPROVED ANTI-FREEZE SOLUTIONS	Smith's Bluecol / BP Anti-Frost	Castrol Anti-Freeze	Duckham's Anti-Freeze	Esso Anti-Freeze	Mobil Permazone	Fina Thermidor	Regent PT Anti-Freeze	Shell Anti-Freeze

WHERE THESE PROPRIETARY SOLUTIONS ARE NOT AVAILABLE, OTHERS WHICH MEET BSI 3151 or 3152 SPECIFICATION MAY BE USED

MAINTENANCE SCHEDULES

RECOMMENDED LUBRICANTS (OVERSEAS) — ANTI-FREEZE SOLUTIONS

(The products recommended are not listed in order of preference)

COMPONENT	AIR TEMP. °C	AIR TEMP. °F	API DESIGNATION	BP	CASTROL	DUCKHAM'S	ESSO	MOBIL	PETROFINA	SHELL	TEXACO CALTEX
*ENGINE OIL CAN	over 20	over 70	MM or MS	Energol SAE40 (Visco-Static)	Castrol 40 HD (Castrolite XL 20W/40)	Q20-50	Esso Extra Motor Oil 20W/40	Mobiloil Special 10W/30 or Mobiloil Super SAE 10W/40	Fina Multigrade SAE 20W/50	Shell Super Motor Oil	Havoline 40 (Havoline 20W/40)
	0 to 20	30 to 70	MM or MS	Energol SAE30 (Visco-Static Long-Life)	Castrol 30 HD	Q20-50	Esso Extra Motor Oil 20W/40	Mobiloil Special 10W/30 or Mobiloil Super SAE 10W/40	Fina Multigrade SAE 20W/50	Shell Super Motor Oil	Havoline 30 (Havoline 10W/30)
	-10 to 0	10 to 30	MM or MS	Energol SAE 20W	Castrol 20 HD (Castrolite 10W/30)	Q5500	Esso Extra Motor Oil 10W/30	Mobiloil Special 10W/30 or Mobiloil Super SAE 10W/40	Fina Multigrade Motor Oil SAE 10W/30	Shell Super Motor Oil	Havoline 20/20W
	below -10	below 10	MM or MS	Energol SAE 10W	Castrol 10 HD	Q5500	Esso Extra Motor Oil 10W/30	Mobiloil Special 10W/30 or Mobiloil Super SAE 10W/40	Fina Multigrade Motor Oil SAE 10W/30	Shell Super Motor Oil	Havoline 10W
GEARBOX O/DRIVE REAR AXLE	over 0	over 30	GL 4	Gear Oil SAE 90 EP	Castrol Hypoy	Duckham's Hypoid 90	Esso Gear Oil GP 90	Mobilube GX 90	Fina Pontonic MP SAE 90	Shell Spirax 90 EP	Multigear Lubricant EP 90
LOWER STEERING SWIVELS	below 0	below 30	GL 4	Gear Oil SAE 80 EP	Castrol Hypoy Light	Duckham's Hypoid 80	Esso Gear Oil GP 80	Mobilube GX 80	Fina Pontonic MP SAE 80	Shell Spirax 80 EP	Multigear Lubricant EP 80
FRONT AND REAR HUBS BRAKE CABLES GREASE GUN				Energrease L2	Castrolease LM	Duckham's LB 10	Esso Multi-Purpose Grease H	Mobilgrease MP	Fina Marson HTL 2	Shell Retinax A	Marfak All Purpose

*WHERE CIRCUIT RACING OR OTHER SEVERE COMPETITIVE EVENTS ARE CONTEMPLATED IT IS ADVISABLE, IN VIEW OF THE INCREASED OIL TEMPERATURE ENCOUNTERED, TO USE OILS OF HIGH VISCOSITY

CLUTCH AND BRAKE RESERVOIRS

CASTROL GIRLING BRAKE AND CLUTCH FLUID CRIMSON. WHERE THIS PROPRIETARY BRAND IS NOT AVAILABLE, OTHER FLUIDS WHICH MEET SAE 70R3 SPECIFICATION MAY BE USED

APPROVED ANTI-FREEZE SOLUTIONS

| Smith's Bluecol | BP Anti-Frost | Castrol Anti-Freeze | Duckham's Anti-Freeze | Esso Anti-Freeze | Mobil Permazone | Fina Thermidor | Shell Anti-Freeze | Startex |

WHERE THESE PROPRIETARY SOLUTIONS ARE NOT AVAILABLE, OTHERS WHICH MEET BSI 3151 or 3152 SPECIFICATION MAY BE USED

OPERATION	DESCRIPTION	SPECIFIED TORQUE lb. ft.	SPECIFIED TORQUE kg. m.
ENGINE		lb. ft.	kg. m.
Alternator mounting bracket to cylinder block	5/16″ UNF. × 1″ setscrew	18—20	2·49—2·77
Alternator to mounting bracket	5/16″ UNF. × 4 7/8″ bolt	18—20	2·49—2·77
Alternator to adjusting link	5/16″ UNC. × 7/8″ setscrew	18—20	2·49—2·77
Camshaft chainwheel attachment	5/16″ UNF. setscrew	24—26	3·32—3·56
Clutch attachment	5/16″ UNC. × 3/4″ setscrew	20	2·77
Coil to cylinder block	5/16″ UNF. × 1/2″ setscrew	16—18	2·21—2·49
Con rod bolt	3/8″ UNF. × 1·65″ bolt	38—42	5·25—5·81
Crankshaft cover to block	5/16″ UNF. × 1 1/8″ bolt	16—18	2·21—2·49
Crankshaft sealing block attachment	5/16″ UNF. × 0·94″ ch. head screw	12—14	1·66—1·94
Cylinder head attachment	7/16″ UNF. × 4·84″ stud	65—70	8·99—9·69
Cylinder block drain tap	1/2″ N.F. tap	18—20	2·49—2·77
Fan attachment	5/16″ UNF. × 1 1/4″ bolt	12—14	1·66—1·94
Flywheel attachment	7/16″ UNF. × 1·06″ bolt	55—60	7·60—8·29
Front engine plate attachment	5/16″ UNF. × 3/4″ setscrew	18—20	2·49—2·77
Front engine plate and cam locating plate attach.	5/16″ UNF. × 7/8″ setscrew	18—20	2·49—2·77
Lifting eye attachment	5/16″ UNF. × 5/8″ setscrew	16—18	2·21—2·49
Main bearing bolts	7/16″ UNF. × 3″ bolt	55—60	7·60—8·29
Mounting rubber bracket to engine	3/8″ UNF. × 3/4″ setscrew	26—28	3·60—3·87
Mounting rubber to engine bracket	3/8″ UNF. mounting	26—28	3·60—3·87
Mounting rubber to frame	3/8″ UNF. × 1 1/8″ bolt	28—30	3·87—4·15
Manifold attachment	3/8″ UNF. × 1·84″ stud	24—26	3·32—3·60
Manifold attachment	3/8″ UNF. × 1·34″ stud	24—26	3·32—3·60
Oil gallery seal	1/8″ N.P.S.I. plug	5—6	0·69—0·83
Oil gallery plug	3/4″ UNF. × 1/2″ plug	25—30	3·46—4·15
Oil gallery plug	1/4″ N.P.S.I. plug	10—12	1·38—1·66
Oil filter attachment		15—18	2·07—2·49
Oil pressure relief valve	5/8″ UNF. plug	30—35	4·15—4·84
Petrol pump attachment	5/16″ UNF. × 1·16″ stud	12—14	1·66—1·94
Rear engine plate attachment	5/16″ UNF. × 7/8″ setscrew	18—20	2·49—2·77
Rear engine plate and gearbox to block	5/16″ UNF. × 1·84″ stud	18—20	2·49—2·77
Rocker pedestal attachment	3/8″ UNF. × 3·89″ stud	24—26	3·32—3·60
Rocker cover attachment	5/16″ UNF. × 4·13″ stud	1 1/2	0·21
Rocker shaft locating screw	No. 12 × 28 UNF. screw	3—4	0·42—0·55
Rocker oil feed plug	5/16″ UNF. × 0·44″ setscrew	16—18	2·21—2·49
Spark plug attachment	14 mm. × 3/4″ plug	14—16	1·94—2·21
Starter motor attachment	3/8″ UNF. × 2 1/8″ bolt	28—30	3·87—4·15
Sump attachment	5/16″ UNF. × 5/8″ setscrew	16—18	2·21—2·49
Note. Above item should maintain a minimum of 8 lb. ft. after settling period.			
Sump drain plug	3/8″ × 18 Dryseal plug	20—22	2·77—3·04
Timing cover attachment	5/16″ UNF. × 1·16″ stud	12—14	1·66—1·94
Timing cover attachment	5/16″ UNF. × 7/8″ setscrew	16—18	2·21—2·49
Timing cover attachment	5/16″ UNF. × 3/8″ pan head setscrew	8—10	1·11—1·38
Note. Above item should maintain a minimum of 4 lb. ft. after settling period.			
Water valve adaptor to cylinder head	3/8″ BSP. adaptor	16—18	2·21—2·49
Water pump pulley attachment	5/16″ UNF. spindle	14—16	1·94—2·21
Water pump attachment	5/16″ UNF. × 1·31″ stud	12—14	1·66—1·94
Water pump to cylinder head	5/16″ UNF. × 1 1/4″ bolt	18—20	2·49—2·77
Water pump to cylinder head	5/16″ UNF. × 3 1/8″ bolt	18—20	2·49—2·77
Water elbow attachment	5/16″ UNF. × 1 7/8″ bolt	18—20	2·49—2·77
Water elbow attachment	5/16″ UNF. × 1″ setscrew	18—20	2·49—2·77

OPERATION	DESCRIPTION	SPECIFIED TORQUE	
ENGINE — PETROL INJECTION VERSION		lb. ft.	kg. m.
Distributor and P.I. pump pedestal attachment	5/16" UNF. × 2½" stud	12—14	1·66—1·94
Distributor and P.I. pump pedestal attachment	5/16" UNF. × 1·31" stud	12—14	1·66—1·94
Distributor to pedestal	5/16" UNF. × 5/8" setscrew	18—20	2·49—2·77
Distributor pedestal end plug	¼" UNF. × ½" setscrew	8—10	1·11—1·38
Emission control valve to bracket	¼" UNF. × 7/8" setscrew	8—10	1·11—1·38
Inlet manifold to stay	¼" UNF. × ¾" setscrew	8—10	1·11—1·38
Petrol injection nozzle attachment	¼" UNC. × 3/8" setscrew	6—8	0·83—1·11
Petrol pump attachment	¼" UNF. × Mounting	6—8	0·83—1·11
Water pump plug	3/8" UNF. Dryseal plug	20—22	2·77—3·04
Water pump plug	5/8" UNF. plug	28—30	3·87—4·15
GEARBOX			
Change speed lever cap to top cover	¼" UNF. × 3/8" setscrew	6—8	0·83—1·11
Change speed lever to top cover	¼" UNF. × 3 3/8" bolt	6—8	0·83—1·11
Clutch housing cover attachment	5/16" UNF. × 1"/1¼" bolt	16—18	2·21—2·49
Clutch slave cylinder attachment	5/16" UNF. × 1 1/8" bolt	18—20	2·49—2·77
Clutch slave cylinder stay attachment	5/16" UNF. × 1 5/8" bolt	18—20	2·49—2·77
Countershaft end cover to gearbox	5/16" UNC. × 7/8" Wedglok setscrew	16—18	2·21—2·49
Countershaft and reverse shaft to gearbox	5/16" UNC. × ·75" Wedglok c/s screw	16—18	2·21—2·49
Extension to gearbox	5/16" UNC. × 2" bolt 1" setscrew	14—16	1·94—2·21
Front cover to gearbox	5/16" UNC. × 7/8" Wedglok setscrew	16—18	2·21—2·49
Gearbox to engine	5/16" UNF. × 1 3/8" bolt	18—20	2·49—2·77
Gear selectors and forks to shaft	5/16" UNF. taper setscrew	8—10	1·11—1·38
Gear lever knob	5/16" UNC. lever	8	1·11
Mounting rubber to gearbox extension	½" UNF. × 1½" bolt	50—55	6·91—7·60
Mounting rubber to frame crossmember	7/16" UNF. mounting	35—40	4·84—5·53
Overdrive adaptor plate	5/16" UNC. × 7/8" Wedglok setscrew	16—18	2·21—2·49
Propshaft flange to mainshaft	¾" UNF. mainshaft	80—120	11·06—16·59
Propshaft attachment	3/8" UNF. × 1 1/8" bolt	24—26	3·32—3·60
Sealing ring cover plate attachment	¼" UNF. × ½" setscrew	6—8	0·83—1·11
Speedometer bearing locking screw	5/16" UNC × 1·56" locking screw	10—12	1·38—1·66
Top cover to gearbox	5/16" UNC. setscrew	14—16	1·94—2·21
Top cover to gearbox	5/16" UNC. × 2 5/8" 2 7/8" bolt	14—16	1·94—2·21
Top up and drain plugs	3/8" UNF. Dryseal plug	20—22	2·77—3·04
REAR AXLE			
Bearing caps to housing	3/8" UNF. × 2" setscrew	34—36	4·70—5·05
Crown wheel to housing	3/8" UNF. bolt	40—45	5·53—6·22
Cover and rear mounting plate attachment	3/8" UNF. × 1·63" stud	26—28	3·60—3·87
Hypoid housing to rear cover	5/16" UNF. × 1" setscrew	18—20	2·49—2·77
Inner driving flange to inner axle	5/8" UNF. axle shaft	100—110	13·83—15·21
Nose plate to axle	3/8" UNF. taper bolt	35	4·84
Note. Tighten above item to 26—28 lb. ft. (3·56 – 3·87 kg.m.) on re-assembly			
Oil seal housing to hypoid housing	5/16" UNF. × ¾" setscrew	16—18	2·21—2·49
Oil level plug	3/8" UNF. Dryseal plug	20—22	2·77—3·04
Prop. shaft flange to pinion	5/8" UNF. pinion	90—100	12·44—13·83
Rear mounting plate to frame	3/8" UNF. weld bolt	26—28	3·60—3·87

OPERATION	DESCRIPTION	SPECIFIED TORQUE lb. ft.	kg. m.
FRONT SUSPENSION			
Brake disc attachment	3/8″ UNF. bolt	32—35	4·42—4·84
Brake caliper and shield attachment	7/16″ UNF. bolt	50—55	6·91—7·60
Brake caliper mounting bracket and tie rod lever attachment	3/8″ UNF. setscrew	26—28	3·60—3·87
Brake caliper mounting bracket and tie rod lever attachment	3/8″ UNF. bolt	26—28	3·60—3·87
Damper to spring pan mounting	7/16″ UNF. × 2 3/8″ bolt	55—60	7·60—8·30
Lockstop bolts	5/16″ UNF. × 1 3/8″ setscrew	18—20	2·49—2·77
Lower wishbone mounting bracket to frame	3/8″ UNF. × 1 1/4″ bolt	28—30	3·87—4·15
Lower wishbone to mounting bracket	1/2″ UNF. × 2 5/8″ bolt	45—50	6·22—6·91
Lower wishbone to vertical link	9/16″ UNF. bolt	45—60	6·22—8·30
Note. Above item to accommodate split pin (Issue 2).			
Lower wishbone to spring pan	3/8″ UNF. bolt/stud	28—30	3·87—4·15
Shock absorber mounting to spring pan	3/8″ UNF. weld bolt	26—28	3·60—3·87
Stub axle to vertical link	1/2″ UNF. stub axle	55—60	7·60—8·30
Stub axle to front hub	1/2″ UNF. stub axle		
Note. Tighten above item to 5 lb. ft., unscrew one flat and insert split pin to give ·003″ to ·005″ end float.			
Top ball joint to upper wishbone	3/8″ UNF. × 2 3/4″ bolt	26—28	3·60—3·87
Top ball joint to vertical link	1/2″ UNF. ball pin	55—65	7·60—8·99
Upper wishbone to fulcrum pin	7/16″ UNF. pin	26—40	3·60—5·54
Upper wishbone fulcrum to chassis frame	3/8″ UNF. × 1″ setscrew	28—30	3·87—4·15
REAR SUSPENSION			
Bump rubber attachment	3/8″ UNF. bump rubber	18—20	2·49—2·77
Damper to mounting bracket	7/16″ UNF. × 1 1/4″ setscrew	55—60	7·60—8·30
Damper link attachment	3/8″ UNF. link	18—20	2·49—2·77
Inner driven flange to outer axles	3/8″ UNF. × 1·13″ bolt	28—30	3·87—4·15
Outer driven flange to axle and hub	1 3/8″ UNF. stub axle		
Note. Above item to be tightened to give ·002″ to ·005″ end float. End float obtained by tightening only. Not by slackening.			
Rear hub assembly	5/8″ UNF. stub axle	100—110	13·83—15·21
Trailing arm to mounting bracket	7/16″ UNF. × 3 5/8″ bolt	45—50	6·22—6·91
Trailing arm mounting brackets to frame	3/8″ UNF. bolt	28—30	3·87—4·15
Trailing arm to brake back plate	5/16″ UNF. × 1 1/2″ stud	16—18	2·21—2·49
Wire wheel extension attachment	7/16″ UNF. stud	65	8·99
Wheel attachment	7/16″ UNF. stud	55—60	7·60—8·30
CHASSIS FRAME AND ATTACHMENTS			
Brake pipe connections and bleed screw	3/8″ UNF. single and double flares	5—7	0·69—0·97
Crosstube to front suspension turrets	3/8″ UNF. × 7/8″ bolts	26—28	3·60—3·87
Chassis to axle note plate front of rear suspension	3/8″ UNF. weld bolt	26—28	3·60—3·87
Chassis to axle back plate back of rear suspension	3/8″ UNF. weld bolt	26—28	3·60—3·87
Exhaust tail pipe attachment to rubber strap	5/16″ UNF. × 1″ setscrew	2—3	0·28—0·42
Exhaust front pipe attachment — petrol injection	5/16″ UNF. × 2 3/4″ bolt	6—8	0·83—1·11
Exhaust intermediate pipe attachment — P.I.	5/16″ UNF. × 3/4″ setscrew	6—8	0·83—1·11
Exhaust pipe silencer attachment — P.I.	5/16″ UNF. × 2 7/8″ bolt	6—8	0·83—1·11
Exhaust front pipe attachment — carburettor	5/16″ UNF. × 1 1/8″ bolt	6—8	0·83—1·11
Exhaust intermediate pipe attachment — carb.	5/16″ UNF. × 2 7/8″ bolt	6—8	0·83—1·11
Exhaust pipe silencer attachment to flexible strip	5/16″ UNF. × 1″ setscrew	2—3	0·28—0·42
Gearbox mounting crossmember to chassis	3/8″ UNF. × 5/8″ setscrew	26—28	3·60—3·87
Oil cooler to radiator shield	1/4″ UNF. × 5/8″ setscrew	8—10	1·11—1·38
Radiator shield attachment	3/8″ UNF. × 3/4″ setscrew	28—30	3·87—4·15
Radiator to chassis	3/8″ UNF. × 1 1/8″ pointed setscrew	12—14	1·66—1·94

TIGHTENING TORQUES

0·113

OPERATION	DESCRIPTION	SPECIFIED TORQUE	
		lb. ft.	kg. m.
CHASSIS FRAME AND ATTACHMENTS—continued			
Radiator stay to crosstube	5/16" UNF. × 3/4" setscrew	18—20	2·49—2·77
Radiator drain tap	1/4" P.T.F. drain tap	12—14	1·66—1·94
Three-way pipe connections to chassis	1/4" UNF. × 1 1/4" bolt	8—10	1·11—1·38
STEERING			
Adaptor to upper and lower column	1/4" UNF. bolt	8—10	1·11—1·38
Adaptor to rubber coupling	5/16" UNF. bolt	14—16	1·94—2·21
Ball joint to tie rod locknut	1/2" UNF. locknut on tie rod	30—35	4·15—4·84
Ball joint tie rod to steering lever	7/16" UNF. ball pin	55—60	7·60—8·29
Lower clamp to outer column and body	1/4" UNF. × 3/4" setscrew	8—10	1·11—1·38
Outer column tie rods to body	1/4" UNF. × 5/8" setscrew	8—10	1·11—1·38
Rack to chassis	5/16" UNF. 'U' bolt	14—16	1·94—2·21
Safety clamp to column	1/4" UNF. × 1 1/4" bolt	6—8	0·83—1·11
Safety clamp grub screw	7/16" UNF. grub screw	18—20	2·49—2·77
Steering wheel attachment	9/16" UNS. inner column	28—30	3·87—4·15
Top clamp to outer column	5/16" UNF. × 1" setscrew	16—18	2·21—2·49
Top clamp to body	1/4" UNF. × 3/4" setscrew	8—10	1·11—1·38
Top clamp to body	1/4" UNF. × 3/4" weld bolt	6—8	0·83—1·11
Universal joint attachment	5/16" UNF. × 1 1/2" bolt	18—20	2·49—2·77
BODY			
Accelerator pedal stop	1/4" UNF. × 1" setscrew	8—10	1·11—1·38
Accelerator control lever to pedal shaft — carb.	5/16" UNF. sq. hd. bolt	16—18	2·21—2·49
Accelerator bearing plate to pedal box — P.I.	1/4" UNF. × 5/8" setscrew	8—10	1·11—1·38
Accelerator anchor bracket to valance — P.I.	1/4" UNF. × 5/8" setscrew	8—10	1·11—1·38
Accelerator countershaft to inlet manifold — P.I.	1/4" UNF. × 5/8" setscrew	8—10	1·11—1·38
Accelerator cam to carrier — P.I.	5/16" UNF. × 1·03" shouldered bolt	16—18	2·21—2·49
Brake servo attachment	5/16" UNF. weld bolts	12—14	1·66—1·94
Brake limiting valve to body	1/4" UNF. × 1 1/8" setscrew	8—10	1·11—1·38
Brake master cylinder to servo	3/8" UNF. weld bolt	20—22	2·77—3·04
Brake and clutch pedal box and clutch master cylinder bracket attachment	1/4" UNF. × 5/8" setscrew	6—8	0·83—1·11
Brake and clutch pedal shaft cover attachment	5/16" UNF. × 5/8" pointed setscrew	16—18	2·21—2·49
Body mounting front side	3/8" UNF. × 2 1/2" setscrew	12—14	1·66—1·94
Body mounting front	3/8" UNF. × 1·63" stud	12—14	1·66—1·94
Body mounting rear cruciform	5/16" UNF. × 1 3/8" spigot point setscrew	8—10	1·11—1·38
Body mounting scuttle brackets	5/16" UNF. × 1 3/8" spigot point setscrew	8—10	1·11—1·38
Body mounting side member sill brackets	5/16" UNF. × 1 3/8" spigot point setscrew	8—10	1·11—1·38
Body mounting rear	5/16" UNF. × 1 1/4" pointed setscrew	18—20	2·49—2·77
Body mounting to rear suspension crossmember	3/8" UNF. × 1 3/8" pointed setscrew	12—14	1·66—1·94
Bonnet hinge to bonnet and body	5/16" UNF. × 1" setscrew	16—18	2·21—2·49
Bonnet fastener to bonnet and body	1/4" UNF. × 1/2" pointed setscrew	6—8	0·83—1·11
Clutch master cylinder attachment	5/16" UNF. × 1" setscrew	18—20	2·49—2·77
Dip switch attachment	1/4" UNF. × 5/8" pointed setscrew	6—8	0·83—1·11
Door hinge attachment	5/16" UNF. × 3/4" pointed setscrew	16—18	2·21—2·49
Door hinge attachment	5/16" UNF. × 5/8" setscrew	16—18	2·21—2·49
Door lock striker attachment	1/4" UNF. × 5/8" Longlok screw	4—5	0·55—0·69
Door lock striker attachment	1/4" UNF. × 1 1/4" Longlok screw	4—5	0·55—0·69
Door lock to door	1/4" UNF. × 1" Longlok screw	4—5	0·55—0·69
Door glass channel and window winder attachment	1/4" UNF. × 1/2" setscrew	6—8	0·83—1·11
Door glass channel attachment	1/4" UNF. × 5/8" pointed setscrew	6—8	0·83—1·11
Engine earth lead to body	5/16" UNF. × 5/8" pointed setscrew	18—20	2·49—2·77

OPERATION	DESCRIPTION	SPECIFIED TORQUE lb. ft.	SPECIFIED TORQUE kg. m.
BODY—continued			
Facia support bracket to chassis	1/4″ UNF. × 1″ pointed setscrew	6—8	0·83—1·11
Facia support bracket to facia	5/16″ UNF. × 7/8″ chrome setscrew	8—10	1·11—1·38
Facia support channel to dash	1/4″ UNF. × 1/2″ setscrew	8—10	1·11—1·38
Facia board bracket attachment	5/16″ UNF. × 3/4″ setscrew	16—18	2·21—2·49
Facia to 'A' post	1/4″ UNF. × 3/4″ setscrew	6—8	0·83—1·11
Facia attachment	1/4″ UNF. × 1/2″ weld bolt	6—8	0·83—1·11
Facia switch plinth attachment	1/4″ UNF. × 1/2″ setscrew	8—10	1·11—1·38
Front bumper to brackets	3/8″ UNF. × 1 3/8″ coach bolt	8—10	1·11—1·38
Front bumper bracket to chassis	3/8″ UNF. × 1 1/4″ bolt	24—26	3·32—3·60
Front overriders to bumper	3/8″ UNF. × 1 3/4″ bolt	8—10	1·11—1·38
Front bumper supports	3/8″ UNF. × 2 3/4″ 3″ bolt	28—30	3·87—4·15
Fuel tank attachment	1/4″ UNF. × 7/8″ pointed setscrew	8—10	1·11—1·38
Fuel trank drain plug	5/8″ UNF.	30—35	4·15—4·84
Gearbox cover attachment	1/4″ UNF. × 3/4″ setscrew	4—6	0·55—0·83
Handbrake fulcrum pin	3/8″ UNF. shouldered bolt	20—22	2·77—3·04
Hardtop to windscreen	5/16″ UNF. × 2 1/2″ domed bolt	6—8	0·83—1·11
Hardtop to backlight	5/16″ UNF. × 1 1/4″ domed bolt	6—8	0·83—1·11
Heater to Plenum chamber	1/4″ UNF. × 1″ bolt	6—8	0·83—1·11
Heater to bulkhead	1/4″ UNF. × 3/4″ weld bolt	6—8	0·83—1·11
Hood to body	1/4″ UNF. × 7/8″ c'sunk hd. point screw	4—5	0·55—0·69
Hood cover angle to rear deck	1/4″ UNF. × 7/8″ plated setscrew	6—8	0·83—1·11
Horn attachment	1/4″ UNF. × 1/2″ setscrew	8—10	1·11—1·38
Petrol pipe to floor	1/4″ UNF. × 1/2″ weld bolt	6—8	0·83—1·11
Rear bumper side fixing	3/8″ UNF × 2″ plated coach bolt	8—10	1·11—1·38
Rear bumper to outer bracket	3/8″ UNF. × 1·38″ chrome bolt	8—10	1·11—1·38
Rear bumper outrigger to shackle bracket	3/8″ UNF. × 5/8″ setscrew	26—28	3·60—3·87
Rear bumper outer and inner brackets to chassis	3/8″ UNF. × 1 1/4″ bolt	26—28	3·60—3·87
Rear bumper outer and inner brackets to chassis	3/8″ UNF. × 2 1/4″ bolt	26—28	3·60—3·87
Rear bumper tie rod attachment	3/8″ UNF. × 3/4″ setscrew	26—28	3·60—3·87
Rear bumper tie rod attachment	5/16″ UNF. × 5/8″ setscrew	6—8	0·83—1·11
Rear overrider and bumper to inner bracket	3/8″ UNF. × 1 3/4″ bolt	8—10	1·11—1·38
Safety harness pivot bolt	7/16″ UNF. × ·96″ chrome bolt	28—30	3·87—4·15
Safety harness eye bolts	7/16″ UNF. eye bolts	28—30	3·87—4·15
Seat slides to floor	1/4″ UNF. × 1″ setscrew	5—6	0·69—0·83
Seat to slide	5/16″ UNF. × 3/4″ setscrew	5—6	0·69—0·83
Seat catch plate to slide	1/4″ UNF. × 5/8″ setscrew	6—8	0·83—1·11
Trunk lid stay to lid	1/4″ UNF. shouldered bolt	6—8	0·83—1·11
Trunk lid stay to bracket	1/4″ UNF. shouldered screw	6—8	0·83—1·11
Valance stay rod attachment	1/4″ UNF. × 1/2″ setscrew	6—8	0·83—1·11
Visor attachment	1/4″ UNF. taper bolt	2—3	0·28—0·42
Wheelarch baffle plate to bulkhead	1/4″ UNF. × 1″ 5/8″ pointed setscrew	6—8	0·83—1·11
Windscreen mounting bracket to 'A' post	1/4″ UNF. × 5/8″ setscrew	6—8	0·83—1·11
Windscreen mounting bracket to 'A' post	1/4″ UNF. × 1″ bolt	6—8	0·83—1·11
Windscreen mounting bracket to 'A' post	1/4″ UNF. × 1 1/4″ setscrew	6—8	0·83—1·11
Windscreen frame to body	5/16″ UNF. × 3/4″ domed bolt	8—10	1·11—1·38
Windscreen wiper motor attachment	1/4″ UNF. × 1/2″ 7/8″ setscrew	6—8	0·83—1·11

TRIUMPH
TR5-PI
WORKSHOP MANUAL SUPPLEMENT

GROUP 1

Comprising:

Engine, Cooling system, Petrol Injection system and Exhaust system

TRIUMPH TR5

WORKSHOP MANUAL

SUPPLEMENT TO GROUP 1

CONTENTS

	Section
ENGINE (Section 1)	
Dimensions and tolerances	1·102
Lubrication	1·107
Removal and installation	1·109
Replacement engine unit	1·111
Dismantling and Reconditioning	1·112
Assembling	1·119
Service operations with engine in place	1·125
COOLING SYSTEM (Section 2)	
Water pump 6	1·201
Radiator	1·202
FUEL SYSTEM (Section 3)	
Description of P.I. Circuit	1·301
Service precautions	1·305
Setting the throttle openings	1·306
Metering Distributor	1·308
Pressure Relief Valve	1·315
Pedestal Seals	1·316
Injectors	1·316
Fault finding	1·317
Air cleaner	1·319
EXHAUST SYSTEM (Section 4)	
Exhaust system	1·401

ENGINE

DIMENSIONS AND TOLERANCES

DESCRIPTION	DIMENSIONS
PISTONS	
Rings	
Top compression:	
Height	0·615″ – 0·0625″ (1·562 – 1·588 mm)
Gap	0·012″ – 0·017″ (0·305 – 0·432 mm)
2nd compression:	
Height	0·615″ – 0·0625″ (1.562 – 1·588 mm)
Gap	0·008″ – 0·013″ (0·203 – 0·33 mm)
Scraper	
Plain: Thickness	0·023″ – 0·025″ (0·584 – 0·635 mm)
Gap	0·015″ – 0·055″ (0·381 – 1·397 mm)
Spacer: Thickness	0·1415″ – 0·1515″ (3·594 – 3·838 mm)
Gap	Ring ends to butt
Groove width	
Top compression:	0·064″ – 0·065″ (1·625 – 1·650 mm)
2nd compression	0·064″ – 0·065″ (1·625 – 1·650 mm)
Scraper	0·1265″ – 0·1275″ (3·213 – 3·238 mm)
Groove root dia.	
Top compression	2·6535″ – 2·6574″ (67·4 – 67·5 mm)
2nd compression	2·6535″ – 2·6574″ (67·4 – 67·5 mm)
Scraper	2·5826″ – 2·5866″ (65·6 – 65·7 mm)
Gudgeon pin	
Length	2·447″ – 2·451″ (62·153 – 62·274 mm)
Dia.	0·8123″ – 0·8125″ (20·632 – 20·645 mm)

PISTON GRADES AND DIMENSIONS (STANDARD BORES ONLY)

	F GRADE	G GRADE	H GRADE
BORE	2·9405″ (74·689 mm) 2·9408″ (74·696 mm)	2·9409″ (74·699 mm) 2·9412″ (74·706 mm)	2·9413″ (74·709 mm) 2·9416″ (74·717 mm)
MAJOR DIA. (measured on ring land at right angles to gudgeon pin).	2·9363″ (74·582 mm) 2·9367″ (74·592 mm)	2·9367″ (74·592 mm) 2·9371″ (74·602 mm)	2·9371″ (74·602 mm) 2·9375″ (74·612 mm)
MAJOR DIA. (measured across skirt at right angles to gudgeon pin).	2·9380″ (74·625 mm) 2·9384″ (74·635 mm)	2·9384″ (74·635 mm) 2·9388″ (74·645 mm)	2·9388″ (74·645 mm) 2·9392″ (74·655 mm)

ENGINE

DESCRIPTION	DIMENSIONS
Oversize pistons	+ 0·020″ (+ 0·508 mm)
Oversize rings	+ 0·010″ (+ 0·254 mm) + 0·020″ (+ 0·508 mm) + 0·030″ (+ 0·762 mm)
CRANKSHAFT	
Journals	
Diameter	2·311″ – 2·3115″ (58·6994 – 58·7121 mm)
Width-intermediate	1·111″ – 1·121″ (28·22 – 28·473 mm)
Width-rear, thrust	1·36″ – 1·362″ (34·544 – 34·595 mm)
Fillet	0·08″ – 0·1″ (2·032 – 2·54 mm) Radius
Undersize bearings	–0·010″ (–0·254 mm) –0·020″ (–0·508 mm) –0·030″ (–0·762 mm)
Crankpins	
Diameter	1·875″ – 1·8755″ (47·625 – 47·638 mm)
Width	0·9066″ – 0·9085″ (23·028 – 23·076 mm)
Fillet	0·1″ – 0·12″ (2·54 – 3·01 mm) Radius
Undersize bearings	–0·010″ (–0·254 mm) –0·020″ (–0·508 mm) –0·030″ (–0·762 mm)
End-float	0·006″ – 0·008″ (0·1524 – 0·2032 mm)
Thrust bearing thickness	0·091″ – 0·093″ (2·31 – 2·36 mm)
CONNECTING RODS	
Internal dia. small end bush	0·8126″ – 0·8129″ (20·64 – 20·648 mm)
Bend and twist	0·0015″ (0·038 mm) Max. – in length of gudgeon pin
CAMSHAFT	
End-float	0·004″ – 0·008″ (0·102 – 0·203 mm)
Journal dia.	1·8402″ – 1·8407″ (46·7411 – 46·7538 mm)
CAM FOLLOWERS	
Dia.	0·799″ – 0·80″ (20·31 – 20·32 mm)
Bore in cylinder block	0·8002″ – 0·8009″ (20·325 – 20·343 mm)

ENGINE

DESCRIPTION	DIMENSIONS
OIL PUMP	
Maximum permissible clearance between outer rotor and body	0·010" (0·254 mm)
Maximum permissible clearance between outer and inner rotors	0·001" – 0·004" (0·0254 – 0·102 mm)
Rotor end clearance	0·004" (0·102 mm)
RELIEF VALVE SPRING	
Free length	1·55" (39·37 mm)
Fitted length	1·25" (31·75 mm)
Load-fitted	14·5 lb. (6·58 kg)
Rate	53 lb/in. (0·611 kg/m)
DISTRIBUTOR AND METERING PUMP	
Distributor drive gear end clearance	0·003" – 0·007" (0·0762 – 0·1778 mm)
ROCKERS	
Bore	0·563" – 0·564" (14·3 – 14·33 mm)
Rocker Shaft dia.	0·5607" – 0·5612" (4·243 – 4·254 mm)
VALVE GUIDES	
Length: Inlet..	2·0625" (52·386 mm)
Exhaust	2·25" (57·15 mm)
External dia.	0·501" – 0·502" (12·725 – 12·751 mm)
Bore	0·312" – 0·313" (7·925 – 7·95 mm)
Height above cylinder head..	0·63" (16·002 mm)

DESCRIPTION	DIMENSIONS
VALVES	
Exhaust	
Head dia.	1·256″ – 1·26″ (31·9 – 32·0 mm)
Stem dia.	0·31″ – 0·3105″ (7·87 – 7·89 mm)
Seat angle	45°
Length	4·597″ – 4·607″ (116·764 – 117·018 mm)
Inlet	
Head dia.	1·441″ – 1·445″ (36·6 – 36·7 mm)
Stem dia.	0·3107″ – 0·3112″ (7·891 – 7·904 mm)
Seat angle	45°
Length	4·597″ – 4·607″ (116·764 – 117·018 mm)
VALVE SEAT INSERTS	
Inlet	
Outside dia.	1·4875″ – 1·4885″ (37·783 – 37·808 mm)
Height	0·247″ – 0·25″ (6·274 – 6·35 mm)
Chamfer (At base)	0·32″ – 0·052″ (0·813 – 1·321 mm)
Exhaust	
Outside dia.	1·2845″ – 1·2855″ (32·626 – 32·652 mm)
Height	0·247″ – 0·25″ (6·274 – 6·35 mm)
Chamfer (At base)	0·032″ – 0·052″ (0·813 – 1·321 mm)
Bore out cylinder head	
Inlet	1·484 (37·69 mm) × 0·25″ (6·35 mm)
	1·485 (37·72 mm) × 0·255″ (6·48 mm)
Bottom radius	0·03″ (0·76 mm)
Exhaust	1·281″ (32·54 mm) × 0·25″ (6·35 mm)
	1·282″ (32·56 mm) × 0·255″ (6·48 mm)
Valve seat angle	89° Inclusive
VALVE SPRINGS	
Inner	
Free length	1·56″ (39·624 mm)
Solid length-max.	0·73″ (18·542 mm)
Outer dia.	0·73″ (18·542 mm)
Wire dia.	0·076″ (1·9304 mm)
Rate fitted	28·5 lb/in.
Outer	
Free length	1·57″ (39·878 mm)
Solid length-max.	0·918″ (23·32 mm)
Inner dia.	0·795″ (20·193 mm)
Wire dia.	0·136″ (3·454 mm)
Rate fitted	150 lb/in ± 3%

ENGINE

Fig. 1. Left-hand view of engine

Fig. 2. Right-hand view of engine

ENGINE

LUBRICATION

Oil circulation (Refer Fig. 3)

Oil drawn from the engine sump by an eccentric rotor type pump (1) is delivered via a non-adjustable relief valve (2) to a full-flow filter (3). Oil which spills from the relief valve returns to the sump; the filtered oil passes to the engine main oil gallery from whence it is distributed to the camshaft and crankshaft journals. Drillings in the crankshaft webs permit oil flow to the crankpins. The cylinder bores and small end bearings are lubricated by splash thrown up by the crankshaft.

A reduced flow of oil to the hollow rocker shaft and valve gear is supplied from, and metered by, a scroll and two flats provided on the camshaft rear journal. Oil from the valve gear spills to the cam followers and cams before returning to the sump.

The timing gear is lubricated by seepage from the camshaft front journal, and by oil mist from the crankcase.

Crankcase oil retention is effected by crankshaft lip type oil seals fitted front and rear.

Oil filtration (Refer Fig. 4)

The full-flow replaceable cartridge type oil filter is secured in position by a single bolt (8) and sealed by a rubber ring (1) interposed between the engine block and the filter body.

Oil is delivered to the outside of the filter element from whence it passes through the element to the engine. A relief valve (5) ensures adequate delivery of oil to the engine under conditions of extreme temperature or filter maintenance neglect.

Crankcase ventilation

Crankcase ventilation is effected by a hose connecting the rocker cover and air intake manifold. A gauze type filter fitted to this hose provides restrictive control and ensures the dissipation of neat oil.

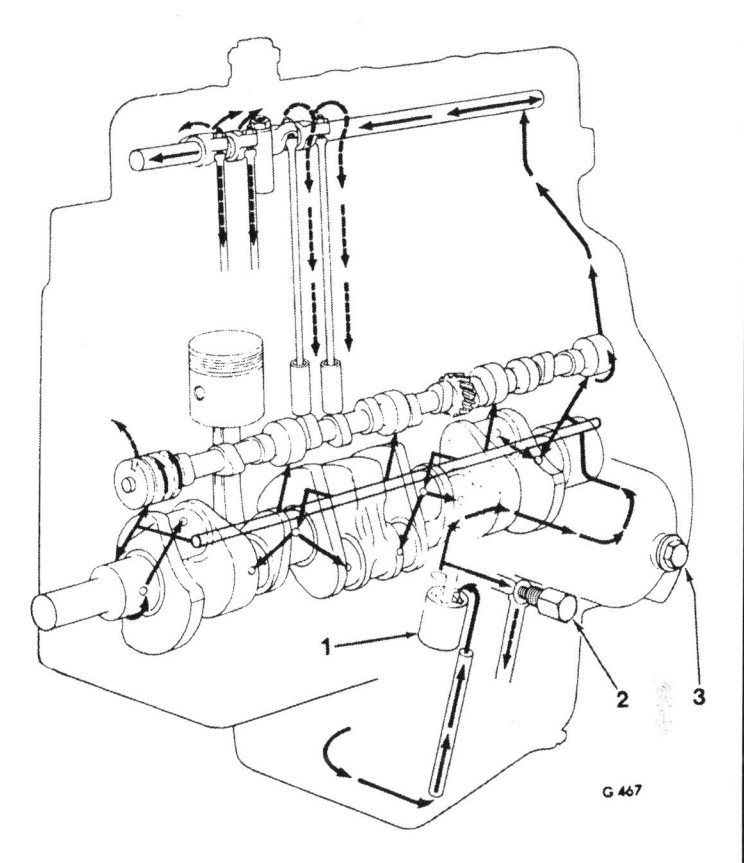

Fig. 3. Diagram of oil circulation

Key to Fig. 4

1	Rubber seal	5	Relief valve
2	Locating washer	6	Spring
3	Filter element	7	Seal
4	Container	8	Securing bolt

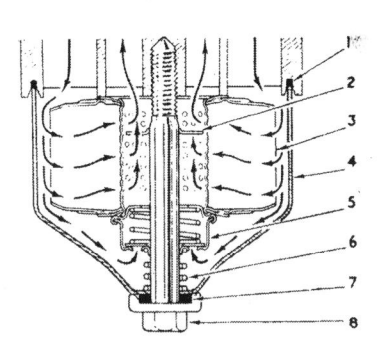

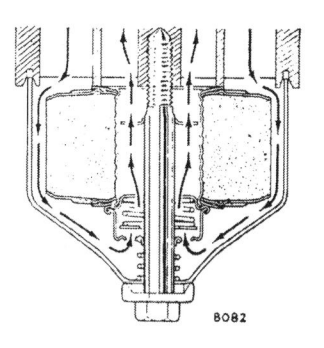

Fig. 4. Circulation of oil through filter

1·108 ENGINE

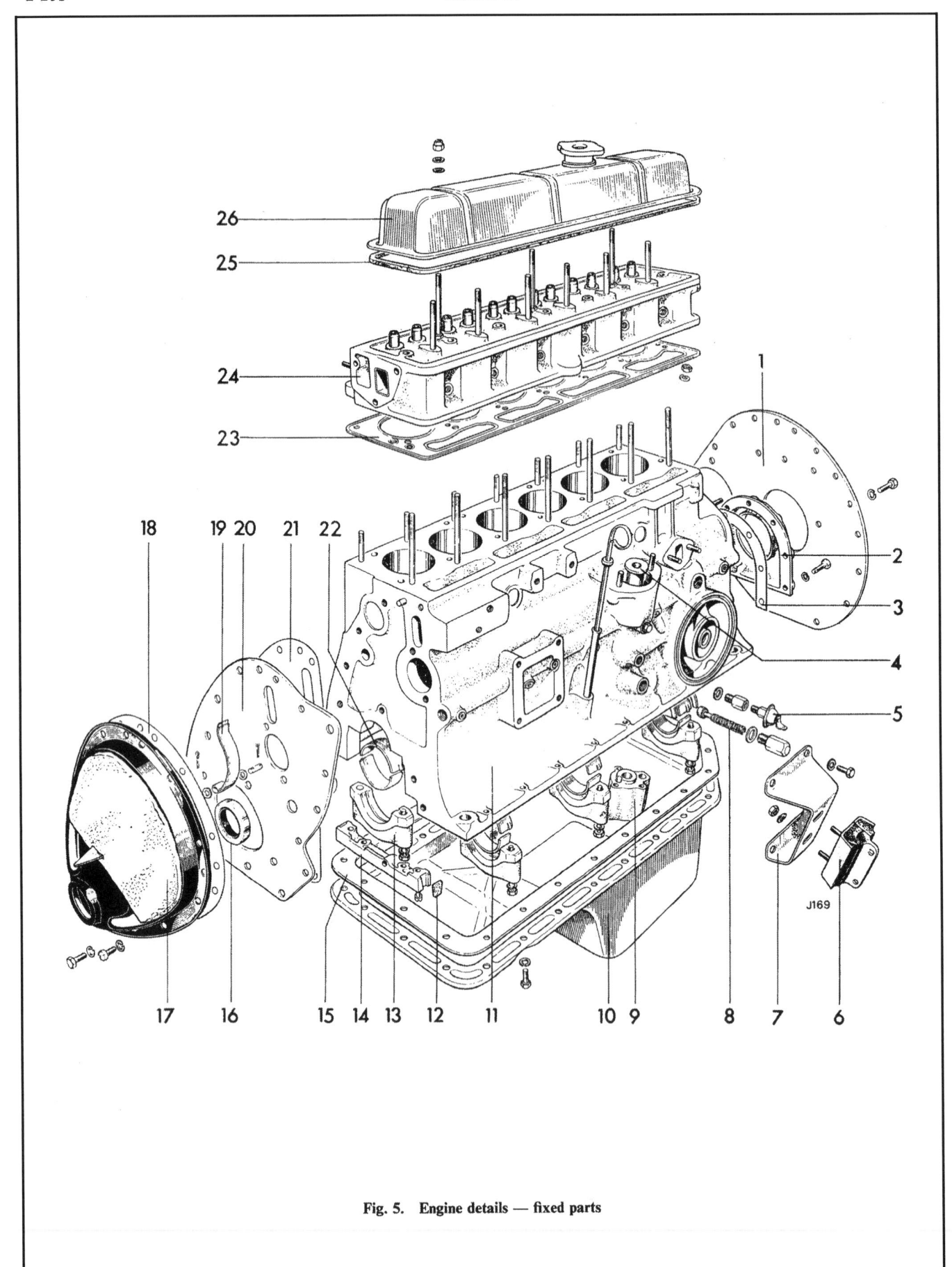

Fig. 5. Engine details — fixed parts

Key to Fig. 5

1 Back plate
2 Rear oil seal and housing
3 Rear oil seal housing gasket
4 Oil pump spindle bush
5 Oil switch
6 Engine mounting
7 Engine mounting bracket
8 Relief valve
9 Oil pump body
10 Sump
11 Cylinder block
12 Front sealing block wedge
13 Main bearing cap
14 Front sealing block
15 Sump gasket
16 Timing case oil seal
17 Timing case
18 Timing case gasket
19 Timing chain tensioner
20 Front plate
21 Front plate gasket
22 Main bearing shells
23 Cylinder head gasket
24 Cylinder head
25 Rocker cover gasket
26 Rocker cover

REMOVING ENGINE AND GEARBOX
(Refer to Figs. 6, 7, 8 and 10)

Drain cooling system.
Remove bonnet.
Remove battery.
Remove air intake manifold.
Remove radiator.
Remove tubular cross member.
Remove U clamps securing steering box to cross-member.
Draw steering box forward to clear crankshaft pulley.
Disconnect the following:
    Servo and ventilating hoses at manifold (1).
    Throttle cable at manifold (2).
    Return spring and wire at manifold and chassis (3).
    Cold start cables at manifold and metering pump (4).
    Heater cable at control valve (5).
    Heater hoses at engine.
    Electrical terminals at coil, temperature transmitter, starter motor, alternator and oil switch (6).
    Engine earth lead.
    Tachometer drive at distributor (7).
    Oil pressure pipe at crankcase (8).
    Excess fuel return pipe at metering unit (9).
    Fuel supply pipe at metering unit (10). (On a vehicle with a full, or nearly full fuel tank the disconnection of the fuel supply pipe at the metering unit will cause fuel to siphon from the tank. To avoid this the tank must be partially drained or the fuel pipe effectively sealed).
Remove inlet and exhaust manifolds.
Remove starter motor.
Remove driver's and passenger's seats.
Remove carpets from footwells and gearbox tunnel.
Remove console.
Remove bolts securing gearbox tunnel.
Disconnect reversing light and overdrive relay cables—if fitted.
Unscrew gear lever knob.
Remove gear lever boot.
Withdraw gearbox tunnel from passenger's side.
Disconnect propellor shaft at gearbox flange (11).
Disconnect exhaust bracket at gearbox mounting (12).
Disconnect clutch slave cylinder bracket from ball housing and remove clevis pin from actuating rod (13).
Slacken gearbox mounting and support bracket (14).
Disconnect speedometer cable at gearbox (15).
Remove gearbox cover (16).

Fig. 6. Right-hand view of engine in chassis

Fig. 7. Left-hand view of engine in chassis

Fig. 8. Left-hand view of gearbox in chassis

ENGINE 1·111

Attach sling to engine lifting eyes.

Take weight of engine on sling.

Remove the engine front mounting bracket adjacent to steering mast and remove the two securing bolts from its opposite counterpart.

Support weight of engine at gearbox.

Remove gearbox mounting and its support plate.

Lower gearbox.

Using lifting gear manoeuvre engine and gearbox clear of vehicle.

Install engine and gearbox by reversing the foregoing procedure.

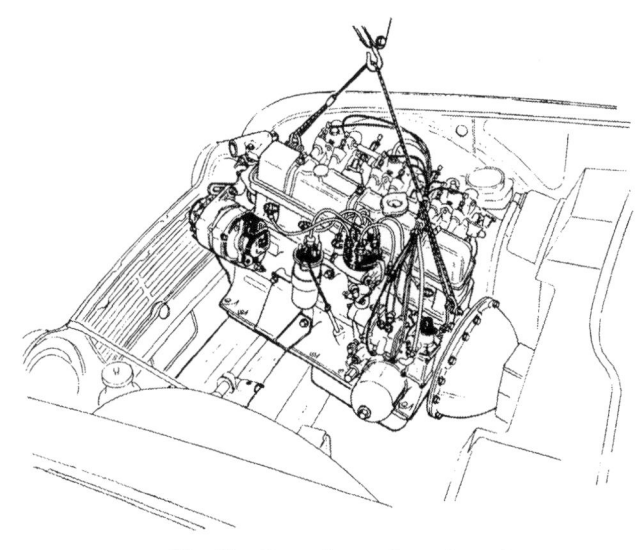

Fig. 10. Removing engine and gearbox

REPLACEMENT ENGINE UNITS

Before despatching an engine withdrawn from service remove the items listed below and seal all apertures. A typical replacement engine unit is shown in Fig. 11.

1. Gearbox and clutch.
2. Alternator and fan belt.
3. Water pump.
4. Fuel metering unit.
5. Distributor.
6. Coil.
7. Engine ventilating hose and filter.
8. Manifolds.
9. Oil filter.
10. Temperature transmitter.
11. Oil switch.
12. Engine mounting brackets.
13. Drain tap.
14. Radiator fan.
15. Engine lifting eyes.
16. Starter motor.

Fig. 11. Right-hand view of a replacement engine

1·110　　　　　　　　　　ENGINE

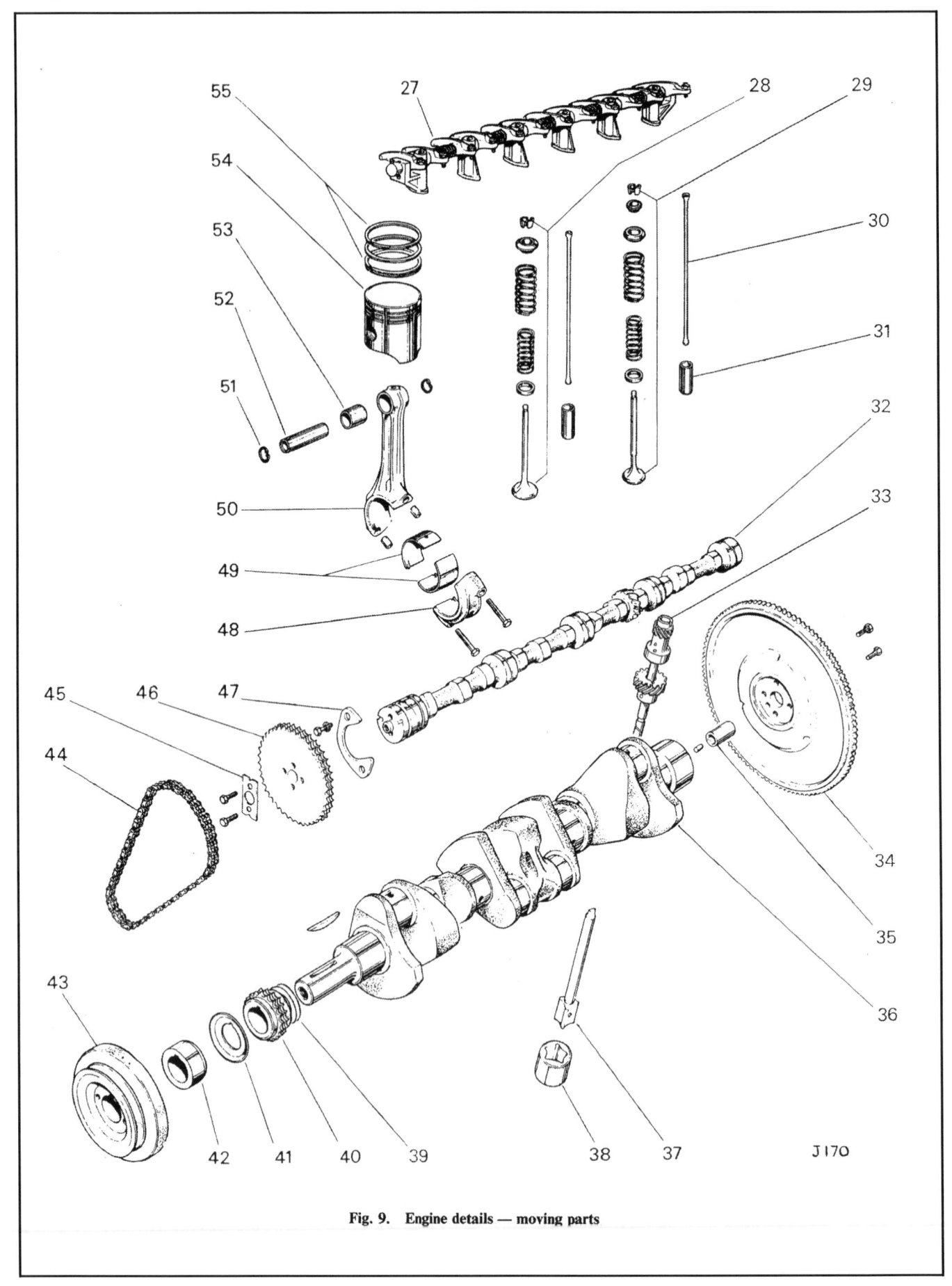

Fig. 9. Engine details — moving parts

Key to Fig. 9

27 Rocker gear assembly
28 Inlet guide assembly
29 Exhaust valve assembly
30 Push rod
31 Cam-follower
32 Camshaft
33 Distributor, fuel metering, and oil pump drive
34 Flywheel and starter ring gear
35 Bush (Crankshaft)
36 Crankshaft
37 Oil pump spindle and inner rotor
38 Outer rotor
39 Shims (Crankshaft sprocket)
40 Crankshaft sprocket
41 Oil thrower
42 Sleeve
43 Crankshaft pulley and damper assembly
44 Timing chain
45 Lockplate (Camshaft sprocket)
46 Camshaft sprocket
47 Keeper plate (Camshaft)
48 Connecting rod cap
49 Connecting rod bearings
50 Connecting rod
51 Circlip
52 Gudgeon pin
53 Bush (Connecting rod)
54 Piston
55 Piston rings

ENGINE DISMANTLING AND RECONDITIONING

Within the following pages will be found all information relevant to engine dismantling, reconditioning and engine assembly procedures. The information given, together with the tolerances which precede this section, relate principally to complete restoration and new engine build. Where partial or temporary repair work is undertaken discretion is left to the experience of the repairer to extract and modify this information to suit his individual requirements and circumstances.

An all too often neglected aspect of engine repair is cleanliness. Maximum engine life cannot be expected where repair work is carried out in an environment that is less than clean.

Fig. 12. Rocker shaft details

Dismantling the engine
Remove sump plug and drain off engine oil.
Remove all auxiliaries.
Remove engine mounting.

Crankshaft pulley
Remove radiator fan.
Remove bolt securing radiator fan mounting and crankshaft pulley.
Withdraw fan mounting and crankshaft pulley/damper assembly.

Flywheel and Backplate
Evenly slacken and withdraw clutch bolts.
Withdraw clutch assembly.
Remove the four bolts securing flywheel to crankshaft flange.
Withdraw flywheel.
Remove bolts securing backplate.
Remove backplate.

Cylinder head
Remove rocker cover nuts and lift off rocker cover.
Evenly slacken and remove rocker pedestal nuts.
Lift off rocker assembly.
Withdraw push rods.
Remove cylinder head nuts in reverse sequence to that shown in Fig. 35.
Lift off cylinder head and gasket.

Rocker gear (Refer Fig. 12)
Withdraw cotter pin at rear end of rocker shaft.
Slide rockers, springs and rear and intermediate pedestals from rocker shaft and place on bench in order of removal. (All components should be restored to their original locations).
Withdraw cotter pin at front end of rocker shaft.
Slacken off and remove the star headed screw securing front pedestal to rocker shaft.
Slide front pedestal and rocker clear of shaft.

Valves

Using a suitable valve spring compressor remove split collets.

Withdraw valve caps, inner and outer valve springs, and spring seats (Fig. 9).

Withdraw valves and place on bench in order of dismantling.

Do not intermix valves.

Timing cover, timing gears and engine front plate
(Refer Figs. 5 and 9)

Remove bolts and screws securing timing case to cylinder block.

Withdraw timing cover.

Withdraw sleeve and oil thrower disc from crankshaft.

Straighten lock tabs on camshaft sprocket bolts and remove bolts.

Ease camshaft sprocket clear of camshaft and detach timing chain from crankshaft sprocket.

Withdraw crankshaft sprocket and its attendant shims from crankshaft.

Remove camshaft keeper plate bolts and keeper plate.

Remove bolts securing front plate to cylinder block.

Withdraw engine front plate.

Camshaft

Lift out cam followers.

Remove distributor pedestal nuts and lift off pedestal.

Carefully withdraw camshaft taking care to avoid damaging cams and journal bearings.

Sump and oil pump

Lift out dipstick.

Remove sump securing bolts.

Withdraw sump.

Remove the three bolts securing oil pump to crankcase.

Withdraw oil pump.

Pistons and connecting rods

Remove bolts securing connecting rod caps.

Remove bearing caps and upper and lower shell bearing halves.

Withdraw connecting rods and pistons from top of cylinder block.

Restore bearings and caps to their respective connecting rods.
(When pistons are to be replaced, i.e. not renewed, they should be marked to ensure return to their original locations).

Remove circlips from pistons.

Press out gudgeon pins.

Separate connecting rods from pistons.

Fig. 13. Removing valves

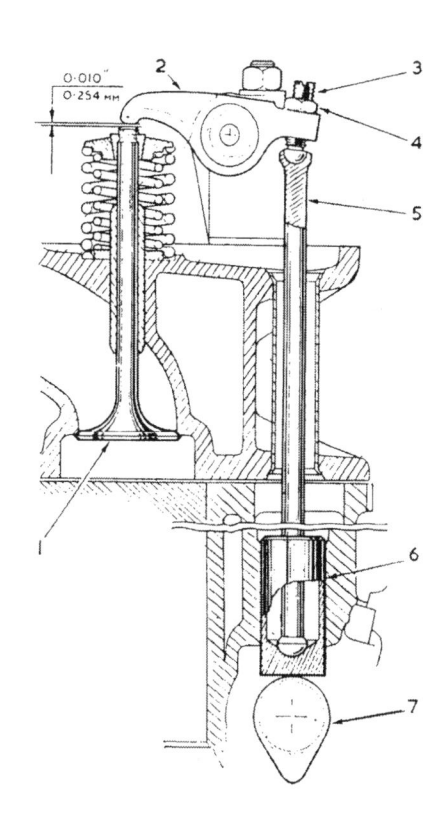

1 Valve	5 Push rod
2 Rocker	6 Cam follower
3 Adjuster	7 Camshaft
4 Locknut	

Fig. 14. Valve operating details

ENGINE

Fig. 15. Position of main bearing cap numbers

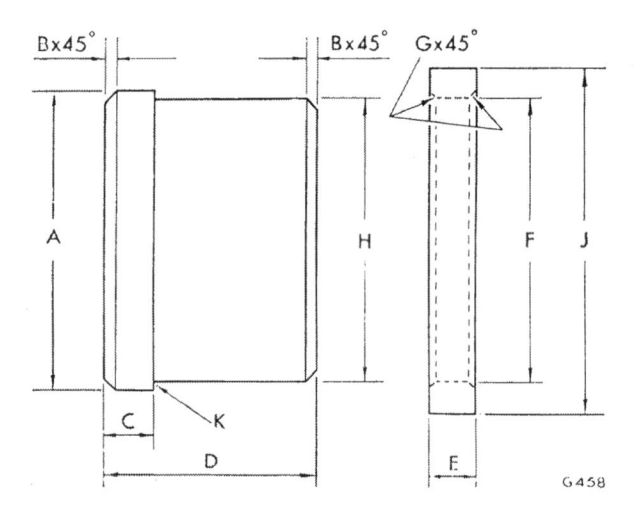

A. 3·0605″ (77·7367 mm)
   3·0615″ (77·7621 mm)

B. ⅛″ (3·175 mm)

C. ½″ (12·7 mm)

D. 2¼″ (57·15 mm)

E. ½″ (12·7 mm)

F. 2·921″ (74·1934 mm)
   2·922″ (74·2188 mm)

G. 1/16″ (1·588 mm)

H. 2·9195″ (74·1553 mm)
   2·9205″ (74·1807 mm)

J. 3½″ (88·9 mm)

K. Max. radius 0·010″ (0·254 mm)

NOTE: Remove all sharp edges.

Fig. 16. Mandrel and limiting ring for removing and installing liners

Crankshaft (Refer Figs. 9 and 15)
Remove bolts securing crankshaft rear oil seal housing to cylinder block.
Withdraw oil seal housing.
Withdraw crankcase front sealing block.
Remove crankshaft bearing bolts.
Withdraw bearing caps.
Slide out thrust bearings from rear bearing.
Lift out crankshaft.

Cylinder bores
Check cylinder bores for scoring and wear.

Cylinder liners
When cylinder bores, already oversize, become worn, cylinders may be restored to standard by boring out and fitting cylinder liners.

Fitting cylinder liners
A mandrel and limiting ring of the dimensions given in Fig. 16 are recommended.
Ensure bores are relieved of burrs.
Thoroughly clean cylinder bores and liners.
Smear bores and outside surface of liner with clean tallow.
Position cylinder block in press.
Enter liner in bore ensuring that it is at right angles to cylinder block face.
Fit mandrel (Fig. 16) into limiting ring and locate on cylinder liner.
Centralise cylinder liner and ram of press.
Ensure ram of press has sufficient travel to insert liner in one continuous movement.
Press cylinder liner into cylinder block until the mandrel makes contact with the limiting ring.
Bore out cylinder liner to required bore size.
Care must be taken to subsequently remove all abrasive dust.

Removing cylinder liners
Place cylinder block on bed of press. (Crankcase towards ram).
Ensure cylinder block is adequately supported and no obstruction is offered to fitted liner.
Insert mandrel (Fig. 16) into liner to be removed. The mandrel ring is not required for this operation.
Check that the ram has sufficient travel to remove the liner in one continuous sweep.
Centralise mandrel under ram.
Press out cylinder liner.

Crankshaft
Check crankshaft for scoring and wear.
Re-grind shaft as necessary.
Undersize bearing sizes are given on Page 1.103

ENGINE

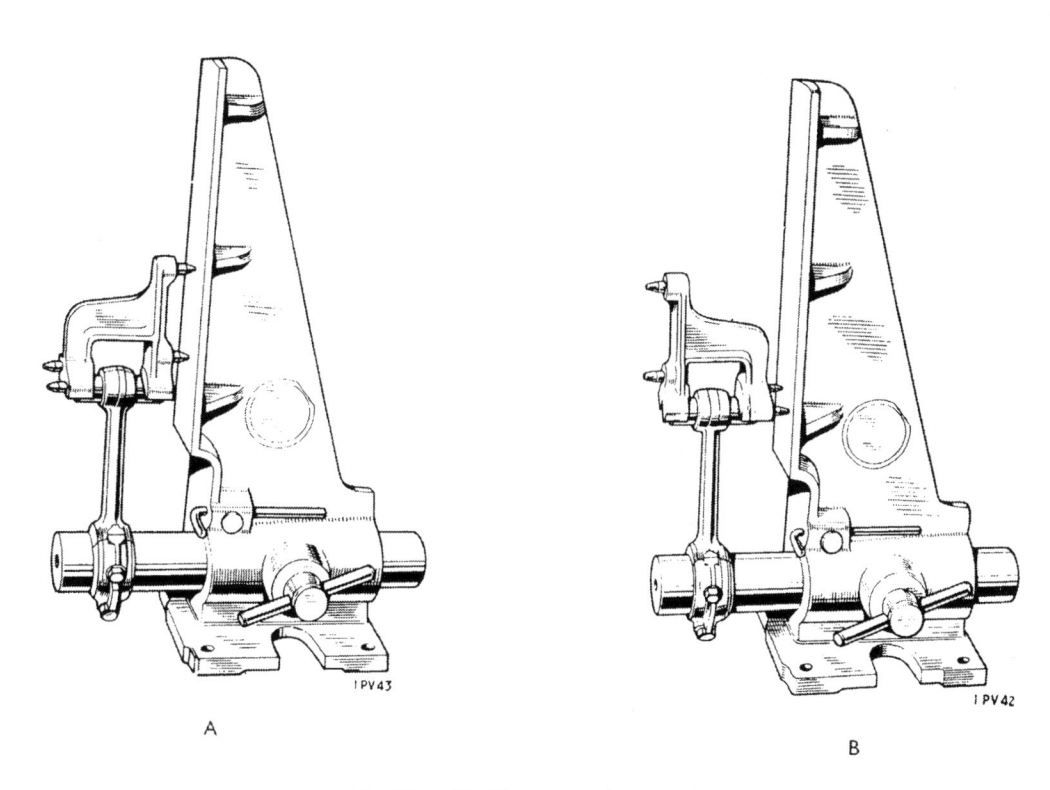

1·115

Fig. 17. Checking connecting rod alignment

Renewing gudgeon pin bushes

Using a suitable adaptor remove bush from connecting rod taking care that no stress is applied to the connecting rod.

Press new bush into position ensuring that the oil hole is properly aligned.

Fine bore or broach the new bush to the size determined by the gudgeon pin. (Refer Page 1·103).

A correctly fitted gudgeon pin (dry) will pass through the bush with a thumb push fit at 68°F. room temperature. If a dry gudgeon pin passes through a bush under its own weight it is too slack.

Connecting rod alignment (Refer Fig. 17)

Connecting rods should be checked both for alignment and twist. In either case a maximum tolerance of 0·0015 in. (0·0381 mm.) over gudgeon pin length should not be exceeded.

Rods found to exceed this tolerance should be corrected or renewed.

Connecting rod balance

The weight variation (lightest/heaviest) in any set of six rods should not exceed four drams (7·09 grams).

Pistons

Pistons and cylinder bores are graded according to their diameter and classified as grade 'F', 'G' or 'H'. The appropriate identification letter is stamped on the piston crown.

Piston balance

The maximum variation in weight existing in any set of six pistons should not exceed 4 drams (7·09 grams). Match pistons and connecting rods (lightest with heaviest) before assembly.

Piston ring gaps (Refer Fig. 18)

Insert each piston ring into the cylinder bore in which it is to operate.

Use a piston to locate the ring squarely in the bore. Measure the ring gap with feelers. Ring gap clearance should be as given on Page 1·102.

Fitting rings to pistons

Piston rings are assembled as follows:—
Bottom: Oil control ring.
Middle: Stepped compression ring (step to skirt).
Top: Plain compression ring.

Fit the oil control ring first. This ring is in three parts.

Take the spacer ring (corrugated member) and slide it over piston skirt into bottom piston ring groove. Ensure that ring ends butt.

Enter a plain, flat, scraper ring over piston skirt, and slide into position between lower corrugated face of spacer ring and piston groove.

ENGINE

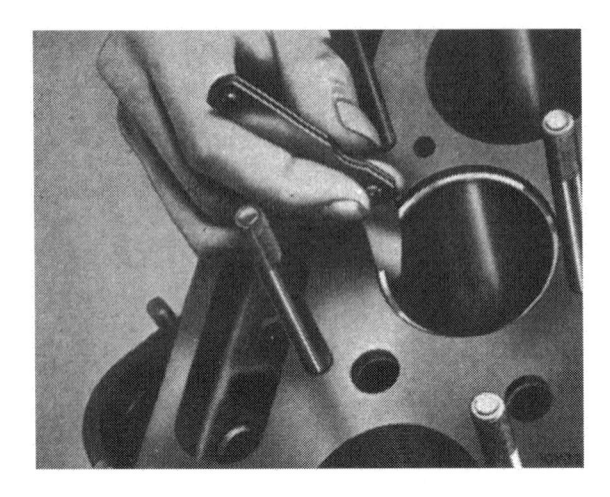

Fig. 18. Checking piston ring gaps

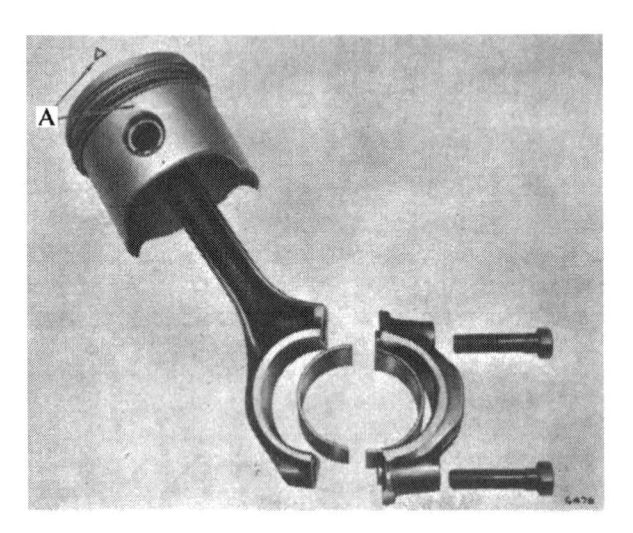

Fig. 19. Piston and connecting rod assembly

Fig. 20. Checking flywheel run-out

Enter remaining plain, flat scraper ring over piston crown and slide into position between upper face of corrugated spacer and piston groove.

Take the stepped compression ring and with the plain diameter uppermost slide gently and evenly into middle piston ring groove.

Employ a circular, gentle movement to ease ring past top groove, or alternatively use three thin, equally spaced strips of tin or plastic.

Slide the plain compression ring over piston crown into position in top groove.

Ensure compression rings are free to rotate.

Stagger all ring gaps before fitting piston to cylinder.

Fitting connecting rods to pistons

Lubricate connecting rod bush.

Offer up connecting rod to piston (the arrow on the piston crown must be fitted pointing to the timing cover, and the connecting rod bearing caps adjacent to camshaft.

Press gudgeon pin through connecting rod bush and centralise in piston between circlip grooves.

Fit circlips ensuring they are properly seated in grooves.

Flywheel (Refer Fig. 20)

A scored flywheel clutch face will necessitate refacing by skimming in a lathe, or alternatively renewing the flywheel.

When skimming is carried out the following tolerances should be observed:—

Run-out at 5 in. (127 mm.) radius
    0·003 in. (0·0762 mm.)
Balance .. .. .. within 1 dram

Renewing flywheel ring gear

Support flywheel (clutch face uppermost) on hardwood blocks, evenly distributed, ensuring that no obstruction is caused to ring gear.

Evenly drive ring gear from flywheel in small movements.

Reverse flywheel on hardwood blocks.

Thoroughly clean flywheel periphery and new starter ring gear.

Expand the ring gear by evenly heating. Uneven heat distribution may create ring distortion.

Remove ring gear from heat source and with chamfered edge of ring teeth adjacent to clutch face place ring on flywheel.

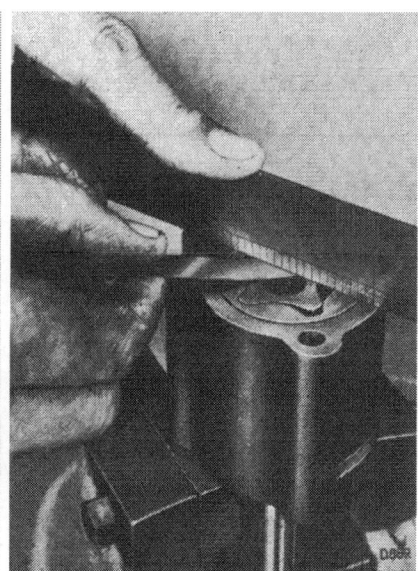

Fig. 21. Checking clearance between inner and outer rotors

Fig. 22. Checking clearance between outer rotor and body

Fig. 23. Checking rotor end clearance

Oil pump (Refer Figs. 21, 22 and 23)

With the oil pump assembled, minus the top cover, and with all components clean and dry check rotor clearances. (Refer to Page 1·104).

Renew worn or unserviceable items as necessary.

Oil pump drive shaft bush (Refer Fig. 5)

Insert the oil pump drive shaft and rotor (37) (Fig. 9), into bush (4) (Fig. 5) and rock the shaft to assess the amount of bearing wear. This bush is readily removed using a stepped drift. Withdraw the bush via the distributor pedestal flange.

Enter new bush from pedestal flange and drive carefully into position.

Timing cover oil seal and chain tensioner

Press out oil seal taking care not to damage timing case.

Evenly insert new seal into timing case ensuring that seal lip is fitted towards the inside of the timing case.

If a new chain tensioner is required remove the spring blades by prising them apart and sliding them out of their retaining pin and bracket.

Fit new spring blades in reverse manner ensuring the convex curvature of the blades is adjacent to chain.

Rear oil seal

Evenly drive out oil seal from housing using a drift through the two holes provided for this purpose.

Thoroughly clean housing and seal recess.

Insert new seal squarely into position in housing ensuring that seal lip is fitted towards cylinder block.

Rocker shaft

Renew rocker shaft if worn or scored. Ensure all oil passages are clear.

Rockers

Renew rockers if bores or tips are worn. Rocker tips are chill-hardened to a depth of 0·060 in. (1·524 mm.) grinding to restore worn profiles is not recommended.

Rocker pedestals will not normally require attention.

Rocker Adjusters

Renew adjusters if ball ends are worn or if the screwdriver slot or threads are damaged.

Renew adjuster nuts if corners are worn or threads strained.

Valve guides

Check valve guide wear by raising the valve from its seat and moving it diametrically in its guide (Fig. 24). If movement of the valve head across the seat exceeds 0·020 in. (0·508 mm.) valve guide renewal is recommended.

When conducting this check a new valve should be employed.

New valve guides can be fitted using tool No. 60A.

Valve guides should project 0·63 in. (16 mm.) above the cylinder head.

ENGINE

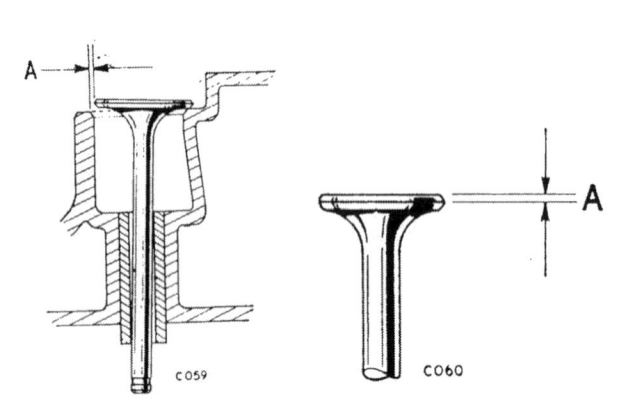

Fig. 24. Assessing valve guide wear

Fig. 25. Valve head thickness

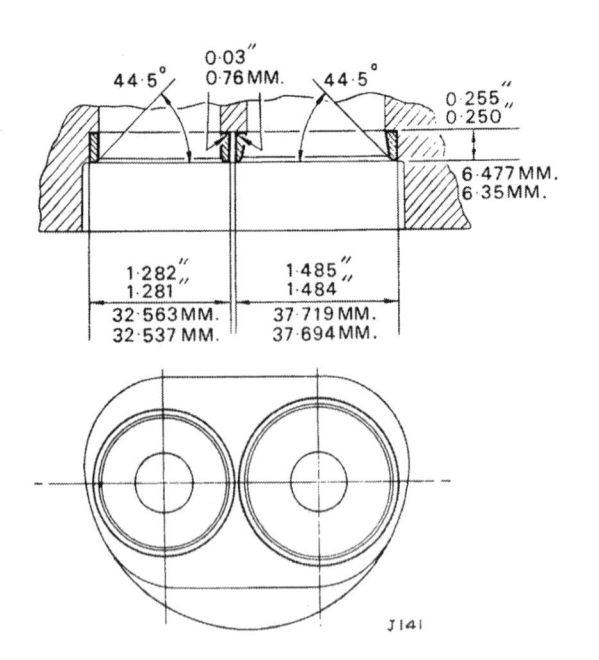

Fig. 26. Valve insert dimensions

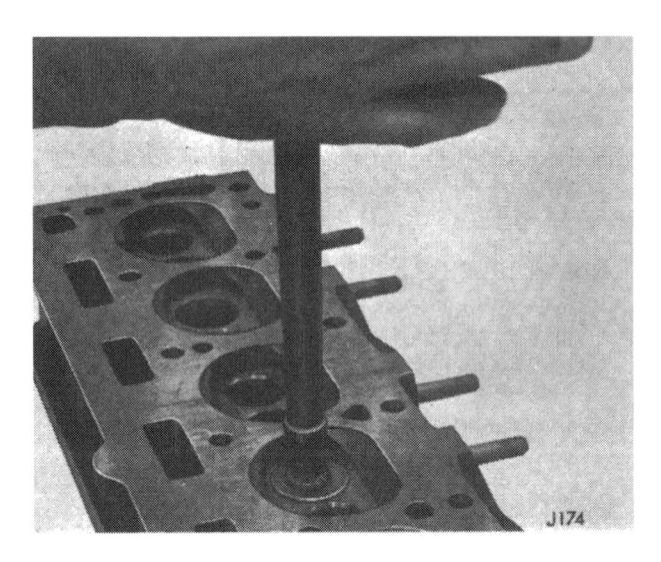

Fig. 27. Grinding-in valves

Valves (Refer Fig. 25)

Check valve faces for wear and damage.

Renew or reface as necessary. A valve should be renewed if, after refacing, its head thickness is reduced below $\frac{1}{32}''$ (0·8 mm.).

Valve seats

Check valve seats for scores, wear and pitting. Reface seats as necessary using conventional reconditioning equipment. Remove only the minimum metal possible to achieve a gas-tight seal.

If a 15° cutter is used to reduce seat width and rectify pocketing the machined diameter **must not** exceed 1·4285″ (36·21) inlet, 1·255″ (31·13 mm.) exhaust. Failure to observe this instruction may render the cylinder head incapable of reclamation.

Valve Seat inserts

When valve seats cannot be restored by refacing, new seat inserts may be fitted.

Cylinder head valve seat pocket dimensions are given in Fig. 25.

Remove all swarf and press the insert squarely into cylinder head.

Secure seats by careful peening.

Cut valve seat faces at an inclusive angle of 89°.

Grinding-in valves (Refer Fig. 27)

Following valve and seat refacing, grind-in the valves to their respective positions. This may be carried out in conventional manner.

Ensure all traces of swarf and grinding paste are removed before commencing assembly.

Valve springs

Check valve springs for cracks, distortion, and free and load lengths. This information is included on Page 1·105.

When defects are found, a complete new set is advised.

Cam-followers

Check cam-followers for chips, scores and wear. Renew as necessary.

Ensure cam-followers are free to slide and rotate in their respective locations before commencing assembly.

ENGINE

ASSEMBLING THE ENGINE

Thoroughly clean cylinder block and engine components and ensure that oilways are clear. Tighten all bolts and nuts to the recommended torque figures given in Group 0.

Crankshaft

Fit main bearing shells to cylinder block and main bearing caps, ensuring bearing caps are properly seated.

Lubricate bearings and crankshaft journals.

Position crankshaft in cylinder block.

Fit thrust bearings to rear main bearing ensuring that thrust faces are adjacent to crankshaft.

Fit main bearing caps and evenly tighten.

Crankshaft end float (Refer Fig. 29)

Check crankshaft end float (Fig. 29), reference Page 1·103.

Front sealing block (Refer Fig. 30)

Smear the ends of the sealing block with jointing compound.

Fit the sealing block and engage its two retaining screws.

Smear the packing pieces with jointing compound and insert them in the slots provided in the sealing block (Fig. 30).

Align faces of sealing block with front of engine and crankcase.

Tighten sealing block retaining screws.

Trim packing pieces flush with crankcase. Do not undercut.

Engine front plate (Refer Fig. 5)

Fit gasket (21) ensuring it properly engages studs and dowels.

Offer up engine front plate (20) to cylinder block.

Retain front plate in position with a single bolt fitted above the crankshaft.

Fig. 28. Inserting crankshaft thrust washers

Fig. 29. Checking crankshaft end float

Fig. 30. Fitting wedges to front sealing block

ENGINE

Fig. 31. Checking camshaft end-float

Fig. 32. Rear oil seal assembly

Fig. 33. Fitting pistons and connecting rods

Camshaft
Lubricate camshaft journals.
Carefully thread camshaft into position in cylinder block.
Fit camshaft keeper plate (Fig. 31).
Check camshaft end float. (Refer Page 1·103).
Excessive end float may be reduced by fitting a new keeper plate.

Crankshaft rear oil seal and housing (Refer Fig. 32)
Lubricate crankshaft flange and oil seal lip.
Using centralising tool No. S.335 carefully insert tool through oil seal.
Offer up tool and housing to crankshaft.
Secure housing in position with its retaining bolts (Fig. 32).
Withdraw centralising tool.

Backplate
Fit backplate and secure in position with its retaining bolts.

Flywheel
Offer up flywheel to crankshaft flanges ensuring that the dowel is properly engaged.
Fit and tighten flywheel bolts.
Using a dial indicator check flywheel run-out (Fig. 20).
If a new flywheel is fitted, mark as follows:—

Marking a new flywheel
The marking of a new flywheel may be carried out at any stage following the fitting of pistons and before replacing the cylinder head.
Using a dial indicator set numbers 1 and 6 pistons at T.D.C.
Scribe a line across flywheel periphery to align with marking on backplate
With a small chisel deepen scribed line.
Using metal types stamp the digits 1 and 6 separated by the marking on the flywheel.

Fitting pistons and connecting rods to engine
Rotate crankshaft until crankpins 1 and 6 are at B.D.C.
Smear cylinder bores and pistons with clean engine oil.
Remove big end bearing cap.
Stagger piston ring gaps.
Fit piston ring compressor tool over piston.
Insert connecting rod and piston into cylinder bore, ensuring that arrow on piston crown points towards front of engine and the connecting rod bearing is adjacent to camshaft.
Gently press piston into bore.
Remove ring tool.
Lubricate crankpin and connecting rod bearings.
Fit shells to connecting rod and cap.
Draw connecting rod through bore and crankshaft webs until bearing is in contact with crankpin.
Fit connecting rod bearing cap.
Tighten connecting rod bearing cap to recommended torque.
Repeat above procedure for remaining pistons.

Oil pump

Lubricate oil pump spindle bush in crankcase.

Lubricate oil pump rotors.

Assemble pump cover to body ensuring bolt holes and inlet passage align.

Insert pump into position in crankcase and fit and tighten securing bolts.

Sump

Fit gasket and sump to crankcase and secure with retaining bolts (do not overtighten).

Relief valve

Insert relief valve into crankcase.

Fit washer to relief valve cap.

Engage spring in cap and relief valve spindle.

Screw cap into crankcase and tighten.

Filter

Fit filter body sealing ring to crankcase.

Insert new filter element into filter body.

Offer up filter body to crankcase and secure with its single fixing bolt, ensuring body rim makes proper contact with sealing ring. Do not overtighten.

Rocker gear (Refer Fig. 12)

Enter front pedestal, rocker and double spring washer on rocker shaft.

Align locating holes in both pedestal and shaft.

Secure pedestal to shaft with star headed screw.

Fit cotter pin to front end of shaft.

Slide rockers, springs and intermediate pedestals on to shaft.

Fit rear pedestal, rocker and double spring washer.

Fit cotter pin to rear end of shaft.

Cylinder head

Thoroughly clean head and all components.

Lubricate valve stems and guides.

Enter valve in guide.

Place inner valve spring seat over guide.

Place inner and outer valve springs in position ensuring that the closed spring coils are fitted adjacent to the cylinder head.

Place valve cap in position (inlet valves) or upper spring seat and valve cap (exhaust valves) (Fig. 9).

Using a valve spring compressor, fit the split collets.

Release spring compressor and check that collets and valve cap are properly seated.

Repeat above procedure for remaining valves.

Fit cam followers ensuring they are free to slide and rotate in their individual locations.

Smear cylinder head gasket with clean grease and place over cylinder head studs.

Fig. 34. The oil pump

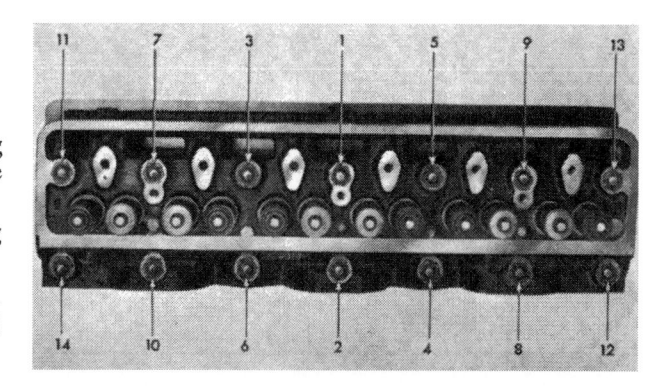

Fig. 35. Cylinder head nut tightening sequence

ENGINE

Fig. 36. Locating rockers in push rods

Fig. 37. Checking sprocket alignment

Fig. 38. Using feeler gauges of equal thickness to determine point of balance

Lower cylinder head into position on cylinder block.

Fit cylinder head washers and nuts and evenly tighten in sequence shown in Fig. 35.

Engage push rods in cam followers (cupped end to rocker).

Fit rocker shaft assembly to cylinder head ensuring that the ball end of each adjuster properly engages its respective push rod cap (Fig. 36).

Enter washers and nuts on rocker pedestal studs.

Evenly tighten rocker assembly in position ensuring that rocker adjusters remain located in push rods.

Sprocket alignment

Fit camshaft sprocket.

Fit crankshaft sprocket.

Place a straight-edge across sprockets (Fig. 37) and check alignment.

Remove crankshaft sprocket, fit shims to crankshaft as necessary and replace sprocket.

Valve timing

Rotate flywheel until T.D.C. mark is approximately 45° before its corresponding mark on engine backplate. This ensures that all pistons are below their T.D.C. positions and eliminates the possibility of valves striking piston crowns when valve clearances are being adjusted.

Set valve clearances of cylinders 1 - 5 to 0·010 in. (0·254 mm.) rotating camshaft in direction of rotation as necessary (clockwise when viewed from timing case).

Set valve clearances of No. 6 cylinder to 0·040 in. (1·016 mm.).

Rotate flywheel to T.D.C. position.

Rotate camshaft until the exhaust valve (No. 12) of number 6 cylinder is almost closed and the inlet valve (No. 11) is about to open. Check this position using feeler gauges of identical thickness (Fig. 38).

Remove camshaft sprocket — if fitted.

Encircle both sprockets with the timing chain and offer up camshaft sprocket to camshaft.

The positions of the camshaft and crankshaft must not be disturbed during this operation.

The four fixing holes in the camshaft sprocket are equally pitched but are offset from a tooth centre. This, together with its ability to be mounted either face out, enables a precise setting to be obtained.

The above procedure enables the fitting of unmarked sprockets to be carried out. It will be found that marked sprockets will align when the camshaft and crankshaft are located as described.

Ensure camshaft lock plates are fitted, tighten bolts, and bend over lock plates.

Adjust valves of No. 6 cylinder to normal clearance.

ENGINE

1·123

Timing case

Check that oil thrower is correctly fitted on crankshaft (angled periphery towards timing case).

Locate gasket in position on engine front plate.

Offer up timing case to engine (Fig. 39) and secure with retaining bolts and screws.

Smear crankshaft spacer and lip of timing case oil seal with clean lubricant.

Engage spacer on crankshaft (tapered edge leading) and gently press through timing case.

Fit crankshaft pulley, radiator fan boss and tighten the single securing bolt.

Fig. 39. Fitting timing case

Replacing distributor drive gear and pedestal

Rotate engine until the 11° B.T.D.C. mark on crankshaft pulley aligns with pointer with No. 1 cylinder on compression.

Engage blades of screwdriver with slot in oil pump drive spindle and rotate to position shown in Fig. 40.

Insert distributor drive gear and shaft so that with the camshaft gears meshed and the tongue on the shaft end engaged in the oil pump spindle the offset drive dog for the distributor is positioned laterally in relation to the engine centre line and the larger half of the dog is rearwards as shown in Fig. 41.

It is important to ensure that the drive gear and shaft are properly seated, i.e. that the oil pump spindle dogs are engaged. When the drive gear and shaft are properly in position the upper face of the gear is approximately level with the pedestal flange on the cylinder block.

Fit gasket to pedestal flange.

Lower pedestal into position ensuring, when properly located, that the slot in the metering pump driving spindle is vertical

Fig. 40. Position of driving dogs in oil pump spindle when fitting distributor gear

Renewing distributor drive gear and/or spindle (Refer Fig. 42).

Following renewal of the distributor drive gear and/or spindle it is important to ensure that end float exists between the distributor drive gear (the gear engaging the camshaft) and the base of the distributor pedestal. The required clearance is 0·003 — 0·007 in. (0·0762—0·1778 mm.) and is obtained by inserting a gasket or gaskets of appropriate thickness below the mounting flange of the distributor pedestal.

Fig. 41. Position of driving dogs on distributor gear when fitting distributor

ENGINE

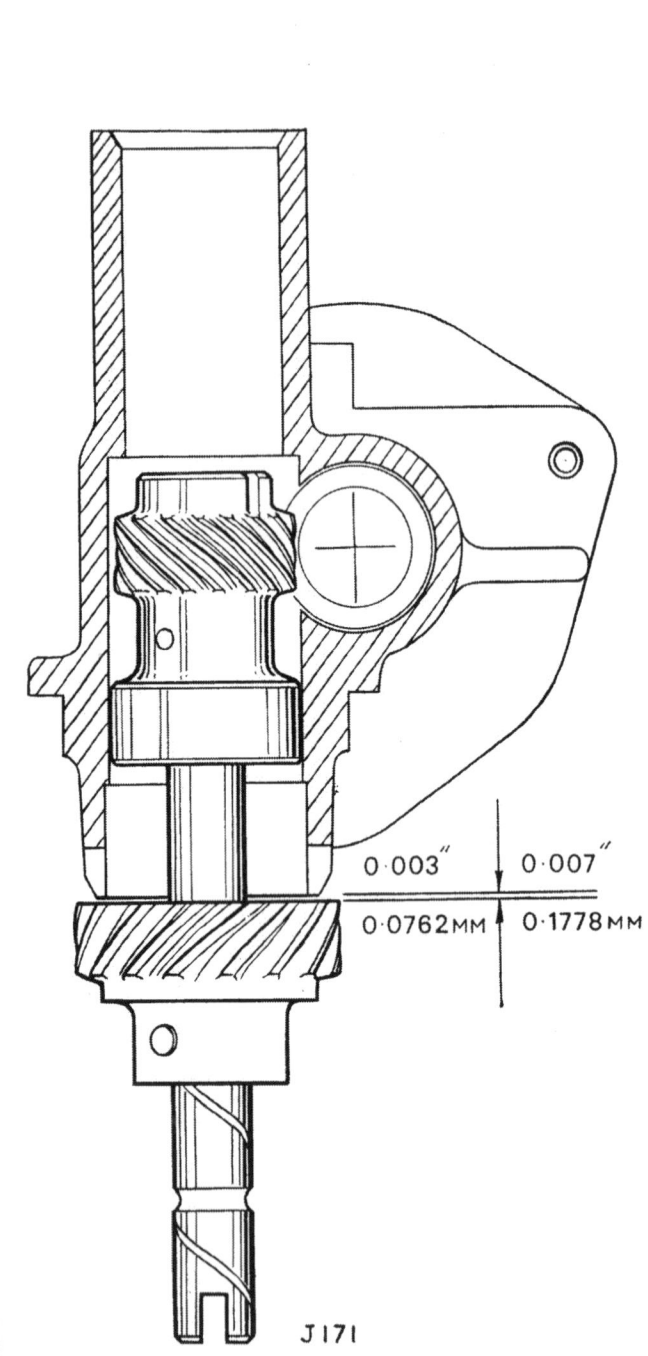

Fig. 42. Distributor drive gear clearance

Fig. 43. Setting the distributor

Timing the ignition

Rotate engine until the 11° B.T.D.C. mark on the crankshaft pulley aligns with pointer when No. 1 cylinder is on compression stroke.

Ensure distributor contacts are clean and are set to ·015 in.

Offer up distributor to engine, turning rotor to engage driving dogs.

Secure distributor clamp bracket to pedestal.

With clamp bracket pinch bolt slackened off, turn distributor body to the approximate position shown in Fig. 43.

Rotate distributor body in clockwise direction, i.e. against the direction of rotor rotation until the distribution points are seen to just break.

(A lamp and battery may be used to more accurately determine the moment of point separation).

The rotor arm will now be opposite the segment in the distributor cap to which No. 1 HT lead is connected.

Gently nip clamp bracket pinch bolt. This bolt must never be tightened or distortion of the clamp bracket will result.

Fit distributor cap and connect up coil lead to distributor.

Connect HT leads to their respective sparking plugs.

To suit individual engine characteristics vernier adjustment is provided. Fine adjustment to the ignition setting may be made during road test or when the engine is connected to electronic tuning equipment.

ENGINE 1·125

SERVICE OPERATIONS WITH ENGINE IN PLACE

Fig. 44. Left-hand view of engine in chassis

Removing cylinder head (Refer Figs. 44, 45 and 5).

Isolate the battery.

Drain cooling system.

Release servo hose at induction manifold, and breather pipe at air intake manifold.

Remove air intake manifold.

Disconnect the following:—

HT leads at sparking plugs.

Fuel lines at injectors.

Water hoses at thermostat housing and water pump.

Heater hoses at engine.

Exhaust pipes at manifold flange.

Throttle linkage at manifold.

Cold start control cable and spring at manifold.

Heater cable at temperature control valve.

Metering pump vacuum hose at manifold.

Slacken alternator pivot bolts.

Remove the following:—

Alternator adjusting link.

Water pump securing bolts.

Fig. 45. Right-hand view of engine in chassis

Rocker cover.

Rocker gear.

Push rods.

Inlet and exhaust manifolds.

Cylinder head nuts.

Lift off cylinder head.

Replace in reverse order.

Removing timing case. (Refer Figs. 46 and 5)

Isolate battery.

Drain cooling system.

Remove radiator.

Remove tubular cross member.

Remove U bolts clamping steering box to chassis.

Move steering box forward clear of crankshaft pulley.

Slacken alternator and remove fan belt.

Remove radiator fan.

Remove the single bolt securing fan extension and crankshaft pulley.

Withdraw extension and crankshaft pulley.

Remove bolts and screws securing timing case.

Withdraw timing case.

ENGINE

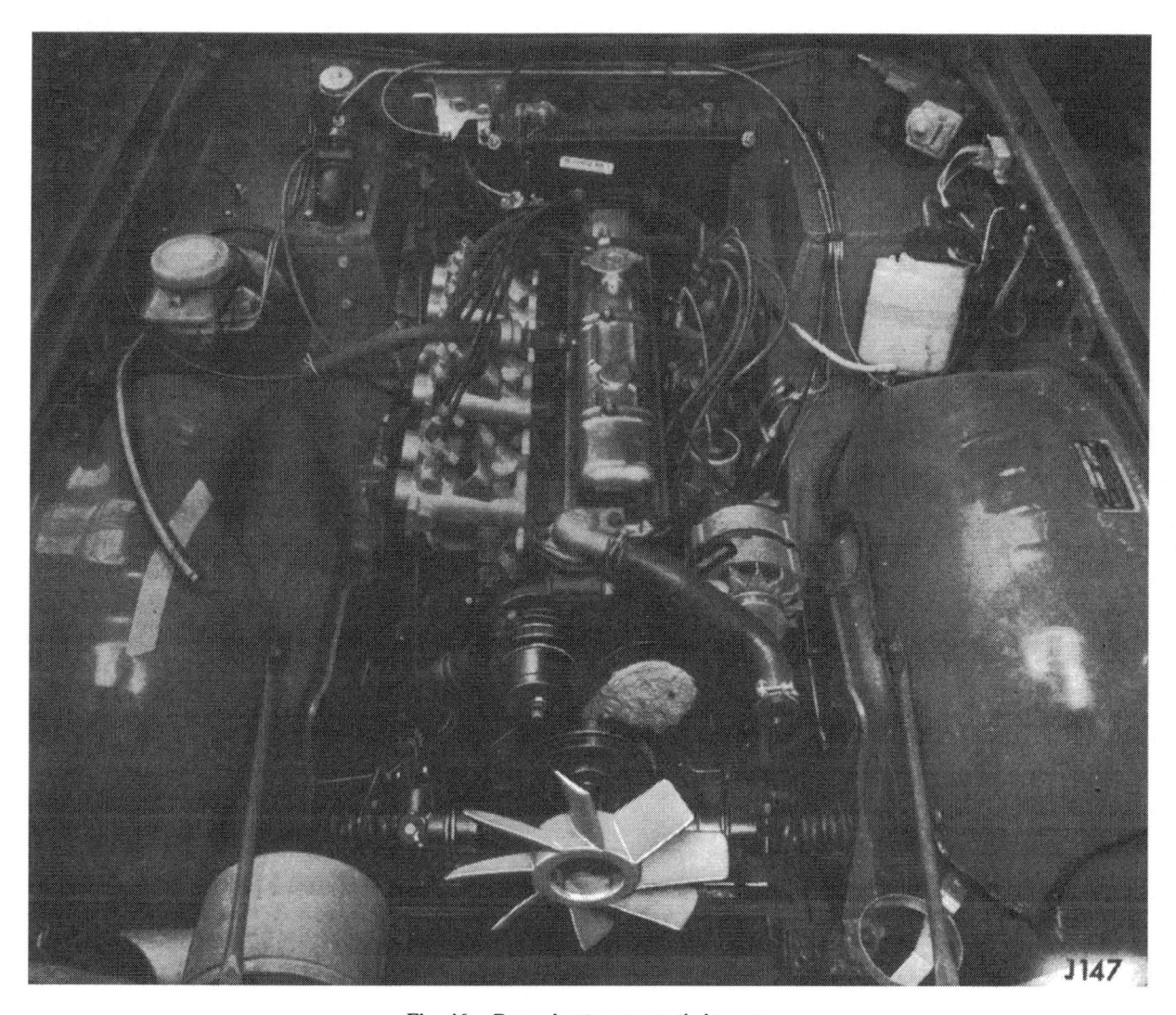

Fig. 46. Preparing to remove timing case

Removing timing chain

Bring 1 and 6 pistons to T.D.C.

Straighten lock tabs in camshaft sprocket bolts.

Remove camshaft sprocket bolts.

Withdraw camshaft sprocket and ease chain clear of crankshaft.

Assemble in reverse order ensuring timing marks are aligned.

To reset timing with unmarked sprockets refer Page 1·122.

Before refitting timing case withdraw spacer from crankshaft.

Replace timing case as described in Page 1·123.

Removing Camshaft

Isolate battery.

Remove grill.

Disconnect metering pump from distributor pedestal

Remove distributor.

Remove distributor pedestal.

Remove distributor driving gear.

Remove cylinder head (Page 1·125).

Withdraw cam followers.

Remove timing case and gears (Pages 1·126 and 1·113).

Remove camshaft thrust plate.

Withdraw camshaft.

Assemble in reverse order resetting valve, fuel and ignition timing (Pages 1·122 – 1·124).

Removing sump (Refer Figs. 47 and 48)

Isolate battery.

Remove sump plug and drain off oil.

Withdraw dipstick.

Remove sump securing bolts.

Withdraw sump.

Replace in reverse order.

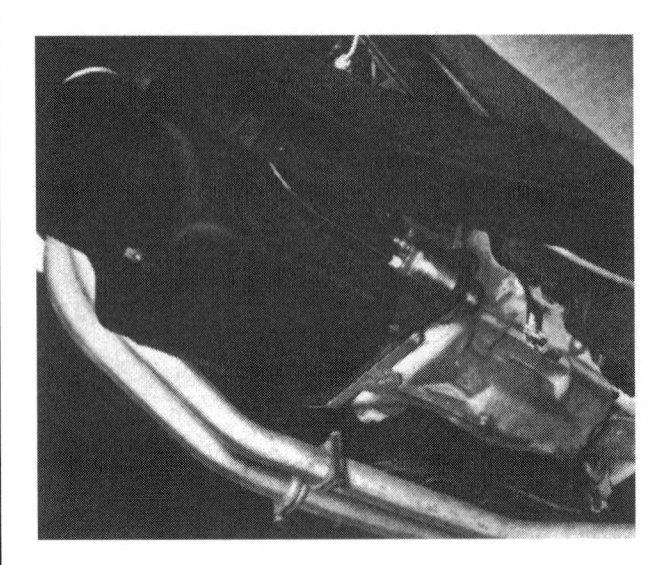

Fig. 47. View of engine sump

Fig. 48. View of engine with sump removed

Removing oil pump, crankshaft and connecting rod bearings

Isolate battery.
Remove sump.

Oil pump

Remove the three bolts securing oil pump to crankcase.
Withdraw oil pump.
Replace in reverse order.

Main bearing shells

Remove lowest bolt in timing cover.
Remove the two screws securing front sealing block.
Remove front sealing block.
Remove main bearing caps.
Slide upper bearing shells out of crankcase (tab end of shell leading).
Slide new upper shells into crankcase (tab end trailing).
Ensure tab ends are properly seated in crankcase.
Renew shells in bearing caps and replace and tighten caps.
Crankshaft thrust bearings may be removed and replaced by removing the rear bearing cap only.
Thoroughly clean front sealing block and crankcase before refitting sealing block as described on Page 1·119.
CAUTION: Do not permit crankshaft to remain unsupported by the main bearing caps for longer than is necessary as compression of the crankshaft oil seal lips may cause subsequent leakage.

Connecting rod bearings

Rotate crankshaft until required connecting rod is at B.D.C.

Remove bearing cap bolts and cap.
Remove shells.
When renewing or replacing shells ensure bearing tabs are properly seated.
Assemble in reverse order.

Connecting rods and pistons

Drain cooling system and engine sump.
Remove cylinder head (Page 1·112).
Remove sump (Page 1·127).
Remove connecting rod bearing caps and shells (do not intermix).
Push pistons and connecting rods through bores in direction of cylinder head.
Refit pistons as described on Page 1·120.
When new pistons and/or piston rings are fitted to worn bores the ridge at the top of bores should be removed. When this operation is performed it is advised that the bores are sealed above the crankshaft or vacuum equipment is used to trap swarf.
Thoroughly clean engine before commencing assembly.
Replace cylinder head and sump in reverse order.

Removing timing case

Isolate battery.
Drain cooling system.
Remove radiator.
Slacken alternator.
Remove fan belt.
Remove the single bolt securing fan boss and crankshaft pulley.
Withdraw fan boss and crankshaft pulley.
Remove bolts and screws securing timing case.
Withdraw timing case.

COOLING SYSTEM

WATER PUMP

To remove (Fig. 1)

Drain the cooling system. Disconnect the two hoses from the water pump.

Detach the Lucar connector from the temperature transmitter (5).

Remove the bolt (28) securing the water pump body and alternator bracket to the engine block.

Remove the fan belt and, supporting the water pump, take out bolts 26 and 27 and lift the assembly clear of the vehicle.

To dismantle

1. Remove three nuts from the studs (10) and withdraw the bearing housing assembly from the pump body.
2. Unscrew the nut (19) remove the washer (20) and extract the pulley (21).
3. Take out the circlip (22) and press the shaft (14) through the impeller (9) towards the pulley side of the bearing housing (13).
4. Remove the following items from the spindle: key (24), bearings (18), spacer (17), washer (16), circlip (23), and spinner (15).
5. Complete the dismantling by removing the sealing gland (11) from the impeller (9).

To re-assemble

1. Fit spinner (15), circlip (23) and washer (16) to the shaft (14). Pack the ballraces (18) with grease (see Recommended Lubricants, Group 0) and press them on to the shaft with the sealed faces outwards and the spacer (17) between them. Fit circlip (22).
2. Using a 0·030″ (0·762 mm.) spacer, press the impeller onto the shaft until the spacer is nipped.
4. Remove the spacer and fit the Woodruff key (24) and pulley (21) to the shaft (14), securing with a Nyloc nut (19) and plain washer (20).
5. Refit the bearing assembly to the pump body (8) using a new gasket (12).

To refit

Reverse the removal procedure, adjust the fan belt tension and refill the cooling system.

KEY TO FIG. 1

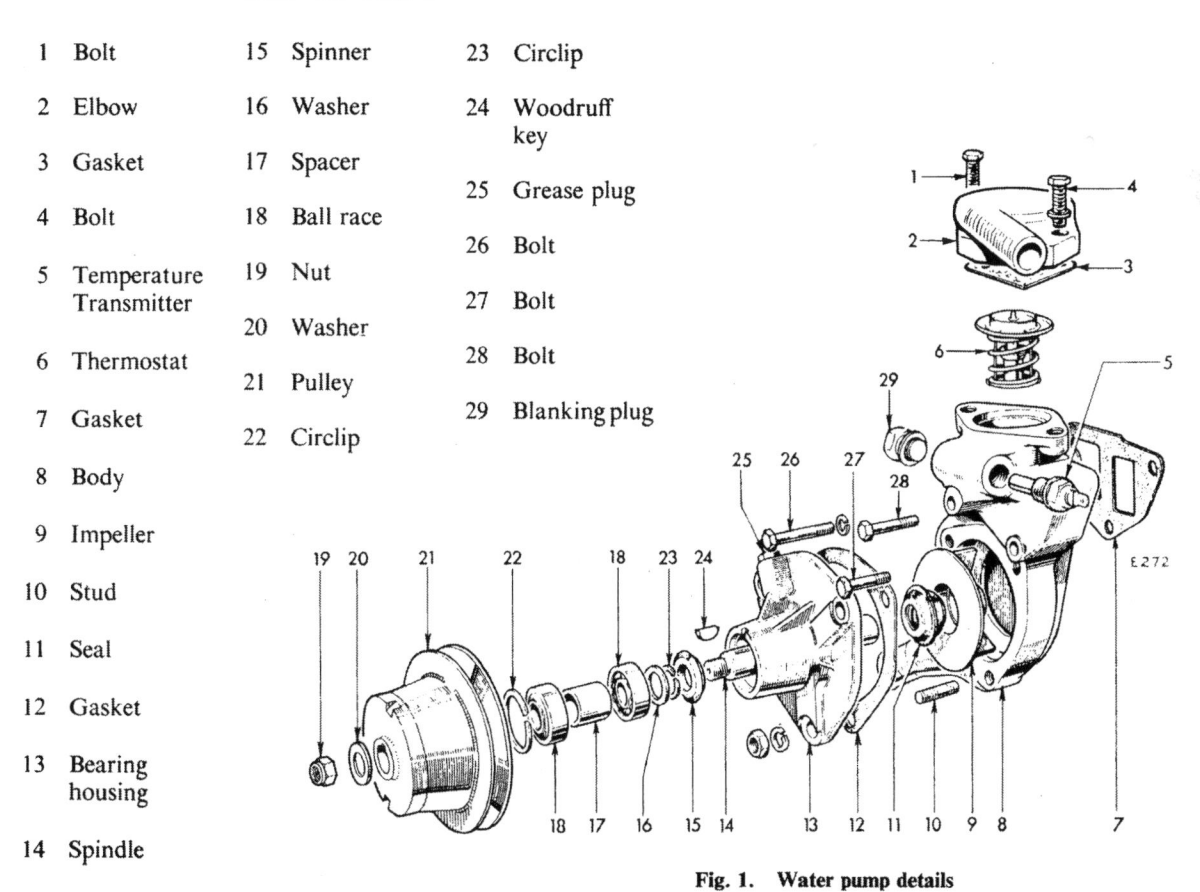

#	Part	#	Part	#	Part
1	Bolt	15	Spinner	23	Circlip
2	Elbow	16	Washer	24	Woodruff key
3	Gasket	17	Spacer	25	Grease plug
4	Bolt	18	Ball race	26	Bolt
5	Temperature Transmitter	19	Nut	27	Bolt
		20	Washer	28	Bolt
6	Thermostat	21	Pulley	29	Blanking plug
7	Gasket	22	Circlip		
8	Body				
9	Impeller				
10	Stud				
11	Seal				
12	Gasket				
13	Bearing housing				
14	Spindle				

Fig. 1. Water pump details

COOLING SYSTEM

THERMOSTAT

Thermostat (Fig. 1)

A wax type thermostat (6) is incorporated in the water pump body (8). To gain access to the thermostat unscrew the bolts (1 and 4), remove the water elbow (2), gasket (3) and lift the thermostat from its housing.

Thermostat opening temperature: Summer condition 82°C. Winter condition 88°C.

RADIATOR

To remove

Drain the cooling system. Referring to Fig. 2, unclip the two side valance panels (2 and 13) from the radiator. Disconnect two hoses (3 and 8) and overflow pipe (9). Undo the four mounting bolts (15 and 16) and nuts (12 and 17) releasing the two securing straps (11) in the process. Lift the radiator from the vehicle.

To refit

Reverse the foregoing procedure and refill the system.

KEY TO FIG. 2

1	Wire clip	10	Rubber washer
2	Side valance sheet	11	Securing strap
3	Top hose	12	Nut
4	Overflow bottle	13	Side valance sheet
5	Setscrew	14	Clip
6	Bracket	15	Bolt
7	Drain tap	16	Bolt
8	Bottom hose	17	Nut
9	Overflow pipe	18	Connecting pipe
		19	Inlet hose

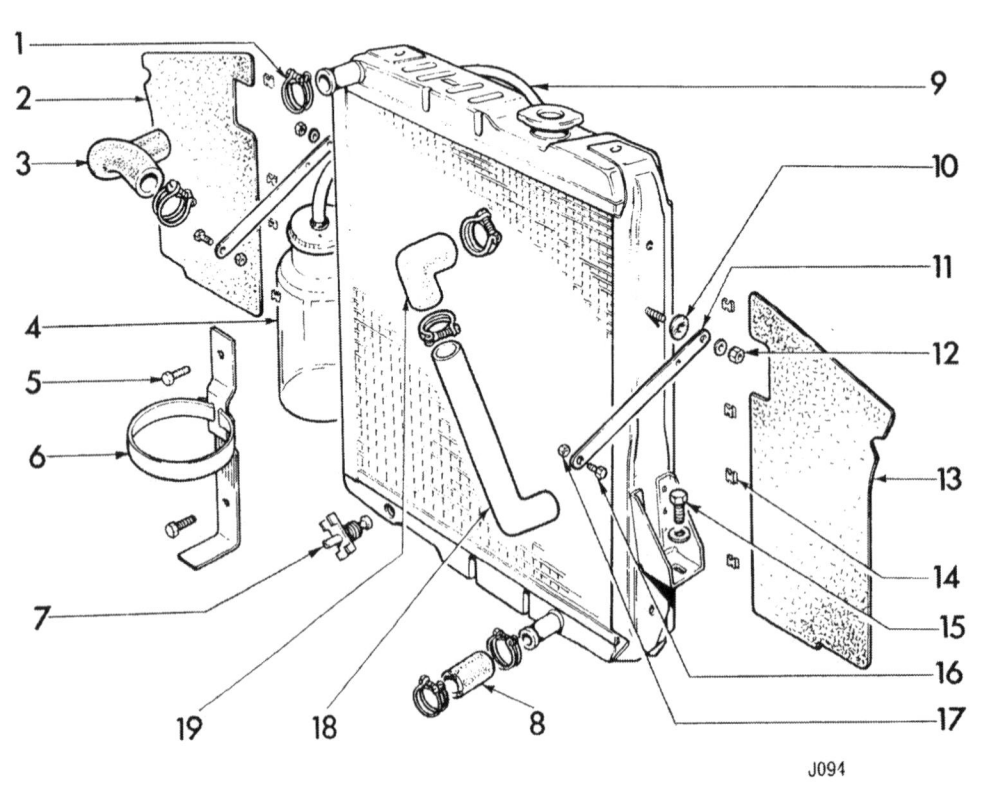

Fig. 2. Radiator details

FUEL SYSTEM

1·301

PETROL INJECTION

Introduction

On the TR5 a Lucas Mk. II petrol injection system replaces carburettors. This system delivers a fine spray of precisely timed and measured fuel to the air intakes via injectors. The mixture is then compressed and spark ignited in the usual manner.

This section of the Workshop Manual seeks to describe the principles of operation as well as the relevant maintenance, overhaul, adjustments and fault finding procedures that can be associated with petrol injection.

It is envisaged that faults such as excess fuel consumption, poor performance, erratic running, etc., will be attributed to the fuel injection system, whereas they are more likely to emanate from other systems of the vehicle. It is, therefore, important to establish the correct functioning of the ignition, electrical, cooling and other systems and that sufficient clean fuel is available.

DESCRIPTION OF P.I. CIRCUIT

Using the schematic illustration (Fig. 1) for reference, a brief description of the system is as follows.

Fuel, gravity fed from the tank to a paper element fuel filter (1), is drawn to an electrically driven gear pump (2) which delivers pressurised fuel to a metering distributor (5). The metering unit measures, subject to engine requirements, and delivers a charge of fuel to each of six injectors at the start of their induction stroke. The injectors, positioned in the induction manifolds, contain a poppet valve which is set to open at 50 p.s.i. and allow the charge of fuel, in the form of a 60° hollow cone spray into the air intake stream.

The metering unit is lubricated by fuel which is then returned to the tank via a leak-off pipe (4).

A pressure relief valve (3) maintains a line pressure of 106 – 110 p.s.i. and allows the return of excess fuel to the filter.

Air trapped in the filter is evacuated from an outlet on top of the filter. The filter unit, being gravity fed, carries a reservoir of fuel that acts as an anti surge device and prevents loss of fuel to the pump on sharp turns, steep hills and sudden stops.

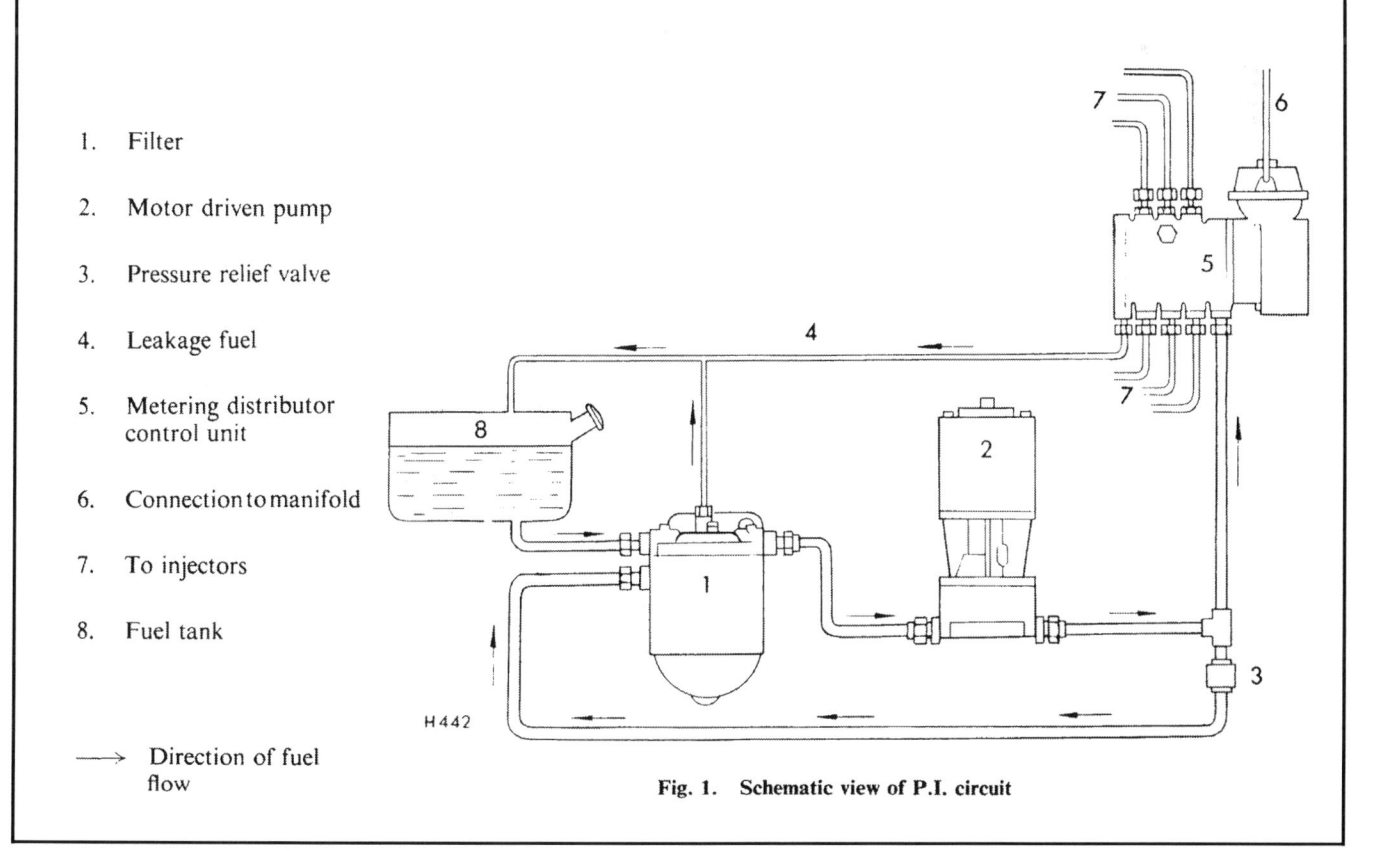

1. Filter
2. Motor driven pump
3. Pressure relief valve
4. Leakage fuel
5. Metering distributor control unit
6. Connection to manifold
7. To injectors
8. Fuel tank

→ Direction of fuel flow

Fig. 1. Schematic view of P.I. circuit

FUEL SYSTEM

DESCRIPTION OF COMPONENTS

Fuel Filter (Fig. 2)

The fuel filter is situated in the luggage compartment and is gravity fed from the fuel tank. The filter comprises a top assembly, with inlet and outlet connections, a bottom bowl and a metal encased paper element. A central bolt locates and clamps the element between 'O' rings sited in the upper and lower casings.

Fuel pump (Fig. 2)

The fuel pump is located at the forward end of the luggage compartment on the left-hand side behind the trim panel.

The unit consists of a composite permanent magnet field motor driving a gear pump.

Full details of the pump and motor are contained in Group 6.

Pressure relief valve (Fig. 3)

The P.R.V. is mounted to the chassis to the rear of the rear axle.

The assembly comprises a simple adjustable spring-loaded relief valve screwed into a brass 'T' piece, a nylon gauze strainer is incorporated into the assembly.

1. Outlet pipe
2. T Junction
3. Valve and strainer holder
4. Pressure relief valve
5. Return to filter pipe
6. Inlet pipe

Fig. 3. Pressure relief valve assembly

1. Pump leak off
2. Inline electrical connectors
3. Pump outlet
4. Pump inlet
5. Filter outlet
6. Filter inlet (from tank)
7. Filter leak off
8. Filter inlet (from P.R.V.)
9. Tank outlet

Fig. 2. Fuel pump and filter

FUEL SYSTEM

Metering distributor assembly

The metering distributor is mounted adjacent to, and driven by, the ignition distributor driving gear.

For ease of description the assembly is dealt with in two parts, namely, the control unit and the metering unit.

Metering unit

Description

A gear drive from the ignition distributor pedestal turns a rotor which has two radial ports to a central bore containing a shuttle which is able to move axially between a fixed and an adjustable stop. The rotor is contained within a sleeve with six outlet and six inlet ports arranged in spaced pairs 60° apart, inlet and outlet alternating. The sleeve is sealed in a cast body having an internal recess which forms a reservoir for pressurised fuel. Sealed outlet valves connect the sleeve to external body connections for the injector pipes.

Operation (Fig. 4A)

When the engine is started and the rotor turns within the sleeve, the rotor port at the control stop end becomes coincident with the port in the sleeve leading to the fuel reservoir in the body casting. Fuel at high pressure enters the rotor bore and drives the shuttle to the right (i.e., towards the fixed stop end of the rotor). This movement of the shuttle displaces fuel in the rotor bore through the ports in the rotor and sleeve to the injector serving No. 1 cylinder.

A further 120° rotation of the rotor (Fig. 4B) causes the rotor ports at the fixed stop end to align with the sleeve port leading to the fuel reservoir. Fuel now enters at the fixed stop end of the rotor and drives the shuttle back towards the control stop end. An identical quantity of fuel is displaced, by the shuttle as it moves to the left, by way of the outlets in the rotor and sleeve to No. 5 injector.

In this way the shuttle continually moves between the two stops displacing an accurate amount of fuel to each cylinder in turn.

The quantity of fuel delivered at each injection is dependant upon the distance the shuttle travels, this distance is adjusted by the control stop.

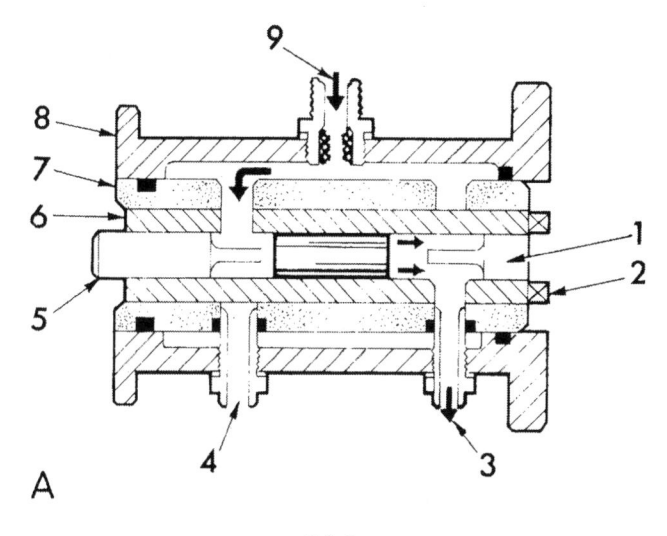

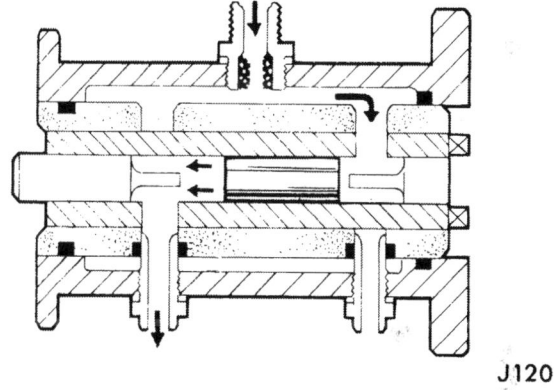

1. Fixed stop
2. Rotor drive
3. Outlet to No. 1 injector
4. Outlet to No. 2 injector
5. Adjustable control stop
6. Rotor
7. Sleeve
8. Body
9. Fuel inlet from pump

Fig. 4. The principle of shuttle metering showing how the shuttle is moved when the rotor is turned

FUEL SYSTEM

Control unit

Description

The control unit is attached to the metering unit by four nuts. A follower (15), with a diaphragm seal set in an annular groove around its periphery, projects through the leading face of the unit. The rear end of the follower bears against the outer two of three rollers (13) carried on the control links (12), whilst the third roller, of smaller diameter, runs against the fuel cam (11).

The control links are pivoted at the top where they are attached to the centre of a spring-controlled rubber diaphragm, the lower part of the control links are free.

Two springs (3) are positioned between the diaphragm and three concentric calibration screws (4). The top of the diaphragm and the calibration screws are in a chamber connected by a pipe to the manifold.

The fuel cam (11) is secured by two screws to a carrier (8) which is in contact with an external control screw (14). The carrier is pivoted at point X, the pivot being extended through the rear face of the metering unit. The excess fuel lever (5) is pivoted at the rear face of the unit and has a cam face at the lower end which contacts the cam carrier pivot.

Operation

Engine fuel demands, according to throttle openings and load, are reflected in changes in inlet manifold depression. The change is sensed by the spring-loaded diaphragm, which takes up a position balancing the loading of the springs (3) against the depression in the chamber.

The control links are thus raised or lowered along the cam track allowing the follower to move further in or out of the forward face of the unit and so regulate the metering unit control stop.

To prevent the full hydraulic force of the control stop from impinging on the control linkage, a balancing spring (2) is fitted on the follower which results in only light pressure between the follower and the rollers.

The control springs at the rear of the diaphragm are chosen to suit the engine requirements. They are adjusted, during calibration, by the manufacturer and the adjustment MUST NOT BE DISTURBED (see note, page 1·310).

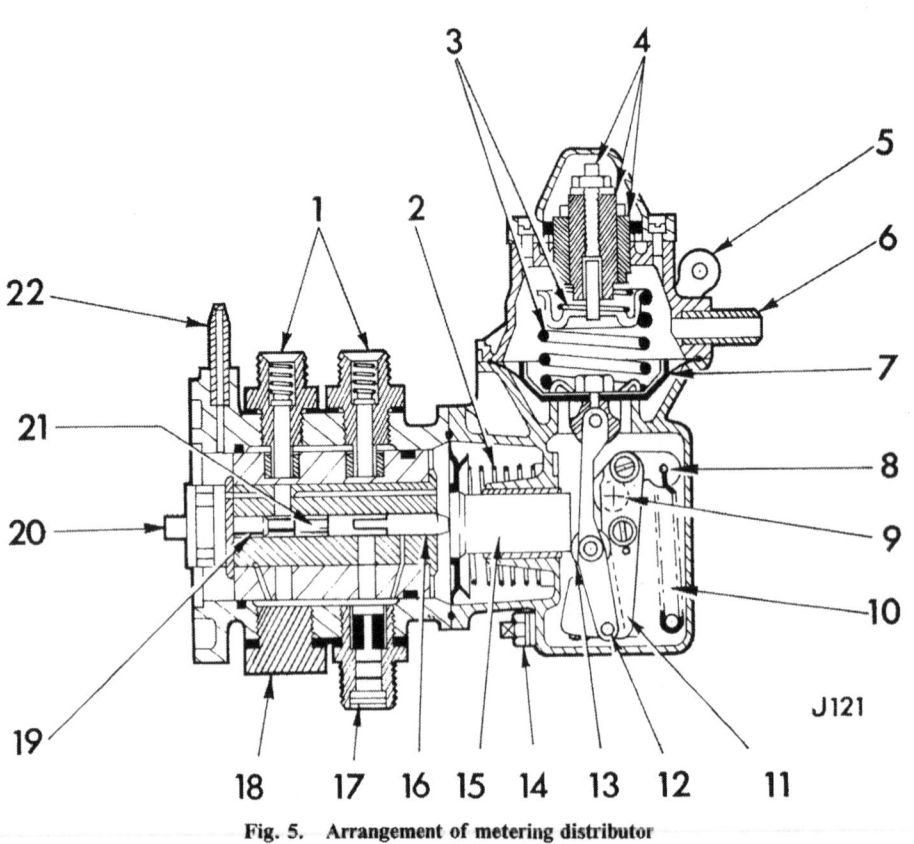

Key to Fig. 5

1. Outlet valves
2. Balance spring
3. Calibration springs
4. Calibration screws
5. Excess fuel lever
6. Connection to manifold
7. Diaphragm
8. Fuel cam carrier
9. Pivot 'X'
10. Return spring
11. Fuel cam
12. Control links
13. Rollers
14. Full load setting screw
15. Follower
16. Control stop
17. Fuel inlet
18. Blanking plug
19. Fixed stop
20. Rotor drive
21. Shuttle
22. Leakage fuel

Fig. 5. Arrangement of metering distributor

FUEL SYSTEM

The fuel cam (11) is secured to the carrier by two screws (C Fig. 18) the holes in the cam are slotted to enable the correct fuel control slope to be set. An external adjusting screw, acting on the fuel cam carrier, determines full load setting. The above adjustments MUST NOT BE DISTURBED (see note, page 1·310).

Movement of the excess fuel lever is transmitted to the fuel cam and carrier which are pivoted at point 'X'. When the lever is turned, the fuel cam and carrier are moved against the tension of the return spring, allowing the rollers, follower and control stop to take up a position providing up to 300% extra fuel.

Injectors

The injectors are fitted into the inlet manifolds and upon their performance depends the correct atomisation of the fuel. A poppet valve in the injector is set to open at approximately 50 p.s.i. and give a 60° hollow cone spray.

SERVICE PRECAUTIONS

In addition to normal service precautions, the following are peculiar to petrol injection engines.

(a) Before subjecting a vehicle to a lengthy overhaul or a prolonged period of idleness, a petrol inhibitor should be added to the fuel and the engine run to ensure complete circulation throughout the system. The gummy residue, from evaporated petrol, is thus prevented from seizing the shuttle and other close-tolerance parts in the system.

(b) The fuel pump must not be switched on whilst any part of the pressurised circuit is disturbed.

(c) The fuel pump must not remain switched on for lengthy periods whilst the engine is stationary. If the ignition circuit is required to be switched on without running the engine for lengthy periods, disconnect the electrical connections to the pump.

(d) Do not re-use sealing rings, always use new ones.

(e) Subsequent to an overhaul it will take some time to re-prime the fuel system, therefore, crank with full choke until the engine starts. Do not attempt to re-prime with a battery in a low state of charge.

1. Retaining bolt
2. Retaining plate
3. Injector
4. Injector pipe union

Fig. 6. Injector in position

Piping and unions

Because of the comparative high pressures used on the fuel system it is imperative that all union connections are securely tightened and that the piping is regularly inspected for fretting, kinking and leaks.

The rubber tubing used on the leak-off return pipe must be carefully replaced to prevent kinking and ensure that the steel pipe does not bite into the rubber and so block the pipe.

The leak-off pipe will, if blocked, cause a pressure build up in the metering unit which will prevent full recuperation of the follower and consequently allow excess fuel to be delivered, resulting in sooting up of the plugs combined with uneven running.

FUEL SYSTEM

MAINTENANCE

Routine maintenance is restricted to renewing the fuel filter element every 12,000 miles as follows:

Remove the spare wheel, place a shallow container beneath the filter. To prevent fuel draining from the tank use a hose clamp, or plug the filter inlet pipes.

Unscrew the centre retaining bolt and remove the element and lower casing (Fig. 7).

Remove the sealing rings in the upper and lower casings (2 and 4) and the bolt sealing washer (1).

Fit a new element, sealing rings and washer, ensuring that the seals are correctly seated and making leak-proof joints.

NOTE: Ensure that the filter element is marked "for petrol" as a diesel fuel filter will break down with the action of petrol on the adhesives used.

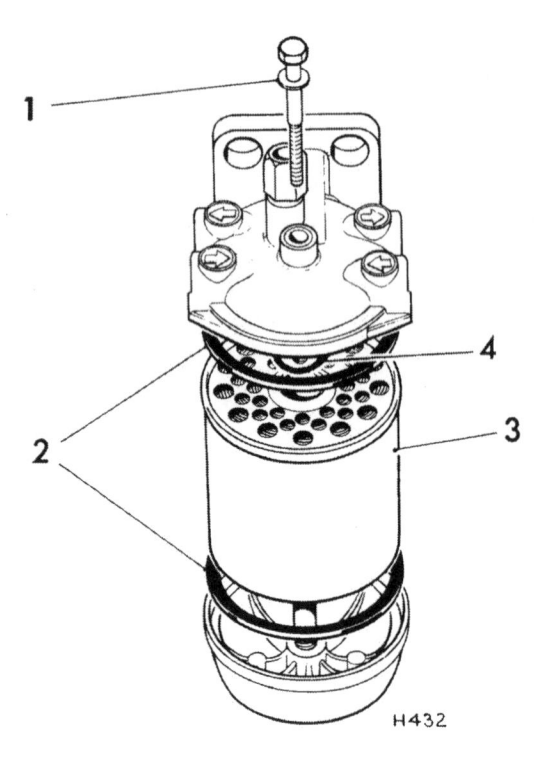

1. Sealing washer
2. Casing seals
3. Element
4. 'O' ring

Fig. 7. Fuel filter-replacement parts

SETTING THE THROTTLE OPENINGS

1. Remove the air intake manifold.

2. Ensure that the cold start knob is fully in, slacken the cam adjusting screw (1) (Fig. 8) until it is clear of the cam.

3. Slacken the accelerator cable adjustment (2).

4. Slacken the slow running screws (3) right back.

5. Slacken the five locknuts (4) on the accelerator adjusting rods (two each on the outer rods and one on the centre rod).

6. Turn the accelerator cross-shaft until it is hard against the backstop.

7. With a screwdriver, adjust the centre rod until the centre pair of butterflies are horizontal to the air flow, i.e., fully open (Fig. 9). Tighten the locknut and allow the cross-shaft to return to the closed position.

8. Adjust the centre control screw (Fig. 10) to give 0·002" (0·05 mm.) clearance at the top and bottom of the butterflies.

9. Adjust the outer control screws to give 0·002" clearance on the outer butterflies.

1. Cold start screw
2. Cable adjuster
3. Slow running screw
4. Adjusting rod locknuts

Fig. 8. Throttle adjustments slackened

FUEL SYSTEM

1·307

10. Tighten the locknuts on the outer control rods.

11. Check the clearance on the butterflies.

12. Take the free play out of the accelerator cable ensuring that the butterfly clearance is not increased.

13. Adjust the cold start cable until the point of the cam is adjacent to the adjusting screw.

14. Start the engine and when normal running temperature is reached adjust the slow running screws to give an idling speed of 750 r.p.m. This can best be achieved with the use of a balancing meter using the centre pair of butterflies as the datum pair and balancing the outers to match.

15. With the engine idling and warm, pull the cold start cable fully open.

    NOTE: This must be done with the cable as pulling the control knob will also increase the fuel quantity.

16. With the cam turned to its fully opened position, turn the adjusting screw (Fig. 11) until the engine speed reaches 2,000 r.p.m.

17. Release the cable and tighten the locknut

18. Adjust the excess fuel lever cable on the metering nut to give full travel on the lever.

    NOTE: The first movement of the cold start knob must take up free play on the lever.

19. Replace air intake manifold.

Fig. 10. Adjusting clearance of butterflies

Fig. 9. Adjusting centre butterflies to fully open position

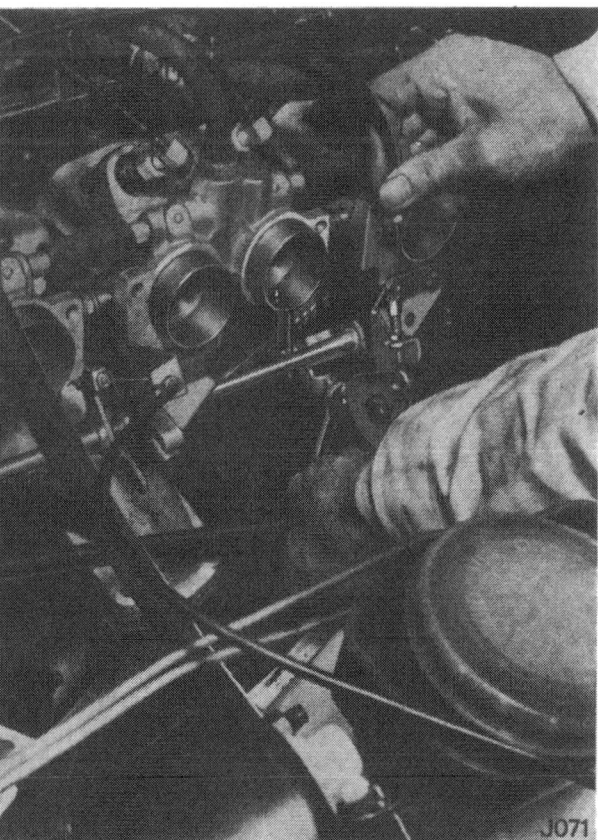

Fig. 11. Adjusting cold start control

FUEL SYSTEM

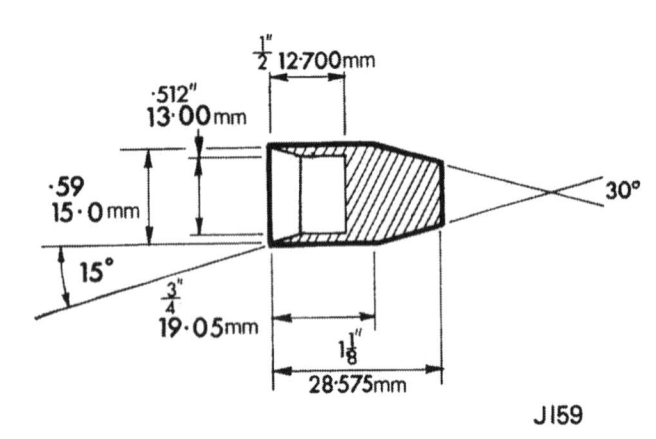

Fig. 12. Protective cover with dimensions

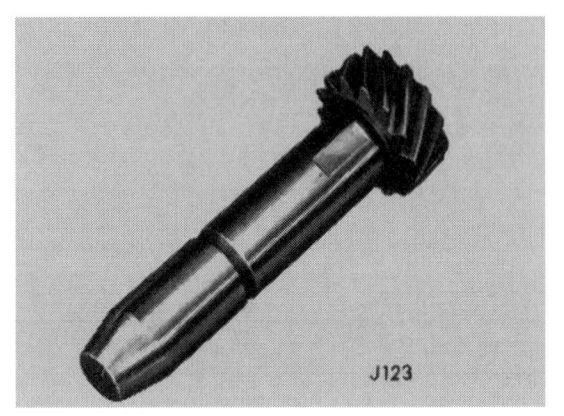

Fig. 13. Protective cover on pinion

Fig. 14. Drive pinion in alignment

METERING DISTRIBUTOR UNIT — REMOVING AND REFITTING

Removing

1. Isolate the battery.
2. Disconnect the injector pipes at the injectors.
3. Disconnect the vacuum pipe at the metering unit.
4. For ease of re-assembly, turn the engine to Nos. 1 and 6 cylinder T.D.C., No. 1 cylinder firing.
5. Disconnect and blank off the fuel inlet pipe and the bleed off pipe.

    NOTE: To prevent loss of fuel when the level of fuel is above the level of the metering unit, use hose clamps or partially drain the fuel tank.

6. Disconnect the cold start cable at the metering unit.
7. Remove the three bolts attaching the metering unit to the drive pedestal.
8. Lift off the unit complete with injector pipes, collect the plastic drive dog.
9. Remove the bolt retaining the sealing plug at the forward end of the pedestal and, with the fingers, push out the drive gear and plug.

It is possible to remove the distributor, pedestal and metering unit as an assembly. It will, however, be necessary to separate them before replacing. Where this course of action has been taken, refer to page 1·124 for re-installation of distributor and pedestal.

Refitting

1. Ensure that the engine is set to No. 1 and 6 T.D.C., No. 1 cylinder firing.
2. To ensure that the seals are not damaged, fit the protective cover (Fig. 12) on the end of the drive gear pinion (Fig. 13).
3. Insert the gear through the pedestal aperture so that, when fitted, the slot in the pinion is aligned vertically (see Fig. 14).
4. Fit a new 'O' ring to the plug (4) (Fig. 15) and insert into the aperture. Lock in position with the retaining bolt (7) and washer.
5. Using a little grease for retaining purposes, fit the plastic drive dog (2) on to the pinion (3).
6. Ensure that the 'O' ring seal (1) is correctly positioned around the pedestal boss.

FUEL SYSTEM

1·309

7. Turn the slotted drive on the metering unit to the horizontal position with the scribed lines on the drive and body coincident, i.e., the drilled hole in the lower half of the drive. (Fig. 16)

   NOTE: Removal of the No. 6 outlet adaptor will show the rotor hole at the start of its injection position.

8. Attach the metering unit to the pedestal, fit and tighten the three bolts.

9. Re-connect the:

   Injector pipes
   Vacuum pipe
   Fuel pipes
   Cold start cable
   Battery.

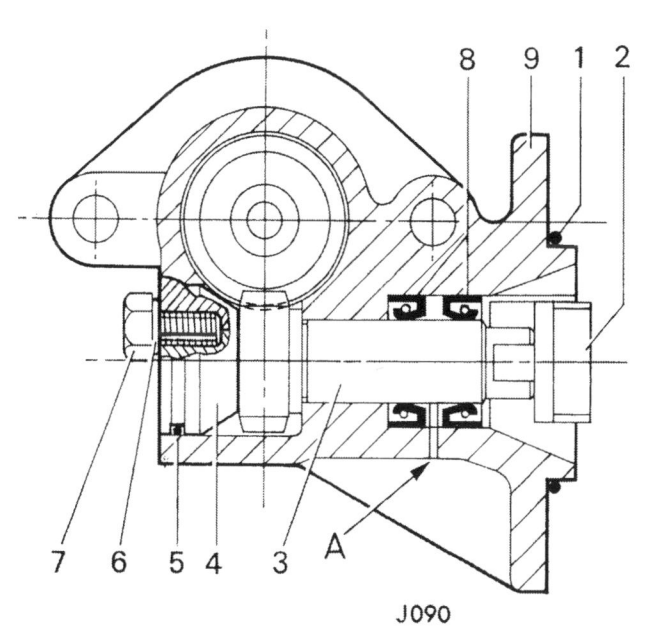

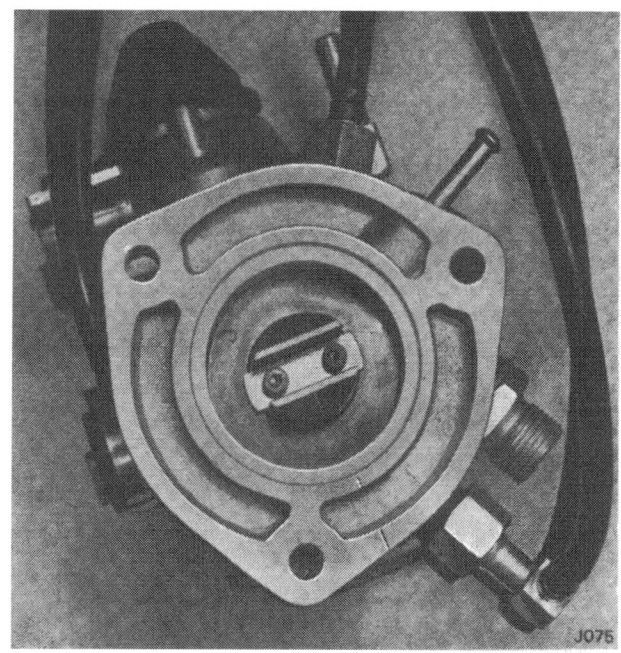

Fig. 16. Metering unit in alignment

1. 'O' ring
2. Drive dog
3. Pinion
4. Plug
5. Plug 'O' ring
6. Washer
7. Retaining bolt
8. Lip seals
9. Pedestal

Fig. 15. Pedestal and drive pinion arrangement

Fig. 17. Metering unit in position

OVERHAUL OF METERING DISTRIBUTOR ASSEMBLY

Under normal working conditions the metering distributor will show only minimal wear, for this reason it will not require maintenance of a routine nature, however, when major overhauls of the engine are undertaken the opportunity to examine the unit for damage and signs of fuel leakage should be taken.

The special tools (Fig. 19), which can be easily made, should be available before stripping the unit.

A clinical state of cleanliness must exist and be maintained during all petrol injection stripping operations, the rotor, sleeve and shuttle assemblies being particularly vulnerable to dirt. All internal parts must be washed in clean petrol before re-fitting, and while dismantled should be handled carefully to prevent damage.

ON NO ACCOUNT MAY THE FOLLOWING ADJUSTMENTS BE ALTERED (Fig. 18)

(a) Calibration screws (A) (3 off) on the end of the depression chamber.

(b) Full load setting screw (B).

(c) Datum track screws (C) (2 off).

The above adjustments are made by using special calibration equipment during manufacture. If the adjustments are disturbed this will necessitate returning the unit for re-calibrating.

FUEL SYSTEM

1·311

Dismantling

1. Unscrew and remove the four nuts securing the mixture control unit to the metering distributor.

    NOTE: The cam follower balance spring is COMPRESSED between these two units, so they must be held together whilst the nuts are undone and then allowed to part slowly and the spring and cam follower removed (Fig. 20).

    Once the two units are separated, the control stop, shuttle and fixed stop are free and may fall out or be washed out with fuel. At this point hold the metering distributor on end and shake out the fixed stop, control stop and shuttle, taking care not to drop or damage them.

The remainder of this instruction is split into two parts, namely, the metering distributor and the control unit.

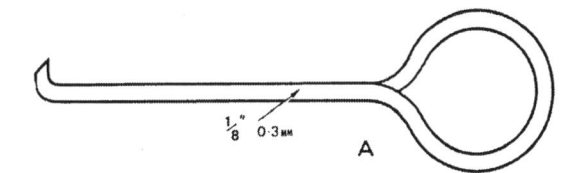

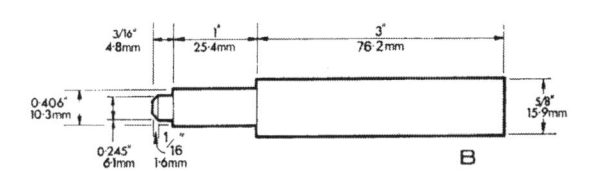

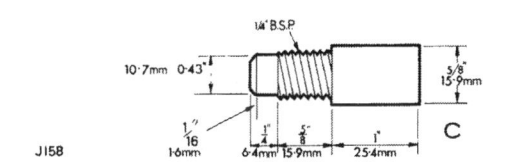

A. Hook for removing sealing rings
B. Tool for fitting sealing rings
C. Alignment tool

Fig. 19. Special tools

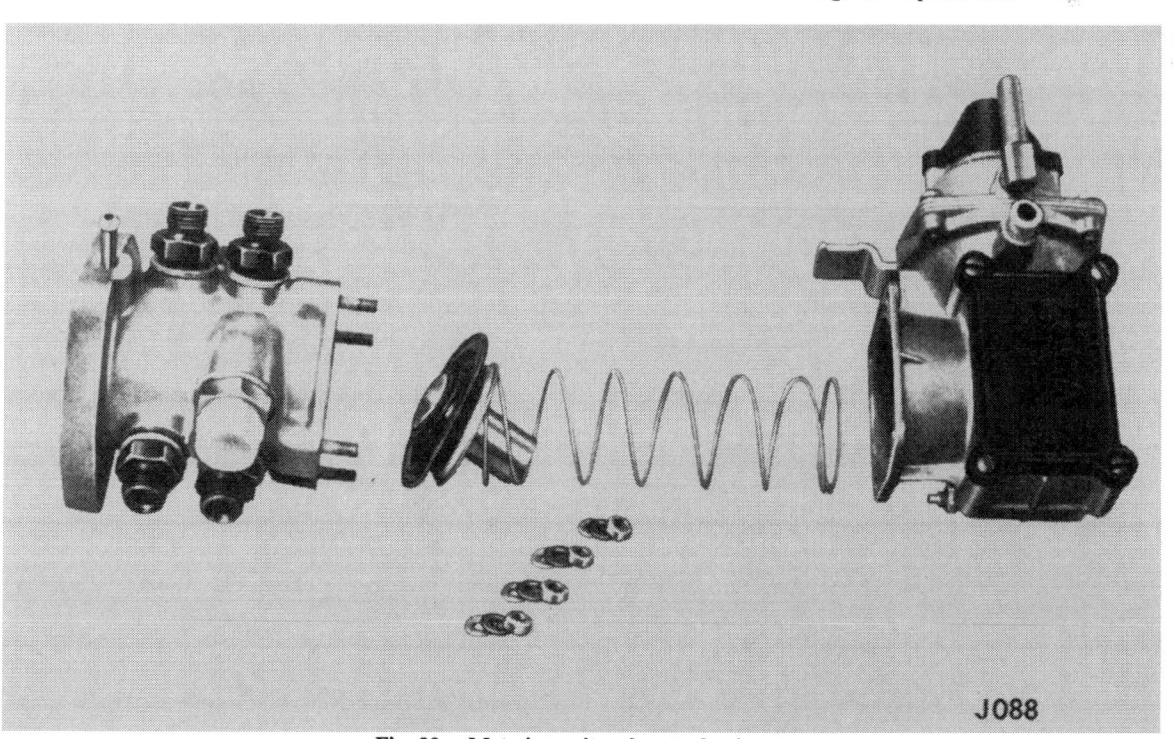

Fig. 20. Metering unit and control unit separated

FUEL SYSTEM

Control unit

2. Remove the cover plate securing screws and lift off the cover plate.

3. Take off the depression chamber after removal of its screws and the overfuel lever cable bracket. The calibration springs, spring carrier, diaphragm and link arm are now free and should be removed (Fig. 21). If the diaphragm assembly and links are to be dismantled, proceed as follows:—
   Hold spherical seat and remove diaphragm securing nut. In the following order, separate the spring seat, diaphragm support, diaphragm and backing plate from the control links (Fig. 22).

4. Place cam follower on the bench with the diaphragm uppermost.

5. Press on inner edge of cam follower diaphragm with the fingers to release the diaphragm from the cam follower.

Metering distributor

6. Remove banjo bolts.

7. Remove all outlet unions—this MUST be done before any further stripping of the metering distributor is carried out.

8. Using the hook (Fig. 19), remove the adaptor seals (6 off) from the outlet adaptor ports.

9. Apply the fingers to the drive end of the sleeve and push out the sleeve from the body (Fig. 23).

10. Remove the fuel inlet union.

11. Push out strainer from inside of fuel inlet union.

12. Remove distributor body 'O' ring and discard.

13. Remove sleeve 'O' ring and discard.

14. Remove rotor stop socket-headed screws. (Note that they may be 'Nyloc' type screws or plain screw fitted with 'Loctite' sealant.)

15. Withdraw rotor from sleeve and place on a clean surface where it will be protected from damage (Fig. 24).

Inspection

Inspect the shuttle, stops, rotor and sleeve for pitting, scoring or any fault that will render the unit unserviceable.

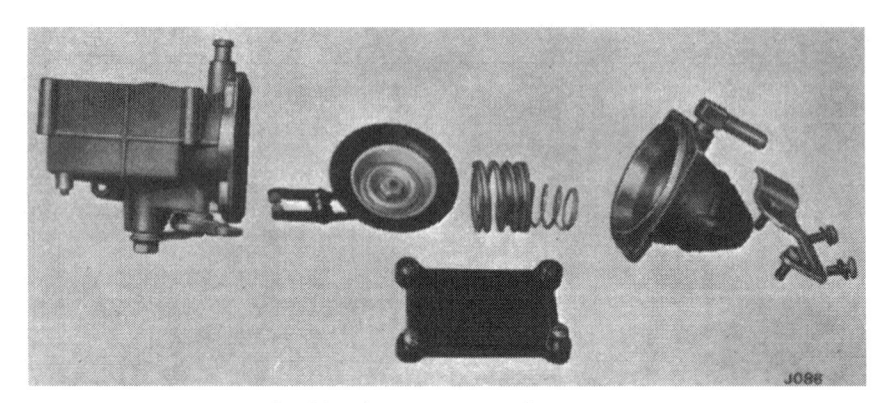

Fig. 21. Diaphragm assembly removed

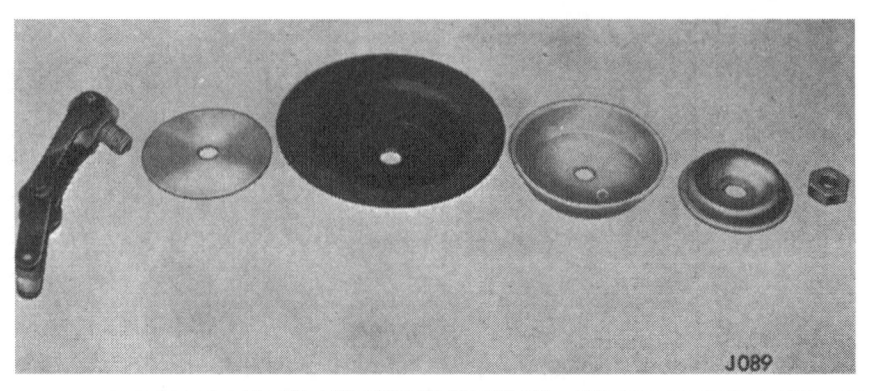

Fig. 22. Diaphragm assembly dismantled

FUEL SYSTEM

Re-assembly

Metering distributor

1. Ensure both countersunk screws in rotor brass thrust plate are tight.

2. Check that non-return valves in each outlet union are not sticking.

3. Fit strainer to fuel inlet union. Strainer should be fitted to end having cone seating rim and longest portion of thread.

4. Fit new seal to fuel inlet union and fit union to body.

5. Wash body in clean fuel.

6. Fit new body 'O' ring.

7. Wash rotor and sleeve in clean fuel and assemble while still wet. Take care when entering rotor into sleeve not to get it jammed. IT IS IMPORTANT THAT THE BRASS THRUST PLATE IS AT 'O' RING END AND THAT ROTOR AND SLEEVE TURN FREELY AFTER ASSEMBLY.

8. Place rotor stop in position with radiused side downwards.

9. Fit new rotor stop securing screws using 'Loctite' sealant to secure and tighten to 16 lb./in. (0·184 kg./m.).

10. Check that the rotor turns freely with an adequate amount of end float.

11. Fit a new 'O' ring to the sleeve.

12. Lightly smear both body and sleeve 'O' rings with clean engine oil.

13. Fit sleeve (without outlet port 'O' rings) with the sleeve ports approximately in line with threaded holes in the body.

14. Fit the alignment tool (Fig. 19) to one of the outlet ports in the body so that it mates with the sleeve port.

15. Fit new 'O' ring to each outlet port using the sealing ring tool (Fig. 19) to ensure each one is firmly home. Remember to fit an 'O' ring to the port containing the alignment tool.

16. Fit washers and outlet unions to each body port.

17. Fit new 'O' rings to banjos and fit banjo bolts.

Fig. 23. Sleeve assembly removed from the body

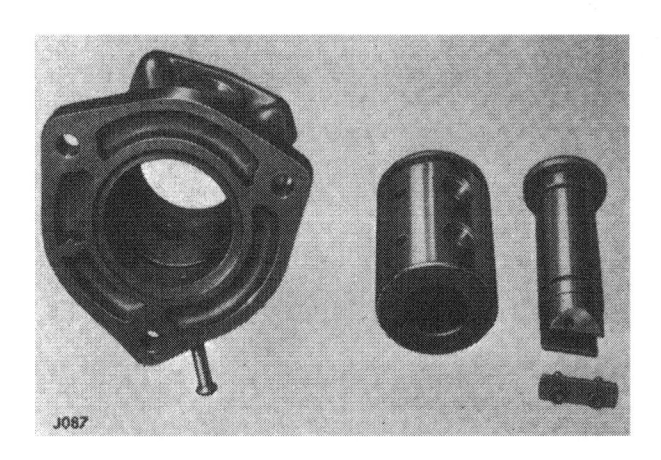

Fig. 24. Sleeve assembly dismantled

FUEL SYSTEM

Metering unit excess fuel lever

The excess fuel lever (Fig. 25), which for cold start conditions allow up to 300% extra fuel, has an adjustment of free play only. With the metering unit removed the adjustment may be checked and adjusted if required, the correct clearance ('A') being 0·006 - 0·008 in. (0·15 - 0·2 mm.).

Adjustment, however, should not be required during normal service. If, for reasons described in 'Fault Finding' (page 1·317) the adjustment is suspect then all that is required is to establish that free play exists at the cable end of the lever. Providing that free play exists (approx. ¼ in; 6 mm.) the excess fuel lever is unlikely to be at fault.

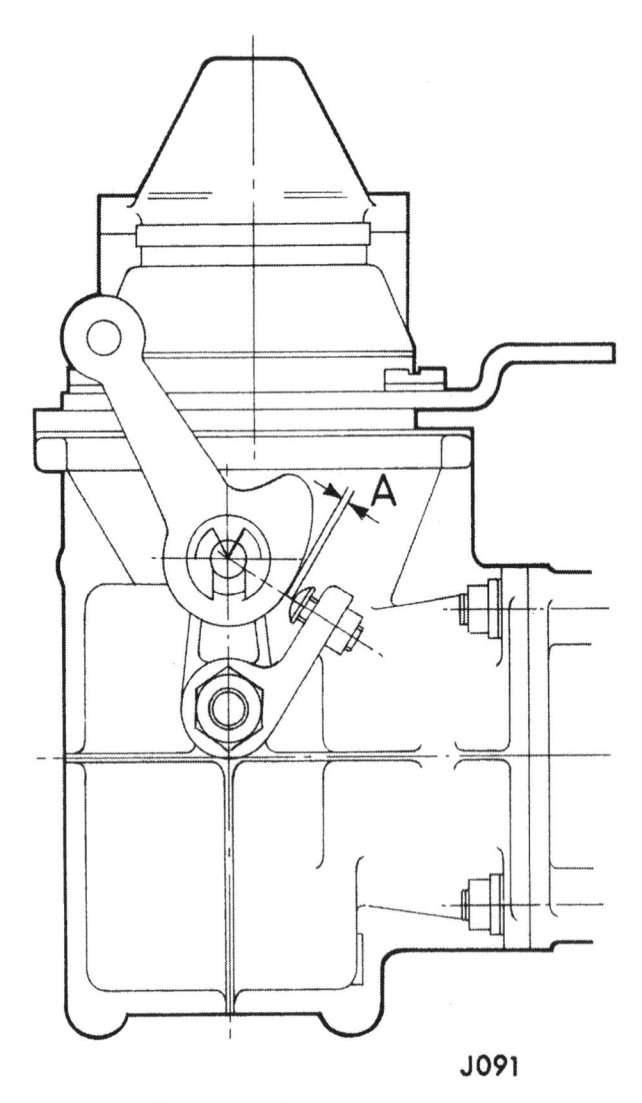

Fig. 25. Setting the excess fuel lever

18. Wash in clean fuel and whilst wet assemble the fixed stop, shuttle and control stop into the rotor. (As an aid to identification, the control stop has the axial hole.)

19. Fit blanking plugs to all unions.

20. Place the metering distributor on one side where the stops and shuttle cannot fall out of the rotor.

Control unit

21. Replace the backing plate, diaphragm, diaphragm support and spring seat in the order given.

22. Screw the depression chamber diaphragm securing nut over a few threads and apply one spot of 'Loctite' Hydraulic Seal to the centre of the nut.

23. Tighten diaphragm locking nut at 4 lb/in. (0·046 kg/m.) and remove surplus 'Loctite'.

24. Lightly smear link rollers with engine oil.

25. Re-fit link arm and diaphragm making sure that spherical seat and link arm are square with the rest of the assembly.

26. Push diaphragm rim into its seating on the body.

27. Assemble calibration springs—large spring on to diaphragm, then spring carrier and small spring.

28. Fit depression chamber cover and overfuel lever bracket, positioning this so that its cranked end is nearest the drive end of the metering distributor. The air inlet connection must be positioned on the opposite side to the banjo connections.

Note that the two longest screws are used on the bracket side of the cover.

29. With the three locating slots of the diaphragm uppermost, feed cam follower through hole in diaphragm—diaphragm can be pushed on to its seating on the cam follower by finger pressure.

Assembly of metering distributor to control unit

30. Fit spring thrust plate over cam follower.

31. Position cam follower and spring between the control unit and metering distributor and secure one to the other with four nuts, plain and spring washers.

32. Refit cover plate, noting that it can only be fitted one way.

FUEL SYSTEM

PRESSURE RELIEF VALVE

Removal

Disconnect the return to filter pipe from the pressure relief valve, plug the ends to prevent dirt entering the system. Using ⅝" AF spanner, remove the pressure relief valve and strainer body. Place the body in a vice and remove the pressure relief valve; the strainer can be removed by hand.

Clean the strainer with dry, filtered compressed air.

Re-fitting is a reversal of removing. Ensure leakproof joints by renewing sealing washers.

Setting

The effects of a pressure relief valve set too low are:

Very low (below 80 p.s.i.) (5624 g/cm²), engine won't pick up at all.

Low (80 - 90 p.s.i.) (5624 - 6328 g/cm²), flat spot on acceleration, erratic running.

At high pressures, excess wear will take place on the control unit linkage.

The correct pressure should be 106 - 110 p.s.i. (7453 - 7734 g/cm²). To check and adjust the pressure proceed as follows:

For this operation a 0 - 120 p.s.i. (0 - 8500 g/cm²) pressure gauge and a 'T' piece with a connection for the gauge and one male and one female outlet of ½" UNF will be required.

1. Remove the two nuts attaching the assembly to the chassis.

2. Disconnect the fuel outlet pipe from the pressure relief valve and connect in the 'T' piece and the pressure gauge (Fig. 27).

3. Disconnect and blank off the return to filter pipe at the pressure relief valve (6).

4. Place a receptacle to catch fuel being discharged from the pressure relief valve.

5. Switch on the ignition and note the pressure gauge reading.

6. Switch off the ignition and adjust the pressure by screwing in the nylon adjuster to increase the pressure and out to decrease the pressure (¼ of a turn equals 5 lb. approx.).

7. Repeat operations 5 and 6 until a pressure of 106 - 110 p.s.i. (7453 - 7734 g/cm²) is attained. If the reading is unstable a new relief valve must be fitted. Further instability indicates a defective pump/motor unit (See Group 6).

8. Re-connect the return to filter pipe and switch on the ignition. Note the pressure gauge reading. An appreciably increased pressure denotes a blocked or kinked return to filter pipe which should be replaced or serviced.

9. Remove 'T' piece and gauge, re-connect the fuel pipe to the pressure relief valve and check to ensure leakproof joints.

10. Refit the unit and tighten the nuts.

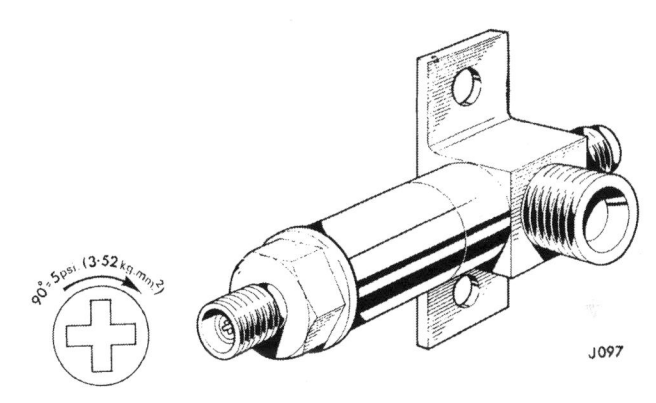

Fig. 26. Adjustment of pressure relief valve

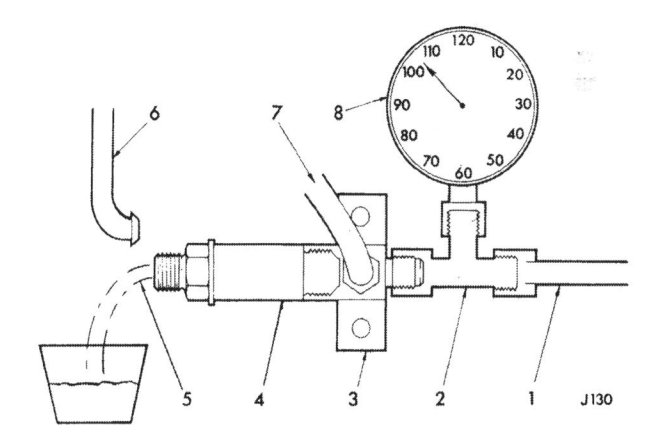

1. Pipe to metering unit.
2. Adaptor.
3. 'T' junction.
4. Valve and strainer holder.
5. Fuel to container.
6. Disconnected return pipe.
7. Inlet pipe.
8. Pressure gauge.

Fig. 27. Checking relief valve pressure

FUEL SYSTEM

PEDESTAL SEALS

Four seals, two 'O' rings and two spring-loaded lip seals are fitted to the pedestal. The 'O' rings can be replaced with the pedestal in situ by:

1. Disconnect the metering unit and replace the 'O' ring on the periphery of the pedestal spigot. The metering unit attachments need not be removed if the unit is suspended, by wire, from a suitable point. Ensure that the drive collar is replaced correctly.

2. Remove the thrust plug at the rear of the metering unit drive gear and replace the 'O' ring on its periphery. The plug is withdrawn by removing its securing screw and easing the plug from the pedestal.

The two spring-loaded lip seals are fitted, back to back, on the metering distributor drive pinion. The function of the seals is to prevent the cross pollution of oil, from the engine, and fuel from the metering unit. A leak bleed hole is provided between the seals (A, Fig. 28) to enable a leak to be noticed before failure of the other seal occurs. If either seal is faulty renew both.

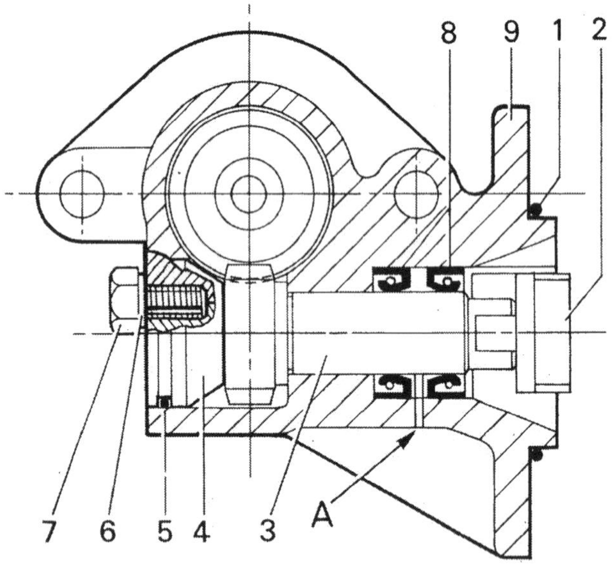

To renew the seals proceed as follows:

Remove the pedestal (see page 1·123), the metering unit may be suspended, on wire attached to a suitable point, during this operation.

Using a screwdriver or hook to remove both seals, ensure that the seal housing is not scored during removal. Inspect the seal housing and remove any burrs or rust spots, etc. Ensure that the leak drain hole is clear and creates no burr into the seal housing.

Prior to fitting, the seals should be coated with grease and, when fitted, grease should be packed between the two seals. Fit the seals using a 0·9" (22·9 mm.) flat ended punch taking care not to damage the seal housing or tilt the seals. The seals are fitted back to back, i.e., the lips facing away from each other. Ensure that the inner seal is correctly seated before fitting the outer, and that, when fitted, the outer seal does not obstruct the drain hole (see Fig. 28).

Refit the pedestal (page 1·123), distributor (page 1·124) and metering unit (page 1·308).

INJECTORS

Testing

A suspect injector may be tested in the following way:

Remove the cleats securing the injector pipes and separate the pipes to prevent the transmission of reflected pulsations from other pipes. Start the engine and hold each injector pipe in turn, a regular pulsation should be clearly felt.

A weak or missing pulsation on one pipe denotes a stuck open injector. No pulse on two consecutive (firing order) pipes indicates that the first injector of the two is blocked, i.e., **1 - 5; 5 - 3; 3 - 6; 6 - 2; 2 - 4; 4 - 1**.

Remove a suspect injector and test in a modified diesel injector test rig. The test should show a 60° hollow cone spray at an opening pressure of approximately 50 p.s.i.

If no rig is available, remove the injector and clean as described below, replace the injector and start the engine. If no improvement is apparent, renew the injector.

To remove an injector

Remove the injector pipe by holding the hexagon on the injector with a spanner and, with another spanner, remove the pipe union.

Remove the bolt securing the injector retaining plate to the inlet manifold. Remove the retaining plate and pull out the injector.

1. 'O' ring
2. Coupling
3. Pinion
4. Plug
5. Plug 'O' ring
6. Washer
7. Retaining bolt
8. Lip seals
9. Pedestal

Fig. 28. Pedestal oil seals

FUEL SYSTEM

1·317

The nylon holder and 'O' ring can be removed, with spanners, if required.

To remove dirt from the injector valve use dry, filtered compressed air at approximately 80 p.s.i. (5·624 kg/cm²) forced through the injector in the direction of fuel flow.

Apart from this, no servicing of the injectors is possible, renew defective injectors.

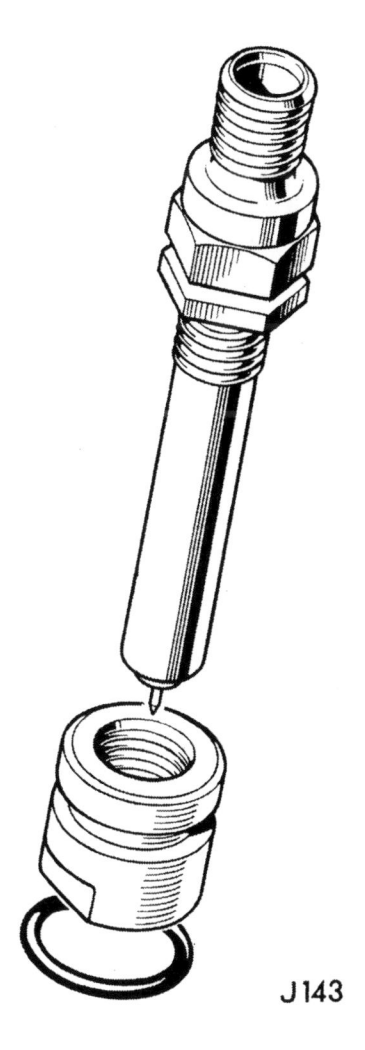

Fig. 29. Injector, holder and 'O' ring

FAULT FINDING

Effects of a fault in the petrol injection system

A fault will usually be revealed in one of four ways:

A. The engine cannot be started or can only be started with difficulty.

B. The engine starts but runs erratically over the whole or part of the speed range.

C. Fuel consumption is excessive.

D. The engine starts but does not respond to movement of the throttle.

Overfuel control lever check

Faults 'A', 'B' and 'C' may be due to incorrect operation of the overfuel control lever. Check that it is fully responsive to manual control over its full range and that when in the 'OFF' position there is a clearance of 0·004 - 0·008″ (0·1016 - 0·2032 mm.) between the lever and the adjustment screw upon which it bears.

A. Engine fails to start or can only be started with difficulty

1. Switch on the ignition and check (audibly or by touch) that the fuel pump motor is running. If it is not, proceed as under "Petrol pump", Group 6.

2. If the pump motor is running, disconnect one of the low tension cable connections at the coil but leave the ignition switch on.

3. Grip each injector feed line in turn lightly with the hand and crank the engine.

   A distinct pulsation should be felt with each line as fuel is injected.

NOTE: The feed lines are cleated together and must be separated to avoid the misleading effect of reflected pulsations.

If obvious pulsations are felt in each line the petrol injection system is unlikely to be the cause of failure to start and some other cause must be found.

If pulsations seem weak or completely absent in one feed line, withdraw and check the associated injector (see fault B, paragraph 4).

FUEL SYSTEM

If pulsations cannot be felt in any line although the pump motor is working apparently normally, check fuel pressure (see page 1·315). If pressure and relief valve setting are satisfactory, switch off ignition and remove metering control unit for examination of the drive coupling, which may have broken.

Finally, remember to restore the coil low-tension connection.

B. Engine starts but runs erratically over the whole or part of the speed range

1. Check the setting of the overfuel control lever (page 1·314). Erratic running may otherwise be caused by:

   An irregularity on the fuel supply to one cylinder only. Some failing which is affecting all cylinders.

   In the former case, the fault is most likely to be a stuck-open injector and fouling of the associated spark plug will almost certainly have occurred.

2. Short circuit each plug to earth in turn and if one does not affect the engine running note when shorted out, remove, clean and re-fit this plug.

3. Withdraw the associated injector from the engine and detach from its feed line.

4. Connect the injector to a dry, filtered air supply at a pressure of 80 p.s.i. (5624 g/cm.^{2}), in the forward (injection) direction. This will invariably cure a faulty injector (sticking open due to a foreign particle becoming trapped) and if it does so the injector can be re-fitted to the engine. If it does not, a new injector must be fitted.

   NOTE: Plastic feed pipes must not be heat treated to enable fitment, but must be put on cold.

5. Where the failure affects all cylinders but is more pronounced with higher speed, check pressure and relief valve setting (see page 1·315). If the metering distributor/control unit has recently been removed, check that it has not been fitted 180° out as regards timing.

6. Provided that the timing is correct, the overfuel control lever working correctly, the injectors are in good order and fuel pressure is satisfactory, then a faulty control unit is indicated. In this instance fit a new complete metering distributor/control unit.

NO ATTEMPT SHOULD BE MADE TO ALTER THE CONTROL UNIT SETTING.

C. Fuel consumption excessive

This may not necessarily arise from a defect in the petrol injection system and the fault must be correctly traced before taking remedial action. The following checks are therefore given on the assumption that other likely causes have been checked first.

1. Check for correct operation of the overfuel control lever (page 1·314).

2. Check the relief valve setting (page 1·315).

If the above (1) and (2) are satisfactory then the control unit is suspect and a replacement metering unit must be fitted. This latter step should be taken only when other likely causes such as plugs, points, leaking pipes, etc., have been eliminated.

D. Engine starts but does not respond to movement of the throttle

1. Ensure that movement of the accelerator pedal is being relayed to the throttle butterflies.

2. Remove and check that the pipe connecting the manifold to the control unit is air tight.

3. Check the relief valve setting.

4. If both the above (1) and (2) are satisfactory, it will be necessary to fit a replacement metering distributor/control unit.

FUEL SYSTEM

1·319

AIR CLEANER (Figs. 30 and 32)

Every 6,000 miles (10,000 km.), or more frequently in dusty conditions, clean the paper element in the air cleaner. To do this proceed as follows:

Remove the nut and bolt fastenings (Fig. 30) attaching the cleaner brackets to their mountings.

Remove the centre retaining nut (1, Fig. 32), take off the cover (2) and remove the element (3).

Clean between the folds of the element with a soft brush or low pressure air line.

Refit the element, cover and unit by reversing the above procedure.

Every 12,000 miles (20,000 km.) renew the paper element using the method described above.

Fig. 30. Air cleaner installed

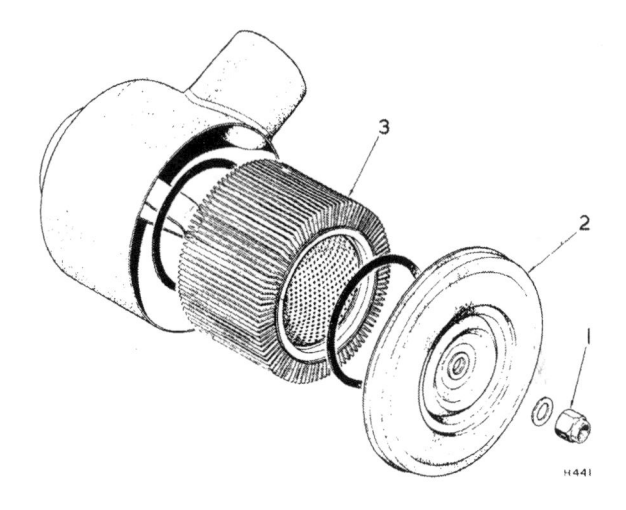

1. Nut 2. Cover 3. Element

Fig. 32. Exploded view of air cleaner

Key to Fig. 31

1. Gasket
2. Manifold clamp
3. Spring washer
4. Nut
5. Exhaust manifold
6. Servo adaptor
7. Washer
8. Balance pipe
9. Washer
10. Meter hose adaptor
11. Balance pipe
12. Washer
13. Plug
14. Inlet manifold front
15. Inlet manifold centre
16. Air inlet tube
17. Screw
18. Butterfly
19. Inlet manifold rear
20. Butterfly spindle
21. Return spring
22. Throttle lever
23. Nut
24. Spring
25. Throttle screw
26. Stud

Fig. 31. Inlet and exhaust manifold details

EXHAUST SYSTEM

The TR5 is fitted with a twin exhaust system utilizing a common silencer.

The pipes are mounted in pairs at three points along the chassis, the two sets of rear mountings are attached by flexible mountings.

The tail pipes and silencer are a welded assembly as are the front pipes and flange; with these exceptions the pipes may be removed and, if necessary renewed independently.

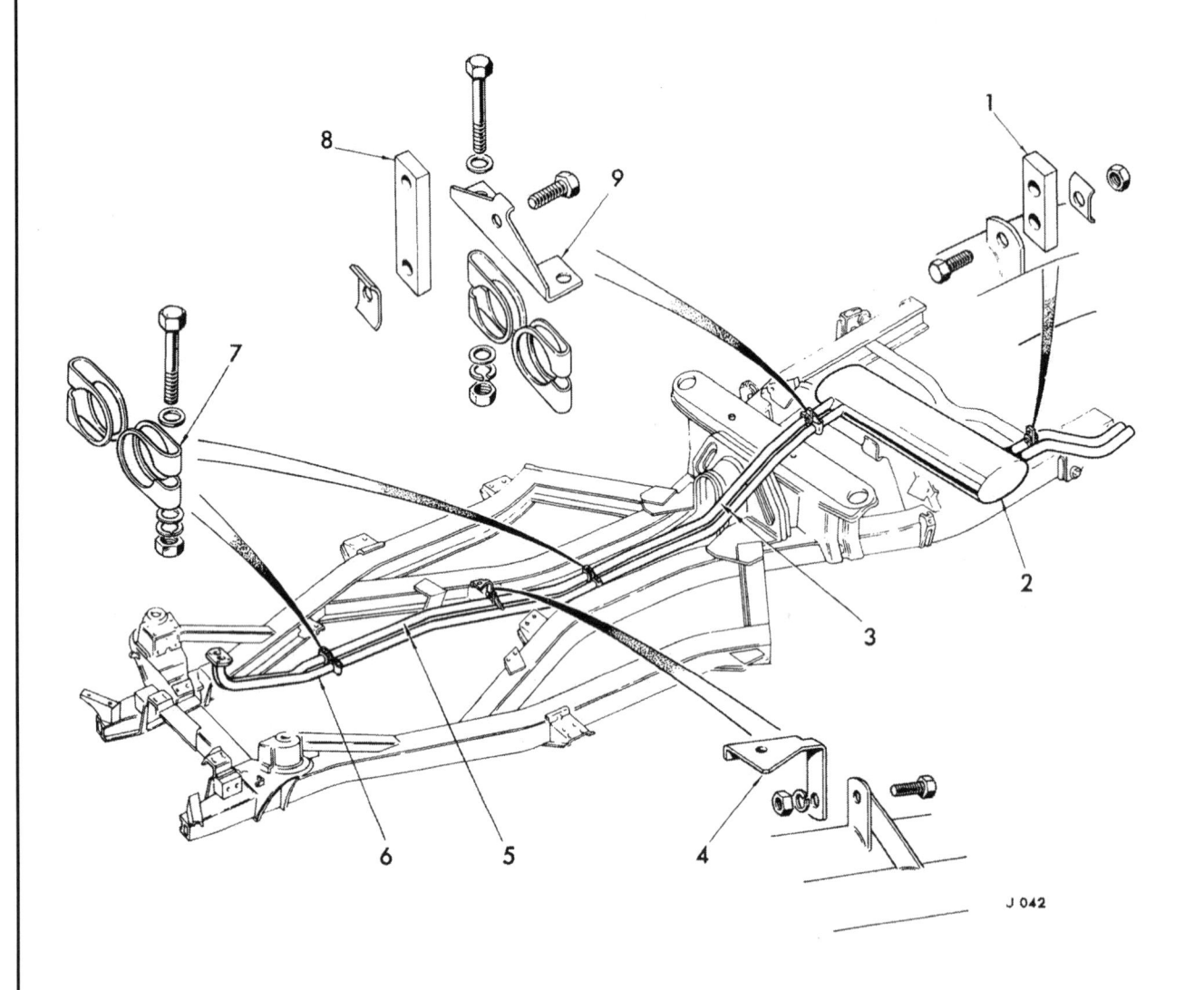

1. Flexible mounting (tail pipes).
2. Silencer and tail pipes assembly
3. Rear intermediate pipes
4. Front mounting assembly
5. Front intermediate pipes
6. Front pipes and flange assembly
7. Pipe clamp assembly
8. Intermediate flexible mounting
9. Intermediate mounting bracket

Fig. 1. Exhaust system details

TRIUMPH
TR5-PI
WORKSHOP MANUAL SUPPLEMENT

GROUP 2

Comprising:

Clutch and Gearbox

TRIUMPH TR5

WORKSHOP MANUAL

SUPPLEMENT TO GROUP 2

CONTENTS

Section

CLUTCH

Slave cylinder	2·102
Master cylinder	2·102
Clutch unit	2·103
Data	2·104

GEARBOX

Gearbox modifications	2·201

CLUTCH

2·102

CLUTCH MASTER CYLINDER

To remove (Fig. 6, Group 3)

Working from inside the vehicle, disconnect the push rod from the clutch pedal sub assembly (11), secured by clevis pin (18), plain washer and split pin.

Disconnect and plug the master cylinder pipe. Remove the two bolts (15) with washers retaining the master cylinder (16) to the bulkhead.

To refit

Reverse the removal procedure, refill the cylinder and bleed the hydraulic system.

SLAVE CYLINDER

To dismantle (Fig. 1)

Remove the dust cover (2) and use a low pressure air line to eject internal components (4), (5), (6) and (7).

To re-assemble (Fig. 1)

Fit the spring (7) into the filler block (6) and insert into the cylinder body (3). Refit the seal (5), piston (4) and dust cover (2).

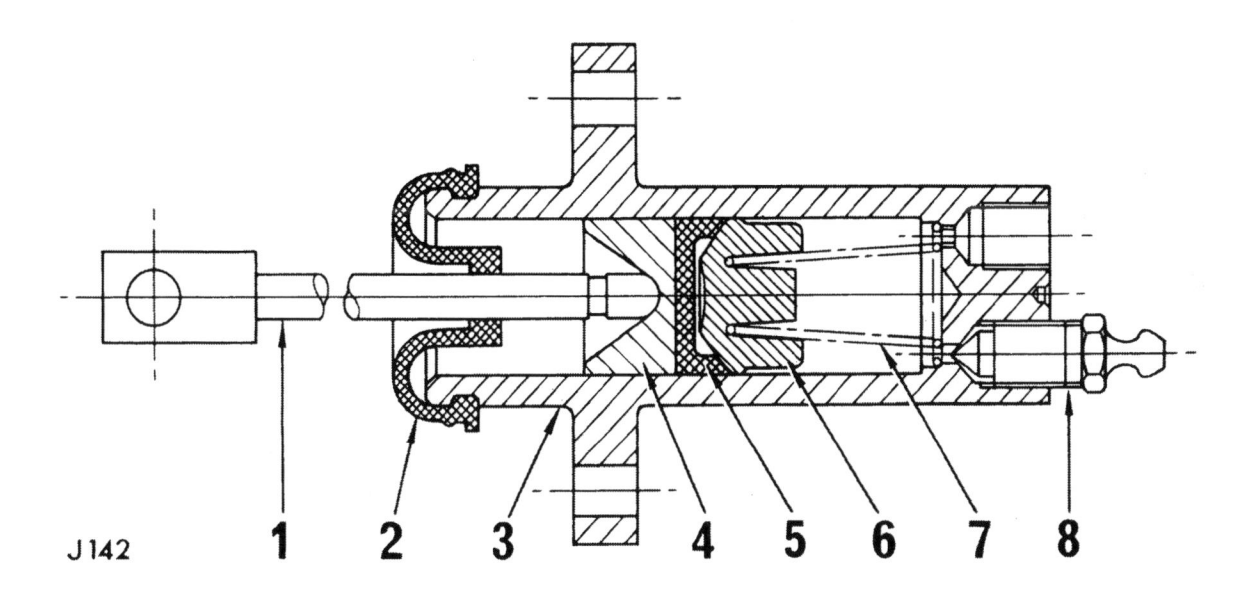

1. Push-rod
2. Dust cover
3. Body
4. Piston
5. Seal
6. Filler block
7. Spring
8. Bleed nipple

Fig. 1. Sectioned slave cylinder

CLUTCH

CLUTCH UNIT

To dismantle (Fig. 2)

A faulty clutch unit should normally be replaced by a new unit, but if dismantling is necessary proceed as follows:

Mark all parts to ensure that they are assembled in the same relative positions.

With the clutch face downwards on a bench:

1. Lift off the outer cover (7).
2. Take out circlip (6).
3. Remove the diaphragm spring (5).
4. Remove the two spring clips (4).
5. Lift the inner cover (3) of the pressure plate (2).

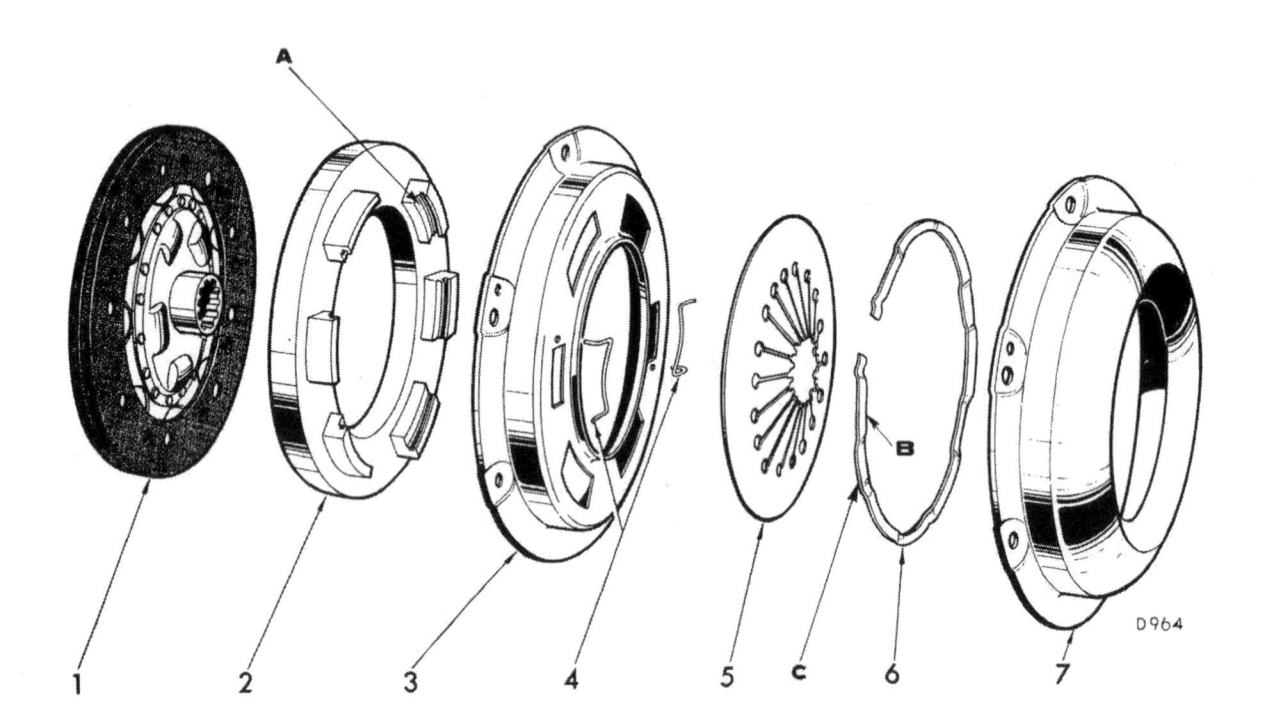

1 Driven plate
2 Pressure plate
3 Driving plate
4 Spring clips
5 Diaphragm spring
6 Circlip
7 Cover pressing

Fig. 2. Clutch unit details

CLUTCH 2·104

To re-assemble

Assemble in the reverse order of above, taking note of the following points:

1. To maintain balance, ensure that all components are assembled in the correct relative positions.

2. Apply a trace of zinc base grease to the inner working faces (A) of the pressure plate lugs.

3. When fitting the circlip ensure that the six flat portions (B) locate in the grooves of the six pressure plate lugs, and that the five undulations (C) bear against the diaphragm spring.

CLUTCH DATA

Type	8½" dia. (21·5 cms.) Laycock diaphragm spring type.
Operation	Hydraulic.
Adjustment	Self adjusting.
Facings	Ferodo RYZ – Mintex H1B.
Travel to release	0·315" (8·001 mm.).
Flywheel to spring tips	1·465" ± ·050" (37·21 ± 1·27 mm.).
Clutch slave cylinder	Lockheed 1" (25·4 mm.) bore.

Fig. 4. Diaphragm spring removed

Fig. 3. Clutch cover assembly

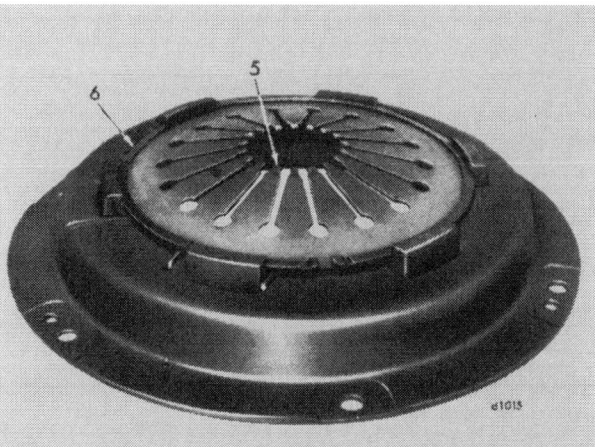

Fig. 5. Cover pressing removed

GEARBOX

Except for the following changes all servicing procedures given in TR4 (Group 2 – Section 2) remain unaltered.

Countershaft hub modification (Fig. 1)

To retain the needle roller bearings (43), (49) in both ends of the countershaft hub (44), circlips (43A), (49B) have been added.

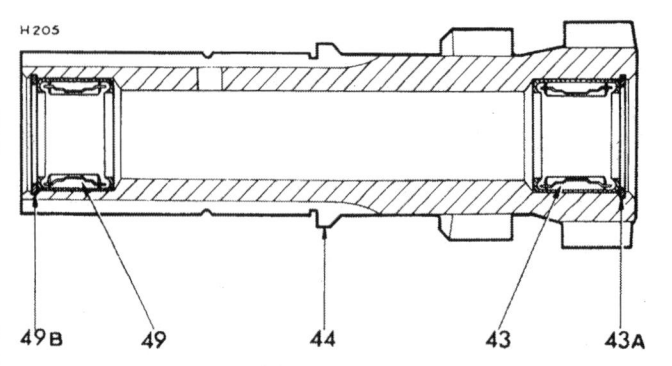

Needle roller bearings

A 'caged type' bearing fitted to the Mainshaft and Countershaft has been introduced replacing the 'full complement' type bearing.

43 Needle roller bearing
43A Circlip
44 Countershaft hub
49 Needle roller bearing
49B Circlip

Fig. 1. Countershaft hub modification

Gear lever modification (Fig. 2)

The gear lever assembly (114) has been modified and a rubber bush incorporated to prevent transference of gear lever noise to the vehicle interior and to overcome the possibility of gear lever rattle. The spring (112) has been strengthened and items (62) and (66) Fig. 2, Page 2·204, deleted and replaced by adjustable locating pins (137 and 138) secured by locknuts (139).

Method of adjustment

Move the gear lever (114) into the 1st and 2nd gate position and screw the locating pin (137) clockwise until slight movement of the gear lever is noticed. From this position, screw the locating pin a half turn anti-clockwise and tighten the locknut (139).

Move the gear lever into the reverse gate position and adjust the pin (138) as described above.

Other items: Alterations have been carried out as follows:

(a) Speedo drive gear, item 136, Fig. 2, Page 2·204. A moulded type of gear has now been introduced to replace the steel type gear.

(b) Mainshaft flange, item 38, Fig. 1, Page 2·202. A circular type flange has now been introduced.

(c) Grease nipple, items 6 and 7, Fig. 7, Page 2·206. These two items have now been deleted.

(d) Front cover, item 83, Fig. 2, Page 2·204. Reduction in length of the front cover nose.

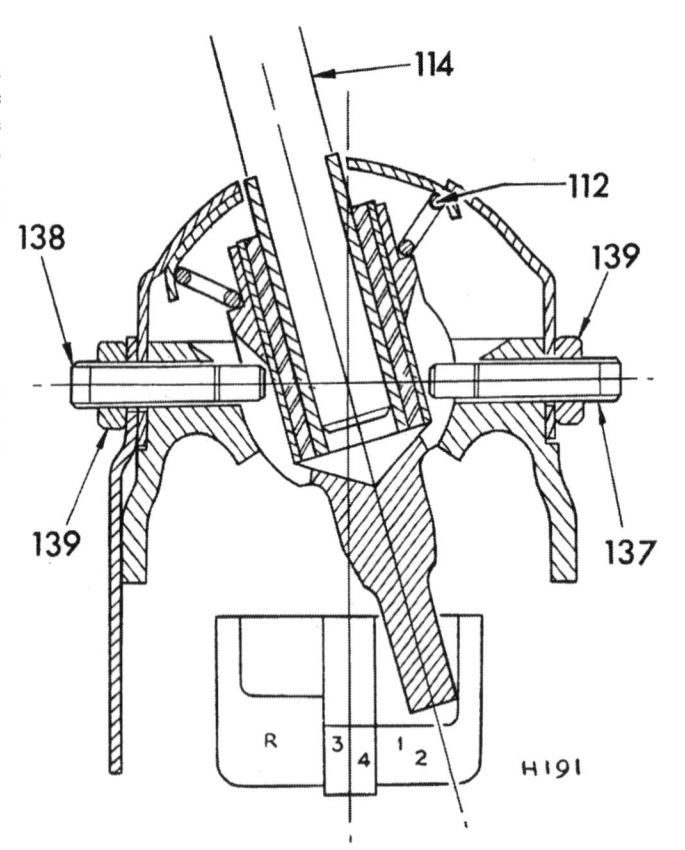

112 Spring
114 Gear lever assembly
137 Locating pins
138 Locating pins
139 Locknuts

Fig. 2. Gear lever modification

TRIUMPH
TR5-PI
WORKSHOP MANUAL SUPPLEMENT

GROUP 3

Comprising:

Brakes

TRIUMPH TR5

WORKSHOP MANUAL

SUPPLEMENT TO GROUP 3

CONTENTS

BRAKES	Section
Hydraulic system	**3·201**
Bleeding procedure	**3·201**
Master cylinder	**3·203**
Pressure differential warning actuator (L.H.D. vehicles only)	**3·206**
Vacuum servo unit	**3·207**
Pedal box	**3·209**
Rear brakes	**3·209**
Regular maintenance—Brakes	**3·210**

BRAKES

Hydraulic system

Description

The foot operated hydraulic braking system employs a tandem master cylinder for transmitting pressure to independent front and rear braking systems. On Left-Hand Drive vehicles both systems are connected to opposing sides of a pressure differential warning actuator (P.D.W.A.) which operates an electrical switch when a pressure drop on one side of the valve causes a shuttle to move from its mid-position. The P.D.W.A. switch operates a warning light on the facia which is series/parallel connected with the oil warning light. Thus when the brakes are working correctly, the brake warning light and the oil warning light are both extinguished as the engine speed is increased from idle (giving regular assurance that the brake warning light is functioning). In the event of a partial brake failure the brake warning system is earthed directly, causing the warning light to glow brightly.

Bleeding the hydraulic braking system

General

If air has entered either of the hydraulic braking systems then only the system affected need be bled. On L.H.D. vehicles during bleeding, exercise care as described in the following procedure to avoid moving the shuttle from its mid-position. However, if the shuttle has moved during bleeding or subsequent to a fault condition, centralise the shuttle by performing operations 5 – 9 on page 3·203.

Preparation for bleeding

Before commencing to bleed the brakes ensure that all the bleed nipples are clean and, taking care to avoid dirt entering the fluid reservoir, remove its filler cap and top-up with new hydraulic fluid. During the bleeding operation keep the level of fluid above the dividing partition in the reservoir. Do not top-up with fluid bled from the system.

Use new fluid from a sealed container, resealing the container after use.

Commence with the brake, of the pair being bled, farthest from the master cylinder. If both systems are to be bled, bleed the rear brakes first. When bleeding the rear brakes, release the handbrake and turn the brake adjusters to lock the shoes against the drums. When the bleeding is completed adjust the brakes.

1. Attach a rubber tube of approx. ¼″ (6 mm.) bore to the brake bleed nipple allowing the other end of the tube to hang submerged in a jar containing a quantity of clean brake fluid.

2. Unscrew the bleed-screw enough to allow the fluid to be pumped out (half a turn is normally sufficient).

KEY TO FIG. 1

1 Cap
2 Baffle plate
3 Seal
4 Reservoir
5 Tipping valve securing nut
6 Tipping valve
7 Seal—reservoir to body
8 Body
9 Screw—reservoir to body
10 Seal
11 Primary plunger
12 Intermediate spring
13 Secondary plunger
14 Seal
15 Spring retainer
16 Secondary spring
17 Valve spacer
18 Spring washer
19 Valve
20 Seal
21 Seal—reservoir to body

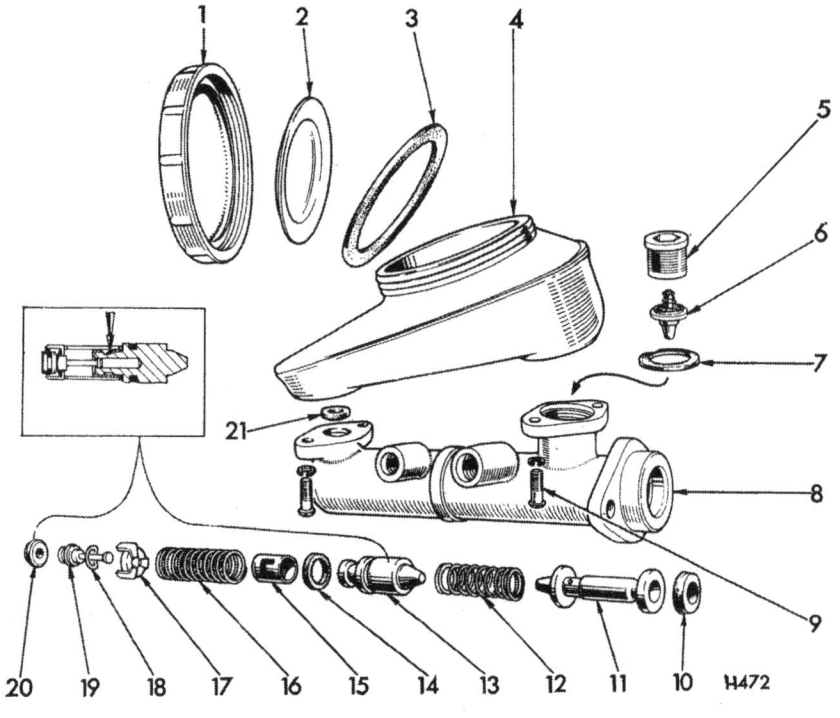

Fig. 1. Exploded View of Master Cylinder

BRAKES

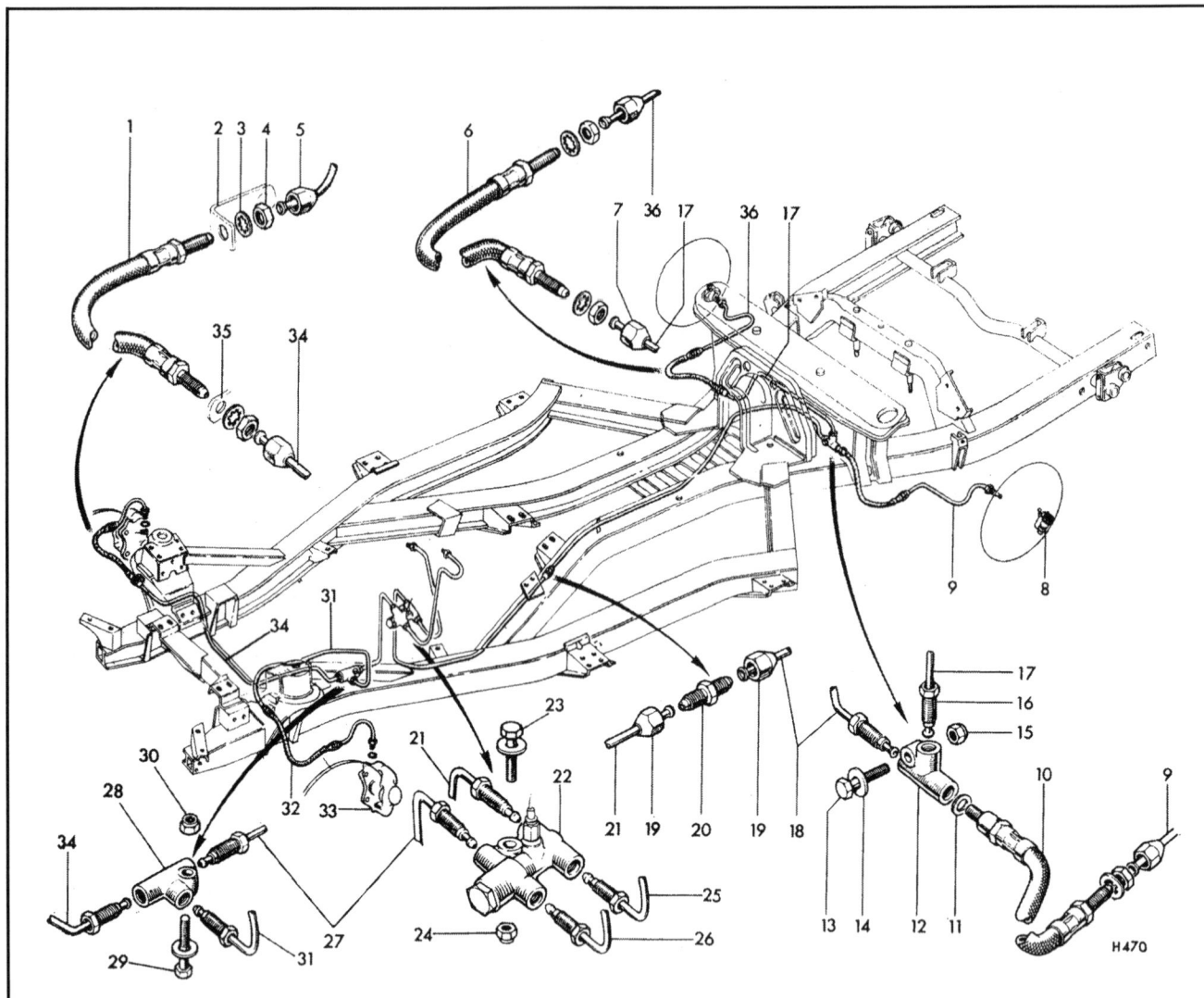

Fig. 2 Hydraulic Piping Layout

KEY TO FIG. 2

1. Flexible hose—R.H. front
2. Support bracket—hose to caliper
3. Shakeproof washer
4. Nut
5. Tube nut—female
6. Flexible hose—R.H. rear
7. Tube nut—female
8. Wheel cylinder
9. Pipe—hose to rear cylinder
10. Flexible hose—L.H. rear
11. Copper washer
12. Three-way union
13. Bolt
14. Washer
15. Nut
16. Tube nut—male
17. Pipe—three way to R.H. rear hose
18. Pipe—connector to three-way
19. Tube nut—female
20. Pipe connector
21. Pipe—P.D.W.A. to connector ⎫
22. Pressure differential warning actuator ⎪ L.H.D.
23. Bolt ⎬ vehicles
24. Nyloc nut ⎪ only
25. Pipe—P.D.W.A. to master cylinder ⎪
26. Pipe—P.D.W.A. to master cylinder ⎪
27. Pipe—P.D.W.A. front three-way ⎭
28. Three-way connector—front
29. Bolt
30. Nyloc nut
31. Pipe—three-way to L.H. front hose
32. Flexible hose—L.H. front
33. Disc brake caliper—L.H. front
34. Pipe—three-way to R.H. front hose
35. Bracket—flexible hose support
36. Pipe—hose to R.H. rear cylinder

BRAKES

3. Depress the brake pedal and allow it to return slowly. Note that on L.H.D. vehicles that only a LIGHT pedal effort is required and the pedal must NOT be pushed through the end of the stroke (in addition, never 'try' the pedal until all air has been dispelled and the system is fully bled, as either action will cause the shuttle to move and actuate the switch). Pausing between each depression of the pedal, continue pumping until all air has been dispelled from the bleed-screw (denoted by the absence of bubbles in the fluid being pumped into the jar).

4. With the pedal depressed, close the bleed-screw nipple and repeat the operation on the other brake.

Procedure for re-centralising the P.D.W.A. piston (L.H.D. vehicles only)

If, for reasons described above, the P.D.W.A. shuttle requires to be re-centralised, adopt the following procedure.

5. Fit a rubber tube, as described in 1 above, to a brake bleed-screw at the opposite end of the car to that which has just been bled.

6. Open the bleed-screw.

7. Switch the ignition on but DO NOT START THE ENGINE. (The brake warning light will glow but the oil warning light will remain extinguished.)

8. Exert a steady pressure on the brake pedal until the brake light dims and the oil light glows. (A click should be felt on the pedal as the shuttle returns to its mid-position.)

9. Tighten the bleed-screw.

NOTE: If the pedal has been pushed too hard the shuttle will move to the other side of the valve, thus requiring the procedure to be repeated on a brake at the opposite end of the car.

MASTER CYLINDER

General

The TR5 employs a tandem master cylinder which consist of two independent and complete hydraulic cylinders in series, one operating on the front brakes the other on the rear. Both cylinders are supplied by a common reservoir divided by a partition.

The master cylinder is mounted in direct line with the brake pedal with a vacuum servo unit interposed, see Fig. 6. Brake pedal pressure is transmitted via a push rod to the vacuum servo unit which in turn transmits the servo assisted pressure via a further push rod to the master cylinder.

Operation of the T.V. C.V. master cylinder (Fig. 3)

Application of pressure on the push rod moves the primary plunger up the cylinder bore and allows a spring-loaded tipping valve to return to centre. The primary supply port is closed by the valve and further movement of the primary plunger results in hydraulic pressure being transmitted to the wheel cylinders of the front brakes. Simultaneously, this pressure acts in conjunction with the increasing force of the intermediate spring to overcome the stronger secondary spring, thus actuating the secondary plunger.

Initial movement of the secondary plunger closes the centre valve supply port and directs hydraulic pressure to the rear brake wheel cylinders.

In case of failure in the rear brake chamber or circuit, the secondary spring is compressed until the coils bind at which point the secondary plunger provides a solid bulkhead for the pressure build up in the front brake chamber.

Failure in the front brake chamber or circuit allows the primary plunger to move forward and contact the secondary plunger which, in effect, provides an extension of the push rod.

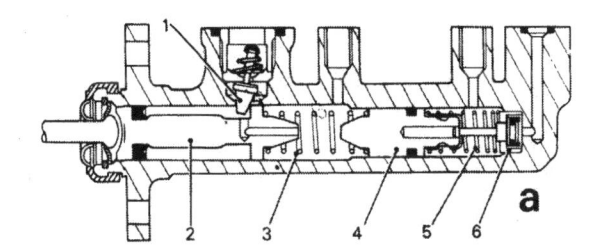

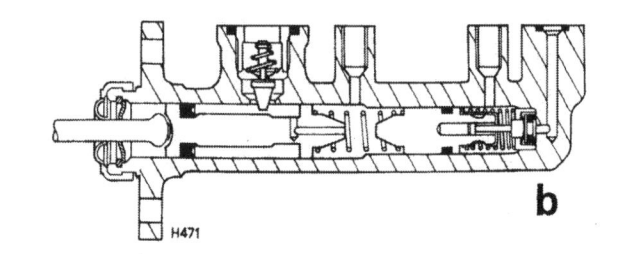

1	Tipping valve	5	Secondary plunger
2	Primary plunger	6	Centre valve
3	Intermediate spring	a	Brake off
4	Secondary plunger	b	Brake applied

Fig. 3. Operation of Master Cylinder

BRAKES

Brake master cylinder — removing (Fig. 6)

1. Detach both fluid pipes from the cylinder body and plug the open holes in the master cylinder to prevent fluid draining on to the paintwork.

2. Remove two nuts (17) retaining the master cylinder assembly to the servo unit.

3. Lift off the cylinder.

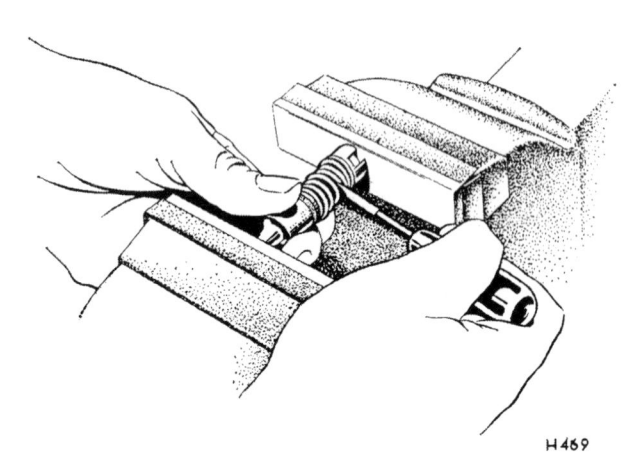

Fig. 4. Pressing the spring retainer back against the secondary plunger

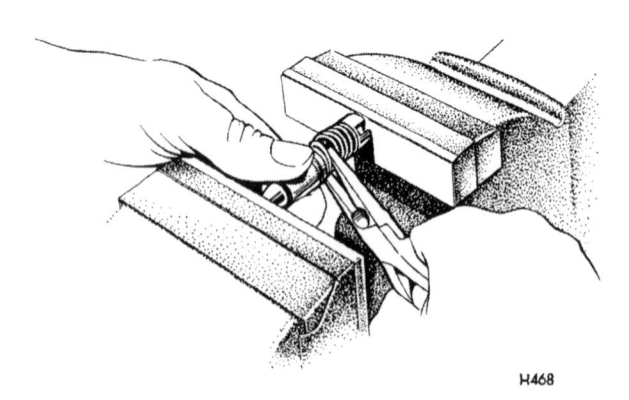

Fig. 5. Depressing the leaf of the spring retainer behind the head of the plunger

Brake master cylinder overhaul (Fig. 1)

Dismantling

1. Drain and discard the master cylinder fluid.

2. Remove four screws (9) attaching the reservoir to the cylinder body.

3. With an Allen key unscrew the tipping valve securing nut (5) and remove the seal (7).

4. Depress the primary plunger and remove the tipping valve (6).

5. Remove the internal parts either by applying low air pressure to the end inlet orifice or by shaking the cylinder body.

6. Separate the plunger and the intermediate spring.

7. Lift the leaf spring of the spring retainer (inset Fig. 1) and remove the spring and centre valve sub-assembly from the secondary plunger (13).

8. Remove the spring (16), valve spacer (17) and spring washer (18) from the valve stem (19), and remove the valve seal (20) from the valve head.

9. Remove the seals from the primary (11) and secondary (13) plungers.

10. Lever out the baffle (2) and remove the cap washer (3) from the filler cap.

Cleaning / examination

Replace all seals by those contained in the service kit. Thoroughly clean all the remaining parts, and the cylinder, with hydraulic cleaning fluid.

Examine the bore of the cylinder, and the plunger, for visible score marks, ridges or corrosion. The slightest imperfection of the bore will necessitate renewing the master cylinder.

Assembling

Prior to assembly lubricate all parts with new hydraulic fluid.

1. Assemble the seals to the primary and secondary plungers.

2. Referring to inset on Fig. 1, fit the valve seal (20), smallest diameter leading, on to the valve head (19).

3. Position the spring washer (18) on the valve stem so that it "flares" away from the valve stem shoulder and follow with the valve spacer (17), legs first.

BRAKES

4. Attach the spring retainer (15) to the valve stem, keyhole first.

5. Slide the secondary spring (16) over the spring retainer, then position the sub-assembly on the secondary plunger (13).

6. The spring must now be compressed whilst the leaf of the spring retainer is pressed down behind the head of the plunger. To do this, position the sub-assembly between the jaws of a bench vice and, to prevent possible contamination, place a clean piece of paper between each end of the sub-assembly and the vice jaws. Close the vice to compress the spring until it is almost coil bound. Use a small screwdriver to press the spring retainer right back against the secondary plunger (Fig. 4). Using a pair of pointed-nose pliers (Fig. 5), depress the leaf of the spring retainer behind the head of the plunger. Ensure that the retainer leaf is straight and firmly located behind the plunger head as shown on Fig. 1 inset.

7. Fit the intermediate spring (12) into position between the primary and secondary plungers.

8. Lubricate the cylinder bore and the plunger seals with hydraulic brake fluid.

9. Insert the plunger assemblies into the bore, valve end leading, easing the entrance of the plunger seals.

10. Press the primary plunger down the bore and fit the tipping valve, securing nut and seal. Tighten to a torque of 35 to 40 lb/ft. (4·84 to 5·53 kg/m).

11. Fit the cap washer and baffle to the filler cap. Screw the cap on the reservoir.

12. Fit the reservoir seals (21 and 7), position the reservoir on the cylinder and secure with the retaining screws.

NOTE: DIFFERENT TANDEM MASTER CYLINDERS HAVE VARYING VOLUME RATIOS (70–30 to 50–50) IT IS THEREFORE OF PARAMOUNT IMPORTANCE TO USE ONLY THE CORRECT REPLACEMENT PARTS OR CYLINDERS.

Brake master cylinder — refitting

1. Place the master cylinder on to the servo unit studs and fit nuts and washers, tightening to a torque of 15·5 to 19·5 lb/ft. (2·14 to 2·7 kg/m).

2. Re-connect both brake pipes and securely tighten.

3. Bleed the system as described on page 3·201.

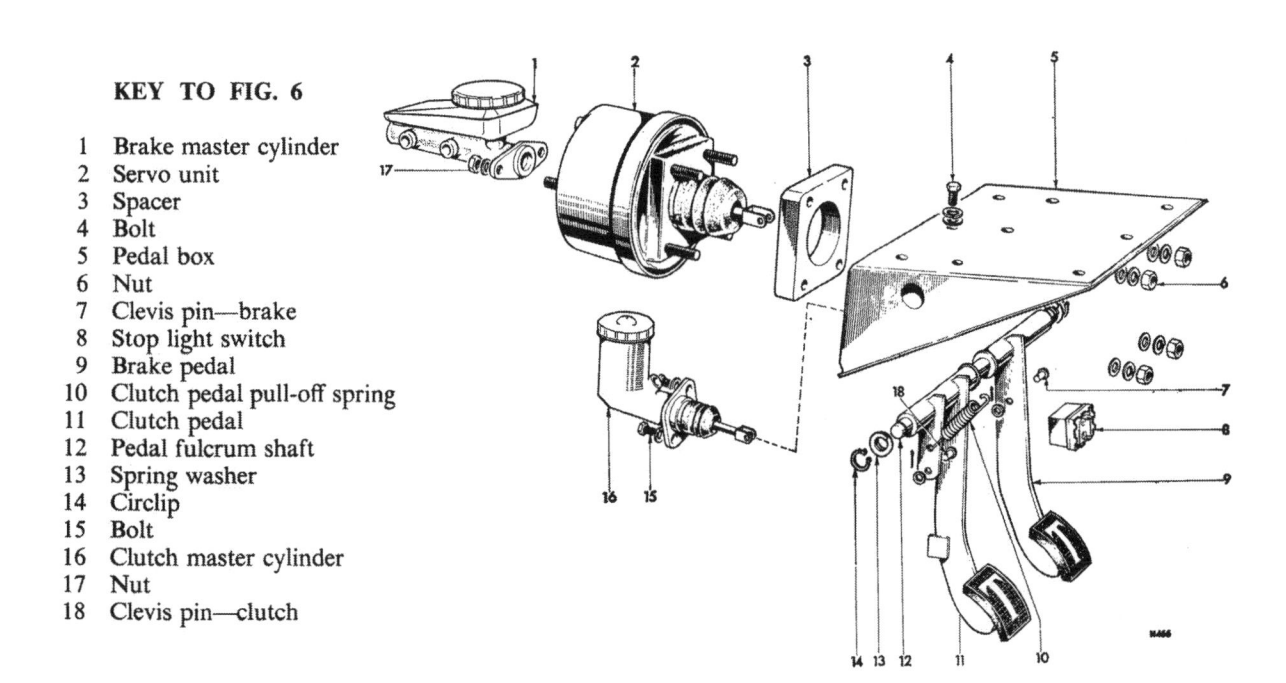

KEY TO FIG. 6

1 Brake master cylinder
2 Servo unit
3 Spacer
4 Bolt
5 Pedal box
6 Nut
7 Clevis pin—brake
8 Stop light switch
9 Brake pedal
10 Clutch pedal pull-off spring
11 Clutch pedal
12 Pedal fulcrum shaft
13 Spring washer
14 Circlip
15 Bolt
16 Clutch master cylinder
17 Nut
18 Clevis pin—clutch

Fig. 6. Master cylinders—servo-pedal box layout

PRESSURE DIFFERENTIAL WARNING ACTUATOR (P.D.W.A.) — L.H.D. VEHICLES ONLY

General (Fig. 7)

The P.D.W.A. is an 'inline' hydraulic valve through which both brake fluid lines are routed. The purpose of the device is to detect failure in either of the systems and to transmit, electrically, warning of the failure, to a light on the facia.

Fig. 7 shows the shuttle valve (4) in the mid-position of the body (2). This is achieved by equalised fluid lines pressure. The switch (1) is in contact with a peripheral groove in the shuttle valve. Lack of pressure in either line allows the pressure in the other line to displace the shuttle and force the plunger to actuate the switch.

Removing and refitting

1. Remove the electrical connection.

2. Disconnect the two inlet and two outlet pipes and plug the exposed ports to prevent loss of fluid and ingress of dirt to the system.

3. Remove the bolt securing the P.D.W.A. to the bulkhead and lift off the unit.

Refitting is a reversal of removing but ensure that all connections are securely tightened before bleeding and, if necessary, recentralise the P.D.W.A. as described on page 3·203.

After bleeding check for fluid leaks with the pedal fully depressed and with the system at rest.

Overhaul

Should an overhaul be necessary, it is advisable to make use of the 'Exchange scheme' and fit a factory reconditioned unit.

Where it is not practicable to fit a replacement unit the following procedure should be adopted for overhauling the unit.

Dismantling (Fig. 7)

1. Remove the unit from the vehicle.

2. Remove the end plug (6) from the unit and discard the copper washer (5).

3. Remove the nylon switch (1).

4. Withdraw the shuttle valve (4) from the bore using, if necessary, a low pressure air line.

5. Remove the two seals from the shuttle valve taking care not to score the piston.

Examination

Thoroughly clean the parts in Ethyl Alcohol or clean brake fluid. Dry the parts thoroughly and inspect the bore of the body and the shuttle valve for scoring or imperfections. The unit must be replaced if the items are found defective.

To test the nylon switch assembly, reconnect to the warning light circuit and actuate the plunger at the base of the switch by pressing it against the earthed frame of the vehicle.

Reassembling

1. Using the fingers only, fit the two new seals on to the piston with the lips facing outwards. Coat the seals with Lockheed Disc Brake Lubricant or equivalent silicone grease.

2. Insert the assembly into the bore, taking care not to bend back the lip of the leading cup.

3. Ensuring that the seating faces on the assembly body and plug are clean and undamaged, fit the new copper washer and screw the plug into the body, tightening to a torque of 16 – 17 lb/ft. (2·21 to 2·35 kg/m).

4. Refit the nylon switch, taking care not to cross the threads. Tighten carefully to a torque of 15 lb/in. (2·07 kg/m). Do not overtighten.

5. Refit the unit to the vehicle.

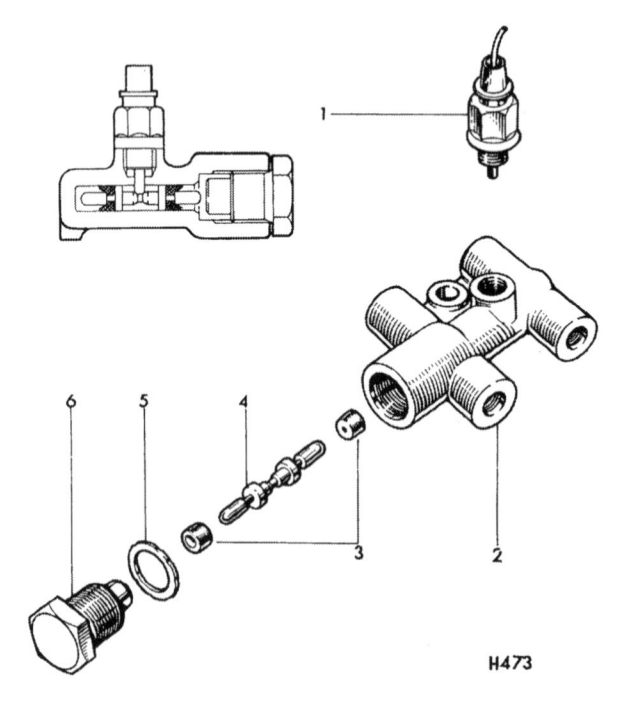

1 Switch	4 Shuttle valve
2 Body	5 Washer
3 Seal	6 End plug

Fig. 7. Pressure differential warning actuator

BRAKES

3·207

VACUUM SERVO UNIT

General

A mechanically operated vacuum servo unit, interposed between the master cylinder and the pedal, assists the driver to apply increased force to the brake master cylinder.

Operation (Fig. 8)

During the normal 'brake off' condition a diaphragm (3) is suspended in a partial vacuum created by the inlet manifold which evacuates air from the servo unit via a non-return valve.

Upon application of the brakes the valve operating rod assembly (8) moves forward to close the vacuum port to the rear of the diaphragm and subsequently to open a port to atmosphere. Mechanical contact then takes place between the valve operating rod and the master cylinder push rod. Consequently, with a vacuum at the front of the diaphragm and atmosphere at the rear, the master cylinder push rod is moved, with assistance, forward.

The brakes are held on by back pressure from the master cylinder push rod (17) acting against the reaction disc (13) and causing the centre of the disc to extrude and push back the valve operating rod (8) which will close the atmospheric port.

When the brakes are released, the atmospheric port is closed, the vacuum port is opened and the diaphragm return spring pushes the diaphragm to the off position. Air is evacuated from the unit to the inlet manifold and the diaphragm is again suspended in a partial vacuum.

In the event of a servo failure mechanical contact between the valve operating rod, reaction disc and master cylinder push rod ensures brake operation without servo assistance.

Servicing

Servicing of the servo unit is restricted to changing the filter (5), the non-return valve (16), the dust cover (6) and the seal and plate assembly (19). Any major failure of the unit necessitates a replacement unit.

Replacing the filter is the only normal replacement required. This should be done when new brake shoes or discs are fitted. Before replacing the filter check the condition of the dust cover, and if necessary, fit a new one.

KEY TO FIG. 8

1. Front shell
2. Rear shell
3. Diaphragm
4. Diaphragm plate
5. Filter
6. Dust cover
7. End cap
8. Valve operating rod assembly
9. Seal
10. Bearing
11. Retainer
12. Valve retaining plate
13. Reaction disc
14. Diaphragm return spring
15. "O" ring
16. Non-return valve
17. Hydraulic push rod
18. Retainer/sprag washer
19. Seal and plate assembly

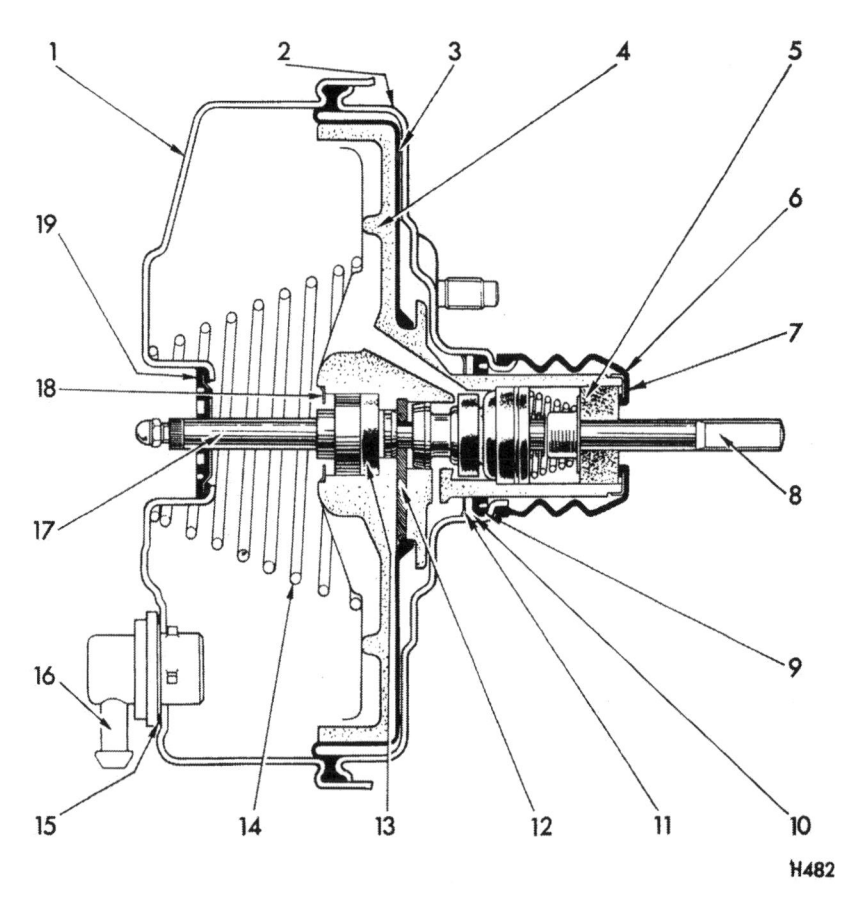

Fig. 8. Vacuum servo arrangement

Removing and refitting the servo unit (Fig. 6)

1. Remove the master cylinder (see page 3·204).

2. Disconnect the vacuum pipe at the non-return valve.

3. Remove the clevis pin (7), secured by a split pin, retaining the operating rod to the brake pedal (9).

4. Remove the four nuts (6) and washers retaining the servo unit to the pedal box (5).

5. Lift out the unit and remove the spacer (3).

Refitting is a direct reversal of removing.

Replacing the non-return valve

Note the angle of the non-return valve nozzle in relation to the shell. Press down on the valve as shown in Fig. 9 and, using a suitable spanner, turn the valve one third of a turn anti-clockwise to release the fixing lugs.

Fit a new 'O' ring on the new valve; place the valve in position on the unit and press the valve to compress the 'O' ring, then turn the valve clockwise one third of a turn to engage the lugs.

Replacing the filter

Pull back the dust cover and remove the filter from the diaphragm plate neck. To facilitate assembly cut the new filter diagonally from the outer edge to the centre hole. Press the new filter into the neck of the diaphragm plate and replace the dust cover.

Renewing the seal and plate assembly

Remove the seal and plate assembly from the front shell recess by gripping the centre rib with a pair of pointed nose pliers.

Using the grease in the replacement kit* lubricate the new seal and plate assembly and press into the recess.

* A service kit, containing a dust cover, end cap, filter, non-return valve, 'O' ring, seal and plate assembly and a tube of Rykon 'O' grease, is available for the limited servicing operations described above.

Push rod

The servo master cylinder push rod is set to the correct length by the manufacturers; it is secured by Locktite and no attempt must be made to alter the setting.

To check the length of a push rod which has become worn or damaged, proceed as follows: Place a straight edge across the front shell recess as shown in Fig. 10 and, with feeler gauges, check the clearance between the end of the push rod and the straight edge. The clearance should be 0·011" to 0·016" (0·28 to 0·41 mm); replace the unit if the setting is incorrect.

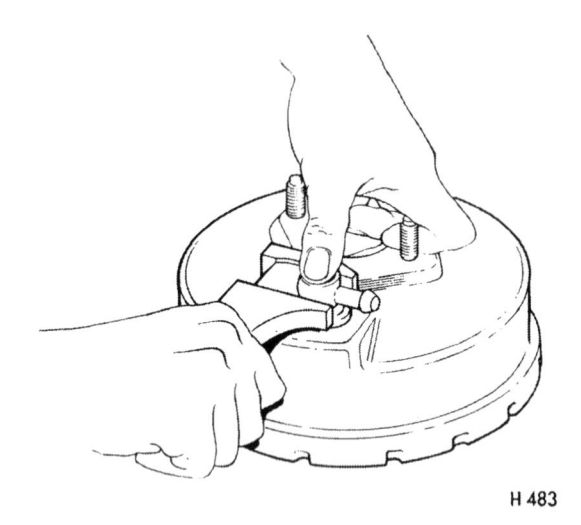

Fig. 9. Fitting the non-return valve

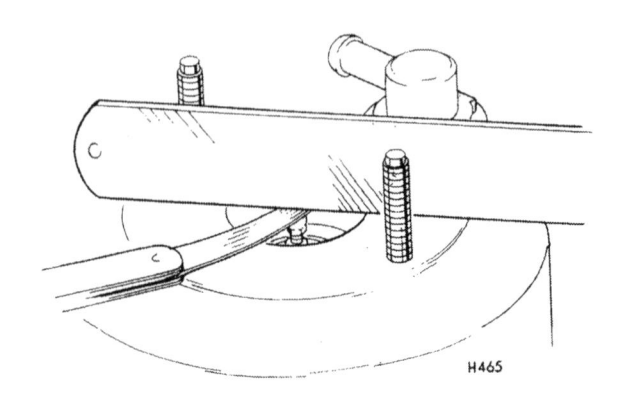

Fig. 10. Checking the clearance between the push rod and the front shell

BRAKES

Pedal Box (Fig. 6)

Removing and dismantling

1. Remove the brake master cylinder, page 3·204.
2. Remove the servo unit, page 3·207.
3. Remove the clutch master cylinder, Group 2.
4. Disconnect the brake light switch.
5. Remove nine bolts (4) on the top of the bulkhead panel, and lift out the box assembly.
6. Remove the clutch pedal return spring (10), brake switch (8), circlip (14) and withdraw the fulcrum shaft (12).

Re-assembling and refitting is a reversal of removing and dismantling. However, ensure that the switch plate is not bent as this will cause the switch to act as a pedal stop and prevent full recuperation of the master cylinder.

Rear Brakes

The rear drum brakes are as fitted to the TR4A detailed on page 3·208 of the manual. However, later models of the TR4A and all TR5's are fitted with a spring pin steady clip as shown on Fig. 12 of this supplement. It is important when fitting this clip that it does not protrude beyond the brake shoe web.

Handbrake

The handbrake unit is as fitted to the TR4A, see page 3·214 of the manual.

Front Brakes

The front disc brakes are as fitted to the TR4A, see page 3·204 of the manual.

Fig. 11. Master Cylinder—Danger line

BRAKES — REGULAR MAINTENANCE

Weekly attention

Every week check the level of fluid in the brake master cylinder reservoir. The fluid level is visible through the translucent casing of the reservoir, **do not remove the cap.** A gradual lowering of the level over a long period is caused by brake pad wear and does not require topping-up. A sudden appreciable drop in the level must be investigated, the cause ascertained and rectified immediately.

Do not allow the level to drop below the danger line on the side of the casing (see Fig. 11).

To avoid dirt entering the system ensure that the reservoir is clean externally before removing the cap. Use only new fluid from a sealed container and re-seal the container after use. Replace the reservoir cap immediately after filling.

Every 6,000 miles

Check and adjust the brakes as necessary.

Every 12,000 miles

De-dust the rear brake linings and examine the linings and the front brake pads for wear or contamination from oil and grease. Renew worn or contaminated pads or linings.

Every 36,000 miles

Thoroughly overhaul the braking system, renewing all seals and defective items. Renew the brake fluid.

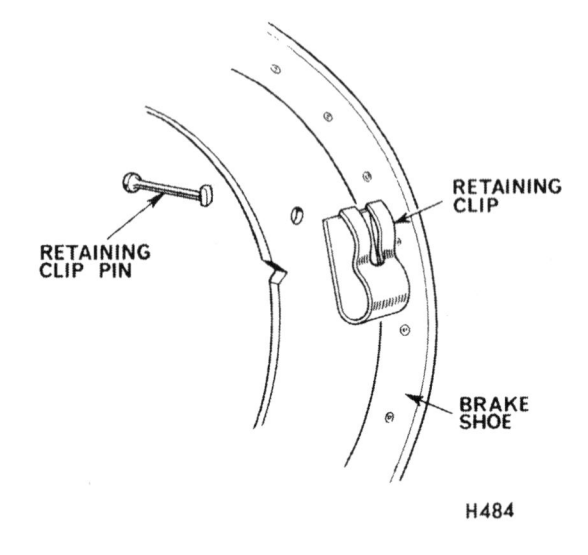

Fig. 12. Brake shoe retaining clip

TRIUMPH
TR5-PI
WORKSHOP MANUAL SUPPLEMENT

GROUP 4

Comprising:

Steering

4·101

TRIUMPH TR5

WORKSHOP MANUAL

SUPPLEMENT TO GROUP 4

CONTENTS

	Section
STEERING COLUMN	**4·102**

STEERING

4·102

STEERING COLUMN

Servicing operations for the TR5 steering column assembly are similar to those described on page 4·207 TR4 Workshop Manual.

Fig. 1 shows revised lower steering column and steering wheel details which replace items 1-19 and 48-52 shown on page 4·206.

NOTE: A cardboard sleeve is now fitted to the upper outer column between the end of the cable trough and the upper clamp. This is to ensure that the correct amount of collapse on impact is available.

All other details for steering and suspension described under Group 4 of the Workshop Manual remain unaltered.

For revised suspension and steering data refer to page 0·103.

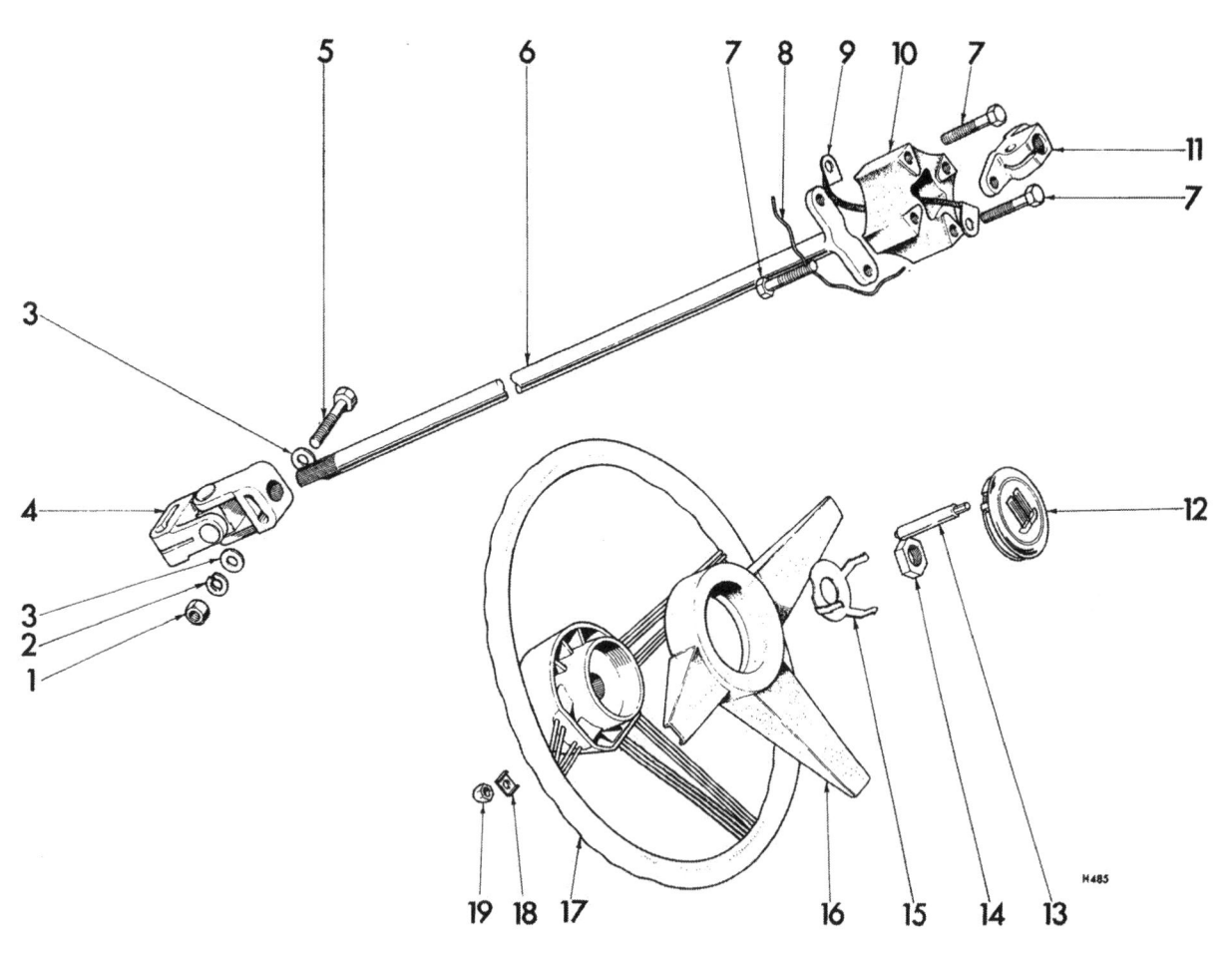

1 Nut
2 Spring washer
3 Plain washer
4 Universal coupling
5 Pinch bolt
6 Lower steering column
7 Bolt
8 Locking wire
9 Earthing cable
10 Rubber coupling
11 Adaptor
12 Horn push
13 Horn brush
14 Nut
15 Clip
16 Wheel trim
17 Steering wheel
18 Clamp
19 "Dotloc" acorn unit

Fig. 1. Steering column details

TRIUMPH
TR5-PI
WORKSHOP MANUAL SUPPLEMENT

GROUP 5

Comprising:

Body

TRIUMPH TR5
WORKSHOP MANUAL

SUPPLEMENT TO GROUP 5

CONTENTS

	Section
Doors	5·201
Door locks	5·201
Facia panel	5·207
Heater Unit	5·209

BODY

DOORS

Lubrication

Before refitting the door casing and other items ensure that all moving parts are adequately greased.

After assembly and once a month, introduce a few drops of thin machine oil into the outside key slots and on to the latch inside the lock case.

IMPORTANT: The private lock cylinder must not under any circumstances be lubricated with grease or graphite.

A. Trim panel

1. **To remove** (Figs. 2 and 4)

    (a) Lever off two buttons (29), unscrew the exposed screws (30) and remove the washers (31).

    (b) Remove the interior handles (26) and (28) by pressing the escutcheons (25) firmly against the trim panel, push out the retaining pins (24) as illustrated in Fig. 5.

    (c) Prise the trim panel from the door.

    (d) Remove the coil springs (23) from the spindles.

2. To refit: Reverse the removal procedure.

B. Remote control

1. **To remove** (Fig. 3)

    (a) Perform operation A1.

    (b) Remove the spring clip (57) and waved washer (56) and release the link arm from the lock.

    (c) Take out three screws (60) with washers and remove the remote control assembly (39) from the door.

2. **To align the unit** (Fig. 3)

    (a) Perform operation A1.

    (b) Manually set the latch-claw into the fully latched position (two distinct clicks will be heard). This enables the remote control mechanism to be set in the locked position whilst the door is open.

    (c) Slacken three securing screws (60) and move the remote control towards or away from the lock until the spring-loaded lever (58) just contacts the spring (59) as illustrated. The holes in the remote control unit are elongated for adjustment purposes. Finally tighten the three securing screws.

3. **To refit:** Reverse the removal procedure.

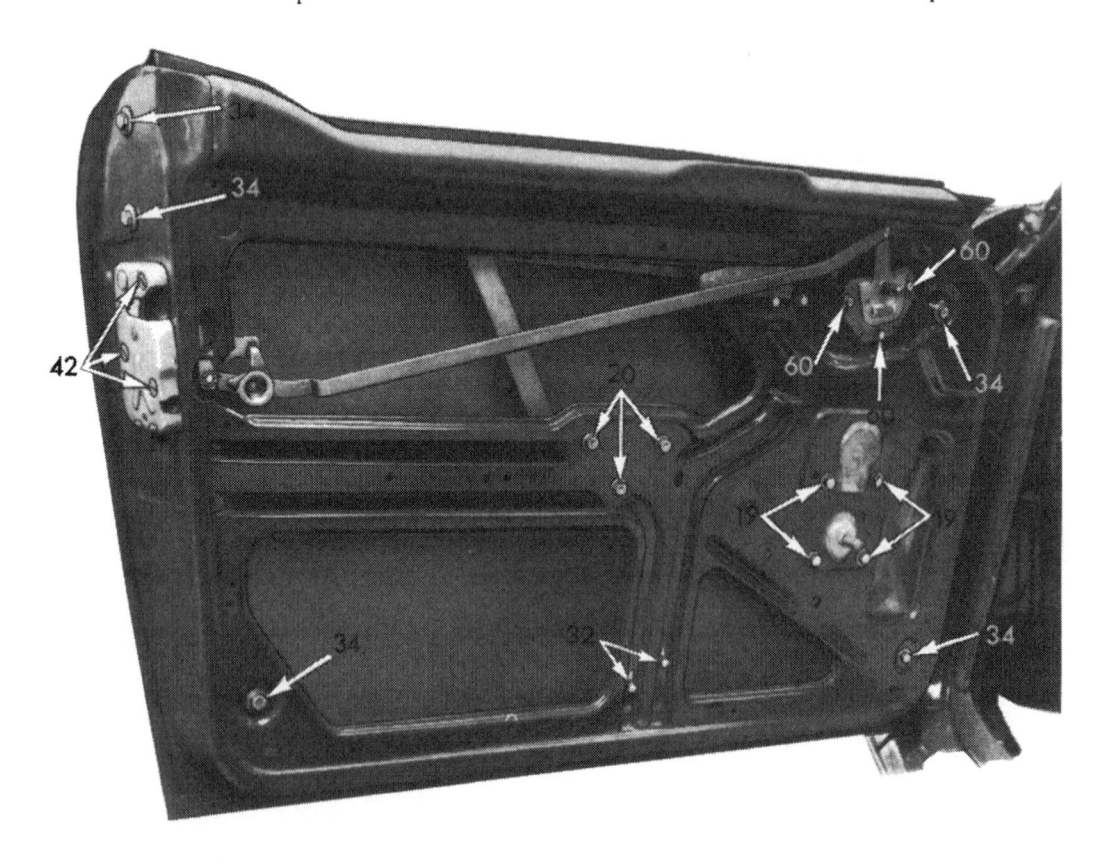

Fig. 1. Door component attachment

BODY

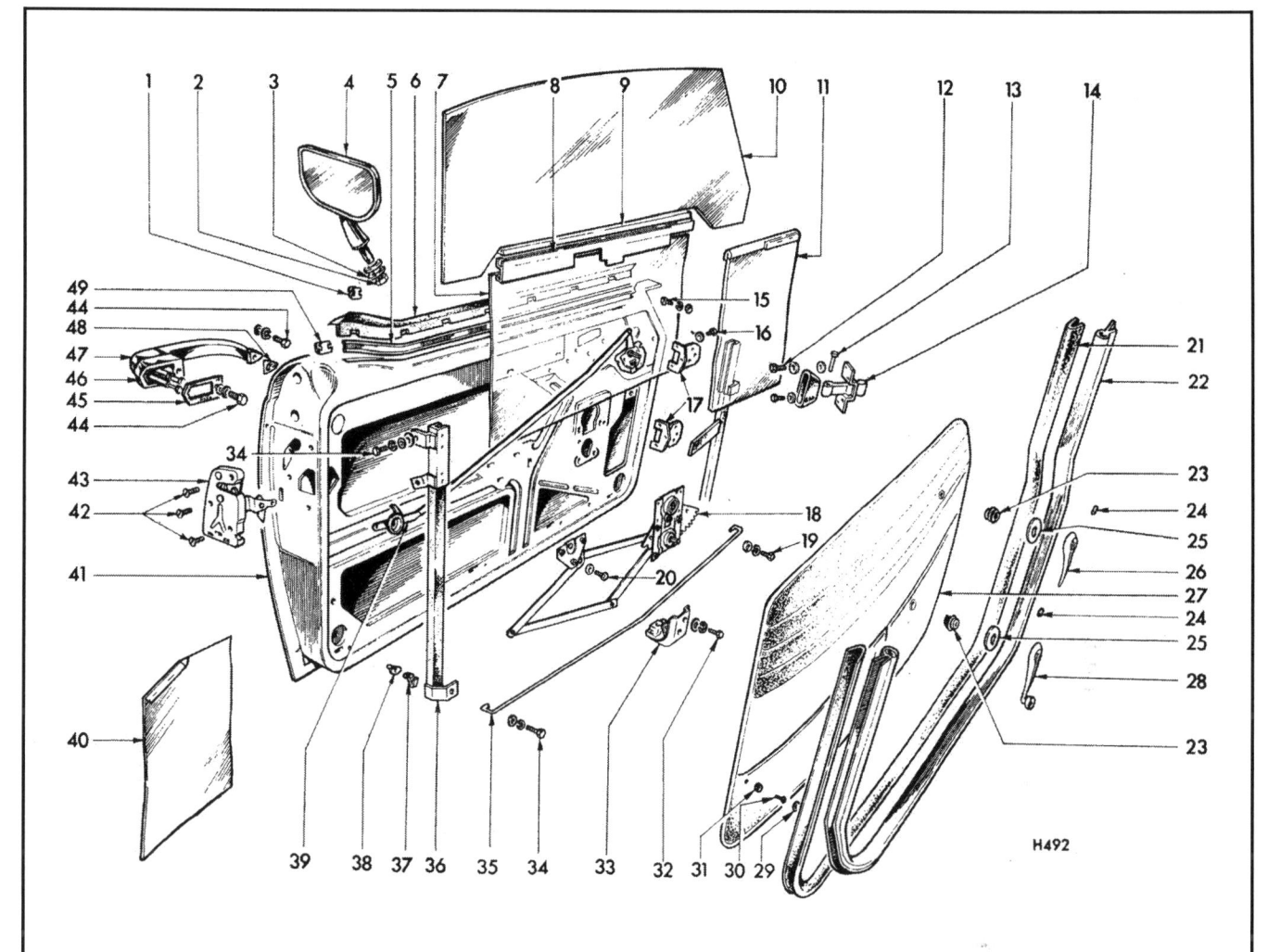

5·202

KEY TO FIGS. 1, 2, 3, 4, 6 and 7

1	Trim clip	23	Spring	44	Setscrew—door handle attachment
2	Nut ⎫ Door mirror	24	Retaining pin		
3	Washer ⎭ attachment	25	Escutcheon plate	45	Seating washer
4	Exterior door mirror	26	Remote control handle	46	Outside door handle
5	Inner weatherstrip	27	Trim panel	47	Push button—door handle
6	Outer weatherstrip	28	Window regulator handle	48	Seating washer
7	Water deflector curtain	29	Cover button ⎫ door pocket	49	Trim-clip
8	Glass channel	30	Screw ⎬ attachment	50	Locknut
9	Glazing strip	31	Retaining washer ⎭	51	Adjustment screw
10	Glass	32	Screw—stop bracket	52	Lock contactor
11	Water deflector curtain	33	Glass—stop bracket	53	Anti-burst strap
12	Screw—check arm	34	Setscrew—glass run channel	54	Screw—striker plate
13	Pin—check arm	35	Tie rod	55	Anti-burst striker plate
14	Check arm	36	Glass run channel	56	Waved washer
15	Bolt—hinge to "A" post	37	Clip	57	Spring clip
16	Bolt—hinge to door	38	Snap-sac	58	Lever
16	Door hinge	39	Remote control unit	59	Spring
18	Window regulator mechanism	40	Water deflector curtain	60	Setscrew—remote control unit
19	Setscrew ⎫ Window regulator	41	Door	61	Lock operating lever
20	Setscrew ⎭ attachment	42	Screw—lock attachment	62	Locking lever
21	Sealing rubber	43	Anti-burst lock	63	Operating fork
22	Draught excluder			64	Spring collar

Fig. 2. Door details

BODY

C. Glass-run channel

1. **To remove** (Figs. 1 and 2)

    (a) Perform operation A1.

    (b) Loosely refit the regulating handle and raise the glass to the fully closed position.

    (c) Remove three hexagon headed bolts (34) and washers. Pull the lower end of the channel (36) away from the tension wire (35).

    (d) Lower the channel into the bottom of the door and manoeuvre it through the lower aperture.

2. **To refit**: Reverse the removal procedure.

D. Anti-burst door lock

In the event of a collision causing severe distortion of the door aperture, this feature resists the separation of the latching elements and the consequent risk of the door flying open.

1. **To remove** (Figs. 2 and 3)

    (a) Raise the glass to the fully closed position and perform operation A1.

    (b) Perform operation B1 (b).

    (c) Take out three countersunk screws (42).

    (d) Lift the lock operating lever (61) sufficiently to allow the lock unit to be withdrawn through its aperture in the door end panel.

    NOTE: No adjustment of the lock unit is required.

2. **To refit**: Reverse the removal procedure.

E. Exterior door handle

1. **To remove** (Fig. 2)

    (a) Raise the glass to the fully closed position and perform operation A1.

    (b) Release the handle by unscrewing two screws (44) and washers located on the inside of the door panel.

2. **To adjust push button** (Fig. 7)

    (a) Perform operation E1 (a).

    (b) Release the locknut (50) and screw the bolt (51) in or out as required; finally re-tighten the locknut.

3. **To refit**: Reverse the removal procedure.

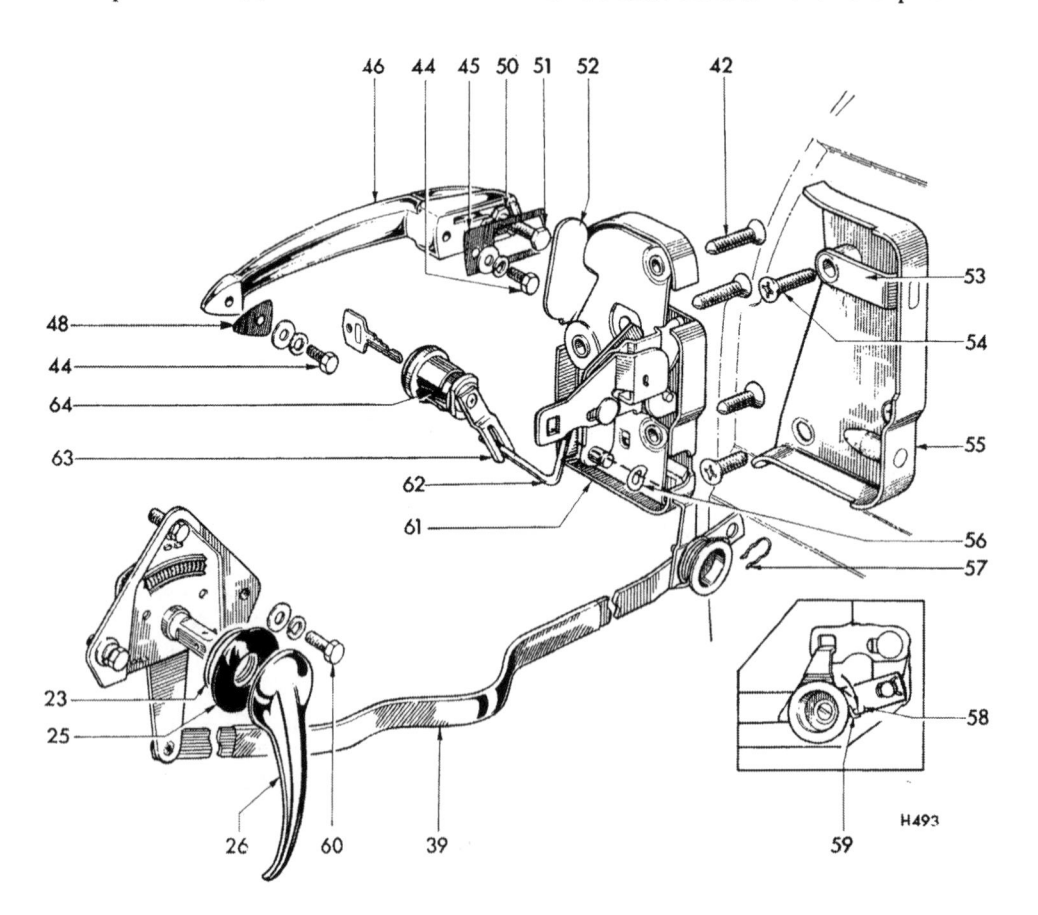

Fig. 3. Anti-burst lock details

BODY

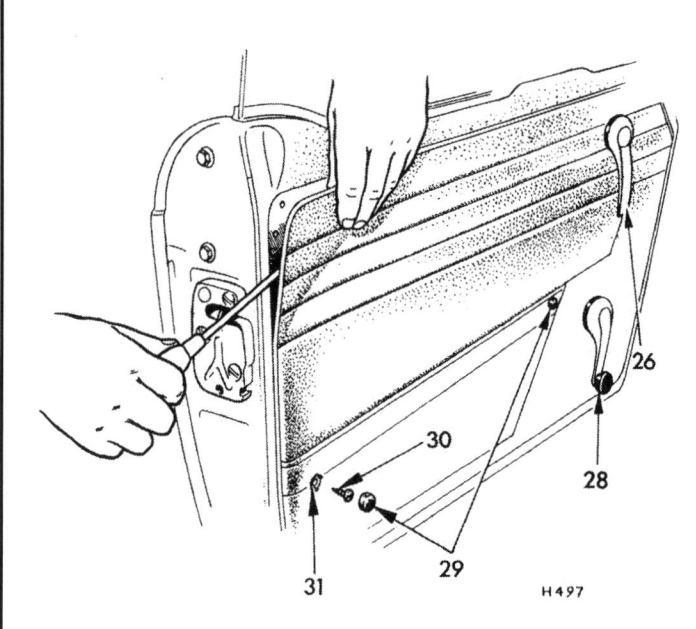

5·204

Fig. 4. Removing the trim panel

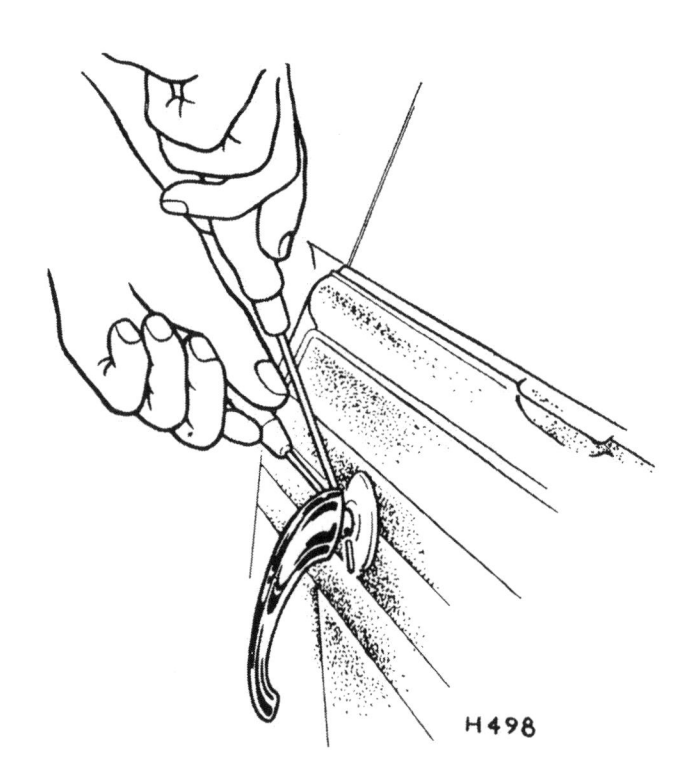

Fig. 5. Removing interior handles

F. Window regulator mechanism

1. **To remove** (Figs. 1 and 2)

    (a) Perform operation A1.

    (b) Loosely refit the regulating handle and raise the glass to the half open position.

    (c) Take out three screws (20) with washers, and four screws (19) with washers securing the window regulator mechanism to the door inner panel.

    (d) Working through the large aperture of the door, slide the complete mechanism to release the two lifting studs from the glass lifting channel.

    (e) Remove the complete regulator mechanism from the door.

2. **To refit:** Reverse the removal procedure.

G. Door glass

1. **To remove** (Fig. 2)

    (a) Perform operation A1.

    (b) Loosely refit the handle and lower the glass.

    (c) Remove the inner weatherstrip (5) by pushing its lower edge upward with a screwdriver from inside the door. This weatherstrip is retained by seven small spring clips (49).

    (d) Perform operation F1 (c) and (d).

    (e) Lift the glass out of the door, taking care not to damage the water deflector panel which is attached to the glass by the channel.

2. **To refit**

    (a) Fold the deflector flat against the inner side of the glass and place the glass into the door.

    (b) Reverse operation F1 (c) and (d), and lower the glass.

    (c) Reposition the deflector panel.

    (d) Using a hooked tool (Fig. 8), hold the spring clips (49) in position and push the inner weatherstrip (5) back into place. The hooked tool may be used to fit any clip which requires renewing.

    (e) Perform operation A2.

H. Anti-burst striker plate

1. **To remove** (Figs. 2 and 6)

    (a) Remove three countersunk screws (42) and release the striker plate (43) from the 'B' post.

2. **To adjust**

    (a) The striker plate (43) should not normally require attention, but when adjustment is required it must be carried out by a process of trial and error proved by checking the door closing action and its position when closed. Ensure that the striker plate is in the horizontal plane relative to the axis of the door movement and that the securing screws are finally tightened.

NOTE: Never slam a door when adjusting the striker plate as any misalignment may damage the components.

Fig. 6. Anti-burst Striker Plate

J. Private lock

The key operated locking barrel is retained by a twin-legged spring collar (64) inside the door.

1. **To remove** (Fig. 3)

    (a) Perform operations A1 and C1.

    (b) Using a suitable tool, compress the collar legs sufficiently to allow the barrel to be withdrawn from the outside of the door.

2. **To refit**

    (a) Ensure that the collar (64) is in place, then insert the key operated locking barrel in the aperture of the door panel, with its operating fork inclined towards the shut face, and press firmly into position.

    (b) Perform operations C2 and A2.

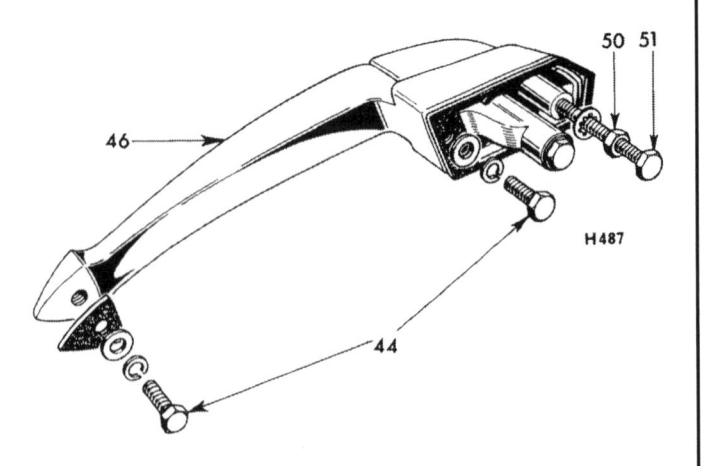

Fig. 7. Push Button adjustment

BODY

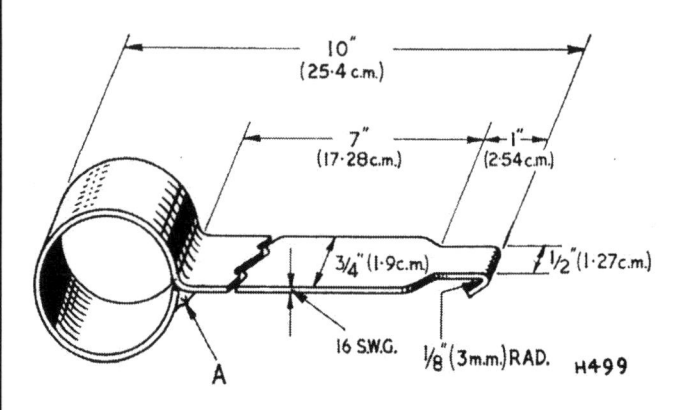

5·206

Fig. 8. Tool for fitting Weatherstrip

Fig. 9. Removing the door

K. Door exterior mirror

1. **To remove** (Fig. 2)

    (a) Perform operation A1.

    (b) Loosely refit the regulator handle and raise the glass to the fully closed position.

    (c) Access to the nut and washer retaining the mirror to the door is gained through the uppermost door aperture.

    (d) Release the nut using a bent shafted ring spanner.

    (e) Withdraw the mirror from the door.

2. **To refit:** Reverse the removal procedure.

L. Door Assembly

1. **To remove** (Figs. 2 and 9)

    (a) Remove four screws securing the dash side carpet to the 'A' post.

    (b) Release the pin (13) from the check arm (14). This pin is retained by a small spring clip.

    (c) Remove six bolts (15) securing the hinges to the 'A' post and lift the door from the vehicle.

2. **To adjust**

    Vertical adjustment of the door is by means of the bolts securing the hinges to the 'A' post. In and out adjustment of the leading edge of the door is by means of the hinge to door securing bolts.

    (a) Slacken the bolts securing the section requiring adjustment and move the door to provide uniform clearance between the contours of the door and the wing.

3. **To refit:** Reverse the removal procedure.

BODY

FACIA ASSEMBLY

To remove (Figs. 10 and 11)

Isolate the battery. Remove the facia support bracket (47) by unscrewing six bolts (46 and 54).

Disconnect the facia ventilation hoses (27) from the heater box and the support clips (37) shown in Fig. 12. Release the heater control cables from the heater box and the water control valve inside the engine bay. Disconnect the drive cables from the speedometer and tachometer and the cold start mixture control cable from the metering unit and butterflies. Unscrew the oil pressure pipe from the gauge unit.

Remove the steering column cowl (see TR4A Manual, Group 4).

Disconnect the facia reinforcement (32) by unscrewing two screws (38) with washers (36) and (37); located in line with the centre of the glove box (18). Slacken the screw (35) and move the reinforcement outward. Unscrew six screws (16) securing the glove box (18) to the facia. Remove the speedometer and tachometer. Disconnect the wiring harness from the switches, instruments and warning lights and slacken the trunnion screw securing the scuttle ventilator rod to the control lever.

Unscrew five nuts (8) with washers (6 and 7) from the studs securing the upper edge of the facia panel to the scuttle top panel and two bolts (27) one each side securing the outer facia to the 'A' post.

Lower the facia panel away from the studs and remove it from the car.

To refit

Reverse the removal procedure and refer to Group 6—Facia connections. Road test the vehicle and check the operation of all instruments and controls.

VENEERED FACIA PANEL

To remove (Fig. 11)

Unscrew five cross/recess screws (5) with washers (4) securing the veneered panel to the facia and two screws (41) securing the glove box check arm (40) to the glove box lid (42).

Unscrew the oil pressure pipe from the gauge unit and disconnect the wiring harness from the instrument cluster, windshield washer switch and windshield wiper switch. Remove the speedometer and tachometer. Lift the veneered panel away from the facia complete with instruments.

To refit: Reverse the removal procedure.

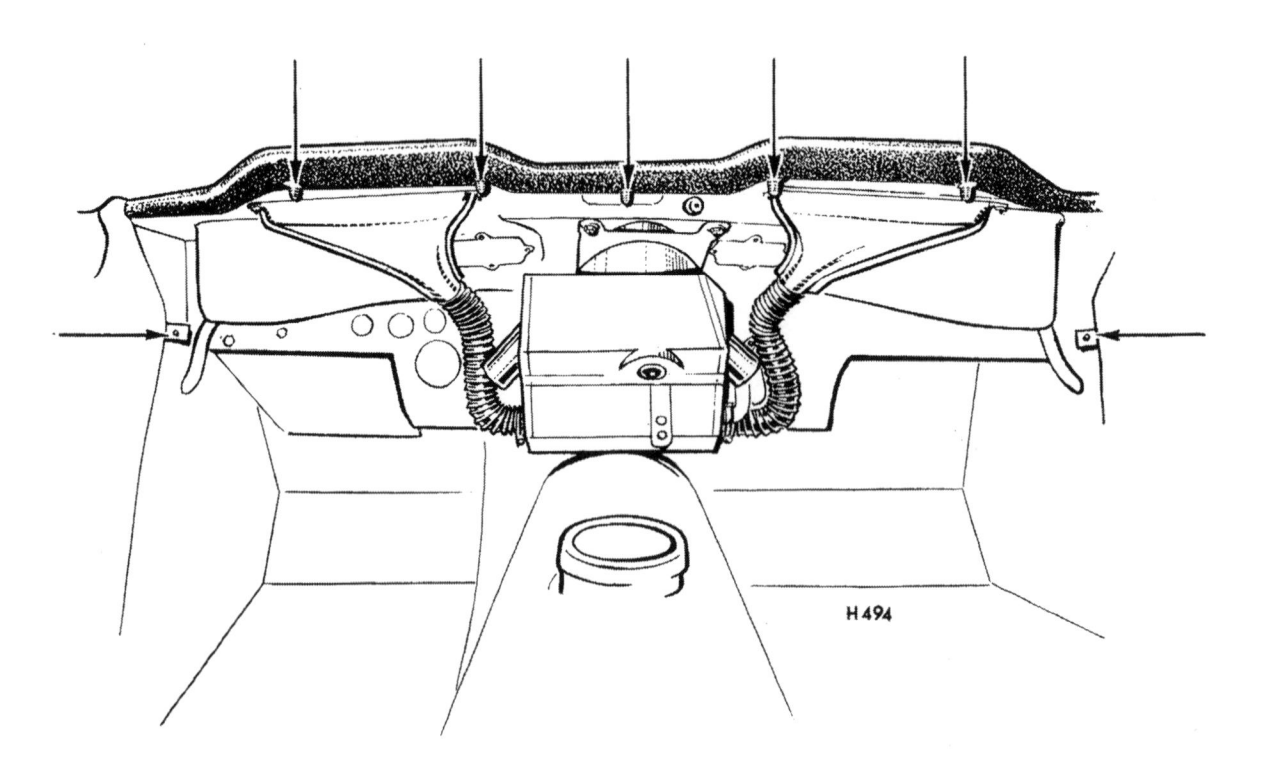

Fig. 10. Facia panel mounting to Body (arrows indicate mounting points)

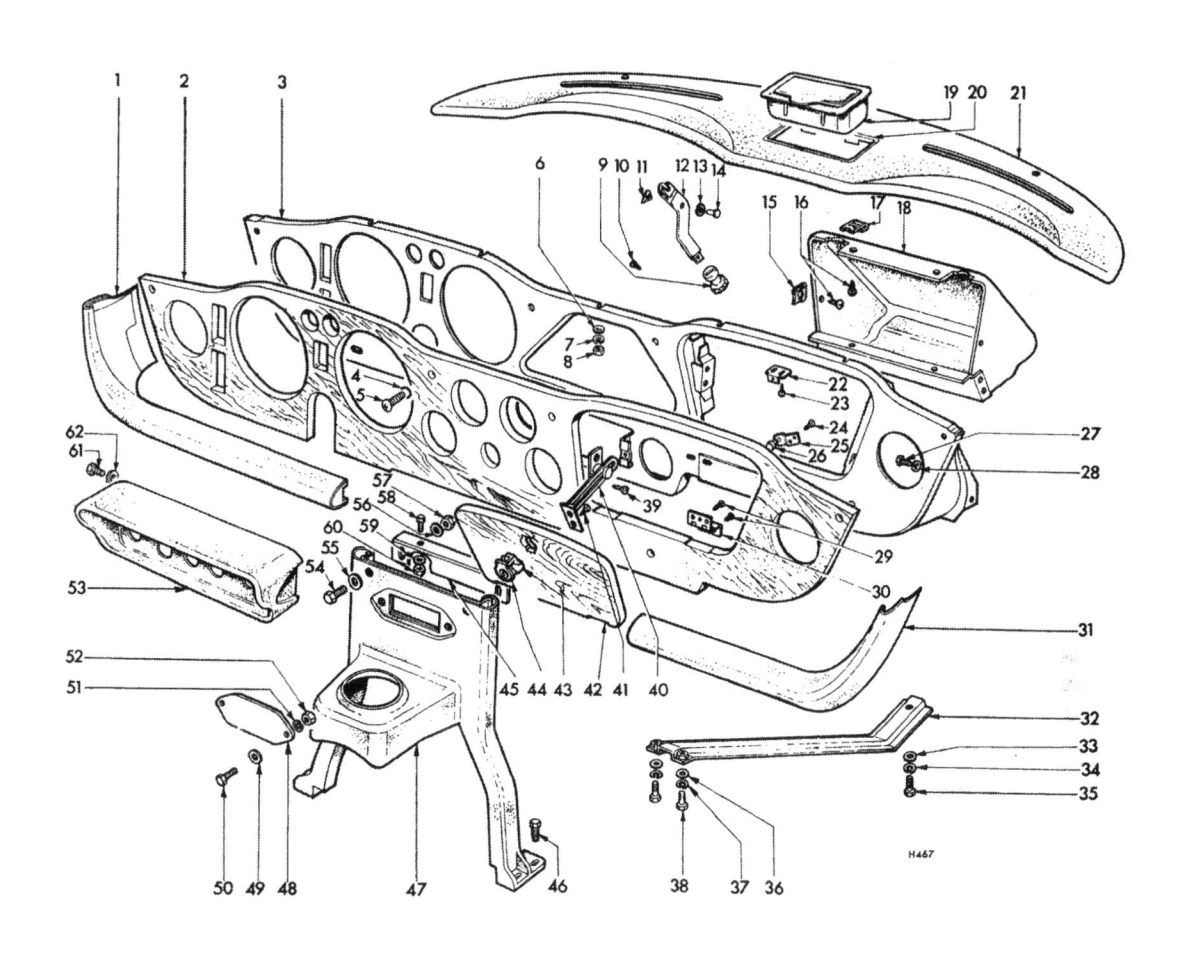

BODY

5·208

1	Crash pad	22	Striker bracket	42	Glove box-lid
2	Veneered facia panel	23	Striker screw	43	Clamp—glove box lock
3	Metal facia panel	24	Screw—buffer bracket	44	Glove box lock
4	Cup washer ⎫ Veneered facia	25	Buffer bracket	45	Bracket
5	Screw ⎭ to metal facia	26	Buffer	46	Bolt—support bracket to floor
6	Washer ⎫ Complete facia	27	Bolt ⎫ Complete facia	47	Support bracket—facia to floor
7	Lock washer ⎬ to scuttle top	28	Lock washer ⎭ to "A" post	48	Cover plate—radio mounting
8	Nut ⎭ panel	29	Screw—hinge	49	Washer ⎫ Cover plate to
9	Vent lever-knob	30	Hinge—glove box	50	Setscrew ⎭ support bracket
10	Screw	31	Crash pad	51	Lock washer
11	Retainer	32	Support channel—facia to dash	52	Nut
12	Vent lever	33	Washer ⎫ Support channel	53	Switch plinth
13	Lock washer	34	Lock washer ⎬ to	54	Bolt ⎫
14	Rivet	35	Setscrew ⎭ dash	55	Washer ⎬ Support bracket
15	Spire nut ⎫ Glove box	36	Washer ⎫ Support channel	56	Washer ⎭ to fixing bracket
16	Screw ⎬ to	37	Lock washer ⎬ to	57	Nyloc nut
17	Spire nut ⎭ facia	38	Setscrew ⎭ facia panel	58	Setscrew ⎫ Fixing bracket
18	Glove box	39	Screw—check link	59	Washer ⎬ to facia
19	Ash tray	40	Check link—glove box lid	60	Nut
20	Ash tray retainer	41	Screw—check link	61	Setscrew ⎫ Switch plinth
21	Scuttle top-crash pad			62	Washer ⎭ to facia panel

Fig. 11. Facia panel details

BODY

HEATER UNIT

To remove (Fig. 12)

Isolate the battery and drain the cooling system. Remove the facia assembly (as described above). Disconnect the ventilation hoses (27) and the outlet and inlet water hoses (25 and 28) from the heater box. Remove three bolts (41) with washers, supporting the heater unit to the scuttle top panel and one nut (38) with washer, supporting the heater unit to the dash front panel.

Lift out the heater unit from the car, taking care not to spill any of the water left in the heater matrix as this will damage carpets, etc.

To refit

Reverse the removal procedure and refer to Group 6 for Facia connections and wiring diagram.

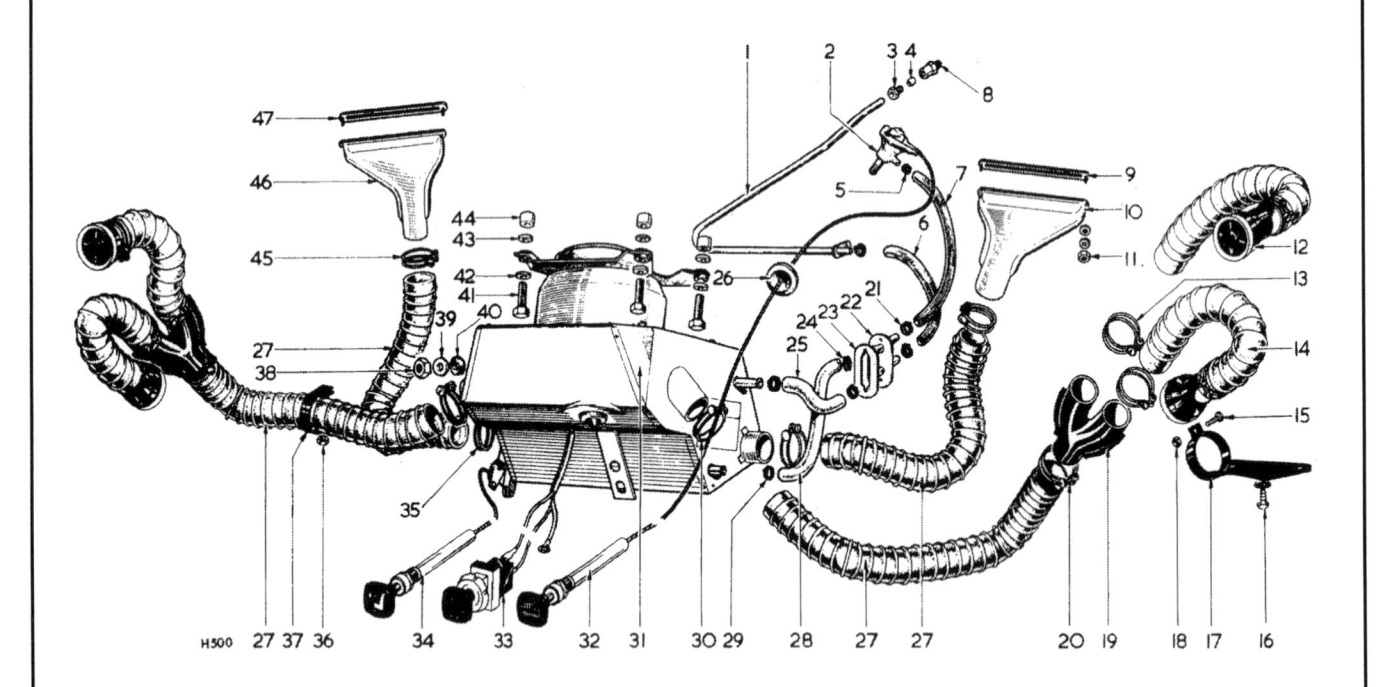

#	Description	#	Description	#	Description
1	Water return pipe	17	Hose bracket	32	Heat control
2	Water control valve	18	Nut—bracket attachment	33	Blower switch
3	Nut	19	Tube "Y" piece	34	Air distribution control
4	Olive	20	Hose clip	35	Hose clip
5	Clip	21	Hose clip	36	Nut—hose
6	Hose	22	Bulkhead adaptor	37	Hose support clip
7	Hose	23	Seal—adaptor	38	Nut ⎫ Heater unit to
8	Adaptor	24	Hose clip	39	Washer ⎬ dash panel
9	Finisher	25	Water hose	40	Washer ⎭
10	Air duct	26	Control cable grommet	41	Bolt
11	Nut—duct attachment	27	Ventilation hose	42	Washer ⎫ Heater unit to
12	Air vent	28	Water hose	43	Washer ⎬ scuttle top panel
13	Hose clip	29	Hose clip	44	Spacer
14	Ventilation hose	30	Hose clip	45	Hose clip
15	Setscrew—hose attachment	31	Heater unit	46	Air duct
16	Screw—bracket attachment			47	Finisher

Fig. 12. Heater arrangement

TRIUMPH
TR5-PI
WORKSHOP MANUAL SUPPLEMENT

GROUP 6

Comprising:

Electrical

TRIUMPH TR5

WORKSHOP MANUAL

SUPPLEMENT TO GROUP 6

CONTENTS

	Section
Wiring diagram	**6·102**
Harness	**6·106**
Facia connections	**6·108**
Fuse box	**6·110**
Alternator	**6·111**
Alternator control unit	**6·118**
Petrol pump	**6·122**
Starter motor	**6·127**
Ignition distributor	**6·134**
Bulb chart	**6·140**
Turn signal flasher unit	**6·141**
Brake line failure indication — left hand steer only	**6·142**
Hazard warning system — left hand steer only	**6·143**
Windscreen washer pump	**6·145**

KEY TO WIRING DIAGRAM — RIGHT HAND STEER

CAUTION: THIS VEHICLE IS FITTED WITH A NEGATIVE EARTH ELECTRICAL SYSTEM. ENSURE THAT THE BATTERY EARTH LEAD IS ALWAYS CONNECTED TO THE BATTERY NEGATIVE TERMINAL.

THE ALTERNATOR AND ALTERNATOR CONTROL UNIT — AND POSSIBLY SOME ACCESSORIES — CONTAIN POLARITY SENSITIVE COMPONENTS THAT MAY BE IRREPARABLY DAMAGED IF SUBJECTED TO INCORRECT POLARITY.

1 Alternator
2 Alternator control unit
3 Ignition warning light
4 Ammeter
5 Battery
6 Ignition/starter switch
6A Ignition/starter switch— radio supply connector
7 Petrol pump
9 Starter motor
10 Ignition coil
11 Ignition distributor
12 Column light switch
13 Dip switch
14 Main beam warning light
15 Main beam
16 Dip beam
17 Fuse box
18 Front parking lamp
19 Rear marker lamp
20 Tail lamp
21 Plate illumination lamp
22 Panel rheostat
23 Instrument illumination
24 Horn
25 Horn push
26 Turn signal flasher unit
27 Turn signal flasher switch
28 L.H. Flasher lamp
29 L.H. Flasher repeater lamp
30 R.H. Flasher lamp
31 R.H. Flasher repeater lamp
32 Flasher warning light
33 Heater switch
34 Heater motor
35 Windscreen wiper motor
36 Windscreen wiper switch

37 Voltage stabilizer
38 Fuel indicator
39 Fuel tank unit
40 Temperature indicator
41 Temperature transmitter
42 Reverse lamp switch
43 Reverse lamp
44 Windscreen washer switch
45 Windscreen washer motor
46 Stop lamp switch
47 Stop lamp
48 Oil pressure warning light
49 Oil pressure switch

A. Overdrive (optional extra)

50 Overdrive relay
51 Overdrive column switch
52 Overdrive gearbox switch— 2nd gear ON
53 Overdrive gearbox switch— 3rd and 4th gear ON
54 Overdrive solenoid

a. From fuse box
b. From fuse box

COLOUR CODE

N	Brown	L/G	Light Green
U	Blue	W	White
R	Red	Y	Yellow
P	Purple	S	Slate
G	Green	B	Black

6·103

ELECTRICAL

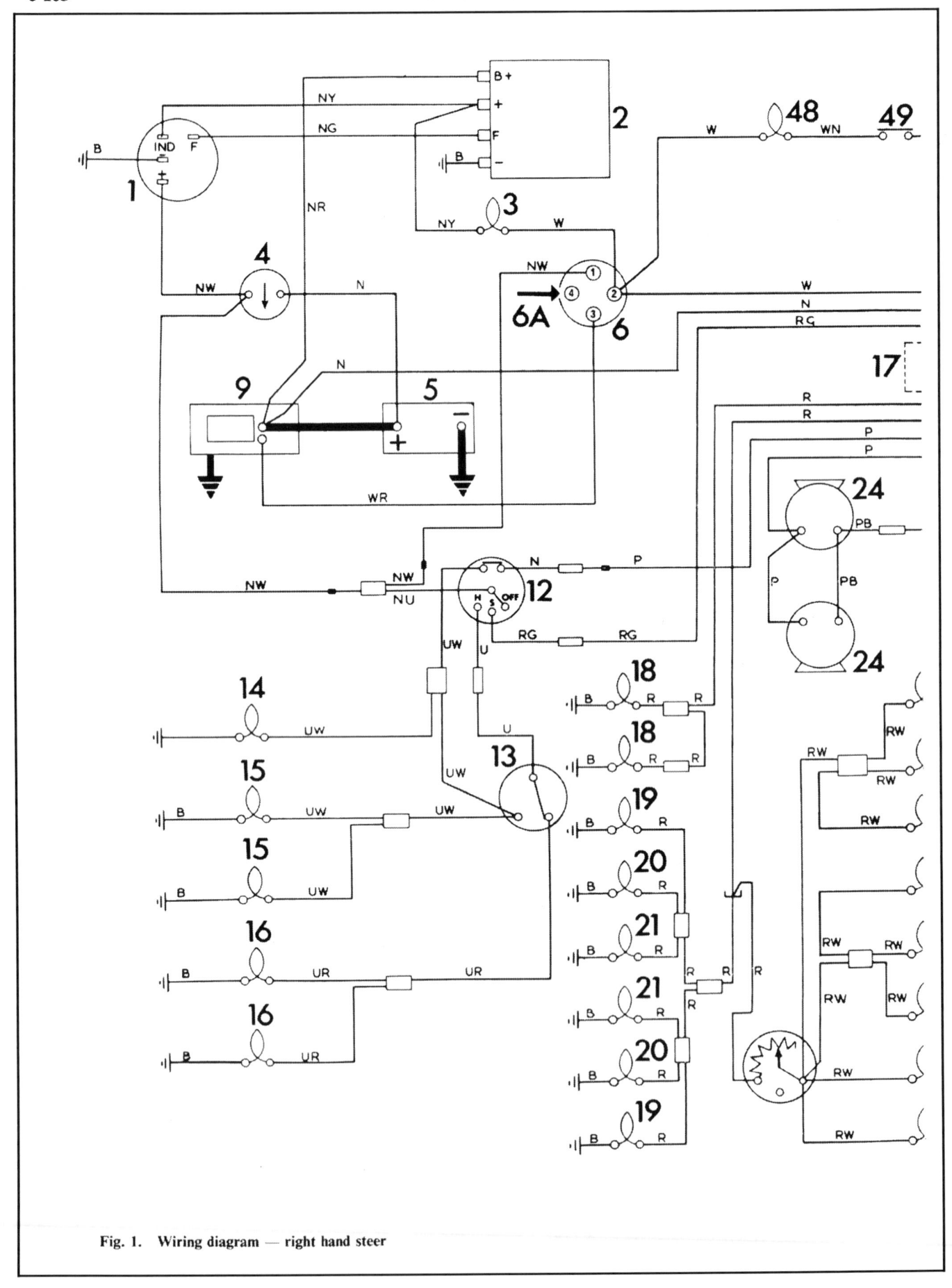

Fig. 1. Wiring diagram — right hand steer

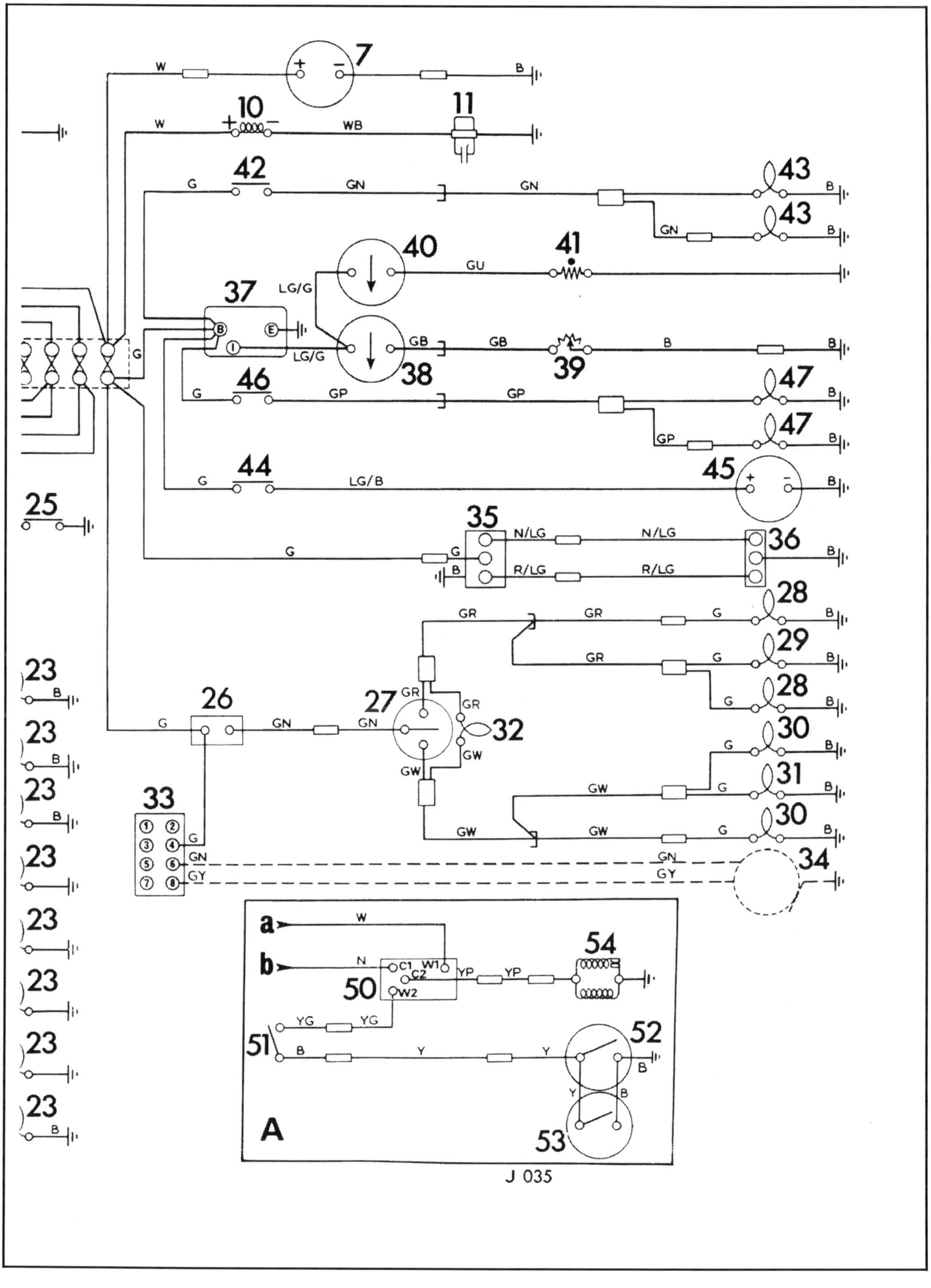

7
W
B
10
WB
11
42
G
GN
43
40
41
GU
37
LG/G
B
E
I
38
GB
39
46
GP
47
44
LG/B
45
25
35
N/LG
R/LG
36
28
GR
29
26
27
32
GW
30
31
33
34
GY
23
A
a
b
50
C1
W1
C2
W2
YP
54
51
YG
Y
52
53
J 035

6·104
ELECTRICAL

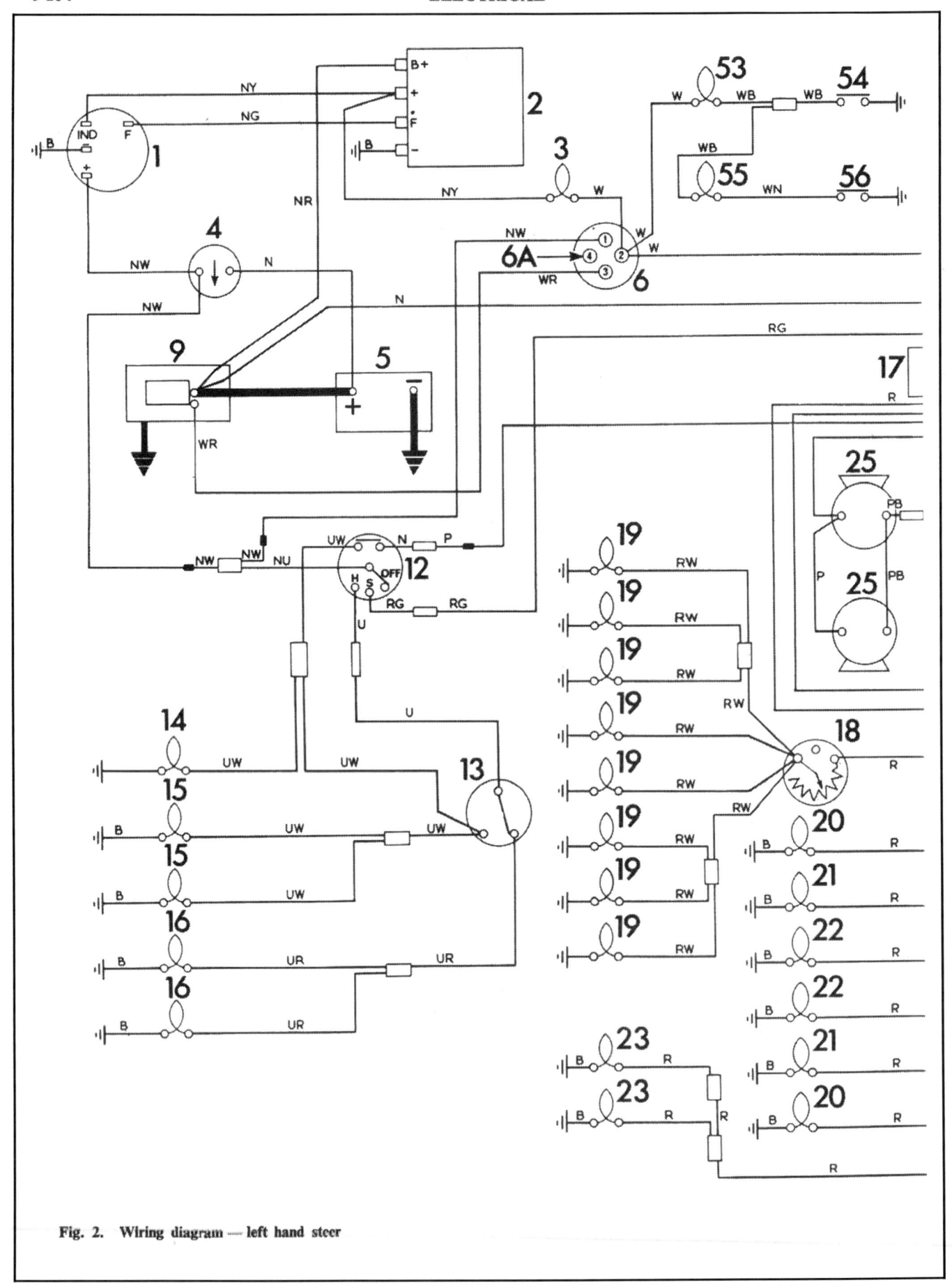

Fig. 2. Wiring diagram — left hand steer

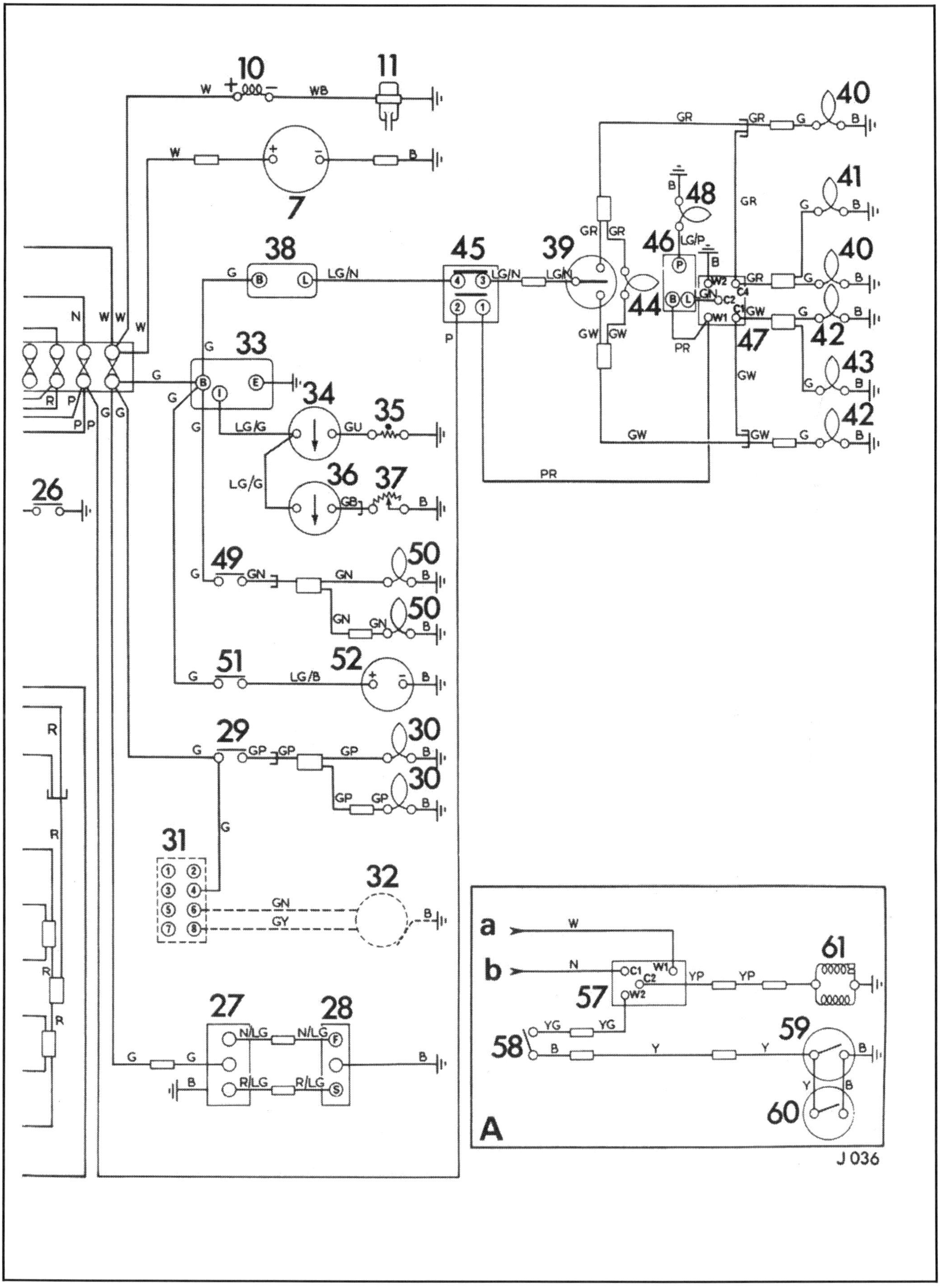

10
11
7
38
45
39
46
48
40
41
40
44
47
42
43
42
33
34
35
36
37
26
49
50
50
51
52
29
30
30
31
32
27
28
A
a
b
57
58
59
60
61
J 036

ELECTRICAL

KEY TO WIRING DIAGRAM — LEFT HAND STEER

CAUTION: THIS VEHICLE IS FITTED WITH A NEGATIVE EARTH ELECTRICAL SYSTEM. ENSURE THAT THE BATTERY EARTH LEAD IS ALWAYS CONNECTED TO THE BATTERY NEGATIVE TERMINAL.

THE ALTERNATOR AND ALTERNATOR CONTROL UNIT — AND POSSIBLY SOME ACCESSORIES — CONTAIN POLARITY SENSITIVE COMPONENTS THAT MAY BE IRREPARABLY DAMAGED IF SUBJECTED TO INCORRECT POLARITY.

1 Alternator
2 Alternator control unit
3 Ignition warning light
4 Ammeter
5 Battery
6 Ignition/starter switch
6A Ignition/starter switch—radio supply connector
7 Petrol pump
9 Starter motor
10 Ignition coil
11 Ignition distributor
12 Column light switch
13 Dip switch
14 Main beam warning light
15 Main beam
16 Dip beam
17 Fuse box
18 Panel rheostat
19 Instrument illumination
20 Rear marker lamp
21 Tail lamp
22 Plate illumination lamp
23 Front parking lamp
25 Horn
26 Horn push
27 Windscreen wiper motor
28 Windscreen wiper switch
29 Stop lamp switch
30 Stop lamp
31 Heater switch
32 Heater motor
33 Voltage stabilizer
34 Temperature indicator
35 Temperature transmitter
36 Fuel indicator
37 Fuel tank unit
38 Turn signal flasher unit
39 Turn signal flasher switch
40 L.H. Flasher lamp

41 L.H. Flasher repeater lamp
42 R.H. Flasher lamp
43 R.H. Flasher repeater lamp
44 Flasher warning light
45 Hazard switch
46 Hazard flasher unit
47 Hazard relay
48 Hazard warning light
49 Reverse lamp switch
50 Reverse lamp
51 Windscreen washer switch
52 Windscreen washer motor
53 Brake line failure warning light
54 Brake line failure switch
55 Oil pressure warning light
56 Oil pressure switch

A. Overdrive (optional extra)

57 Overdrive relay
58 Overdrive column switch
59 Overdrive gearbox switch—2nd gear ON
60 Overdrive gearbox switch—3rd and 4th gear ON
61 Overdrive solenoid

a. From fuse box
b. From fuse box

COLOUR CODE

N	Brown	L/G	Light Green
U	Blue	W	White
R	Red	Y	Yellow
P	Purple	S	Slate
G	Green	B	Black

KEY TO HARNESS

Left hand steer shown — right hand steer similar

MAIN HARNESS

1. Plug connection to body harness
2. Dip switch
3. Windscreen wiper motor
   Hazard relay—left hand steer only
   Fuse box
4. Fuse box
   Alternator control unit
   Hazard flasher unit—left hand steer only
5. Brake line failure switch—left hand steer only
6. Oil pressure switch
   Ignition coil
   Alternator
   Temperature transmitter
7. Horn push—earth return wire connected to steering unit
8. Flasher repeater lamp
   Front parking lamp
   Front flasher lamp
9. Horn
10. Headlamps
11. Horn
12. Front flasher lamp
    Front parking lamp
    Flasher repeater lamp
13. Column light switch
14. Turn signal flasher switch
    Horn push
15. Stop lamp switch
16. Windscreen wiper switch
    Windscreen washer switch
17. Speedometer—flasher warning light
    Speedometer—main beam warning light
    Speedometer—instrument illumination
    Voltage stabilizer
18. Brake line failure warning light—left hand steer only
    Hazard warning light—left hand steer only
    Hazard switch—left hand steer only
19. Tachometer—ignition warning light
    Tachometer—oil pressure warning light
    Tachometer—instrument illumination
20. Ignition/starter switch
    Heater switch
21. Ammeter
    Fuel indicator
    Panel rheostat
    Oil pressure indicator—instrument illumination
    Temperature indicator
22. Battery
23. Starter motor
24. Reverse lamp switch
25. Turn signal flasher unit
26. Windscreen washer pump

BODY HARNESS

27. Plug connection to main harness
28. Petrol pump
29. Rear marker lamp
    Rear flasher lamp
    Tail/stop lamp
    Reverse lamp
    Plate illumination lamp
30. Fuel tank unit
31. Rear marker lamp
    Rear flasher lamp
    Tail/stop lamp
    Reverse lamp
    Plate illumination lamp

OVERDRIVE HARNESS (Optional Extra)

32. Fuse box
    Overdrive relay
33. Overdrive column switch
34. Overdrive gearbox switch—2nd gear ON
    Overdrive gearbox switch—3rd and 4th gear ON
    Overdrive solenoid

6·107 ELECTRICAL

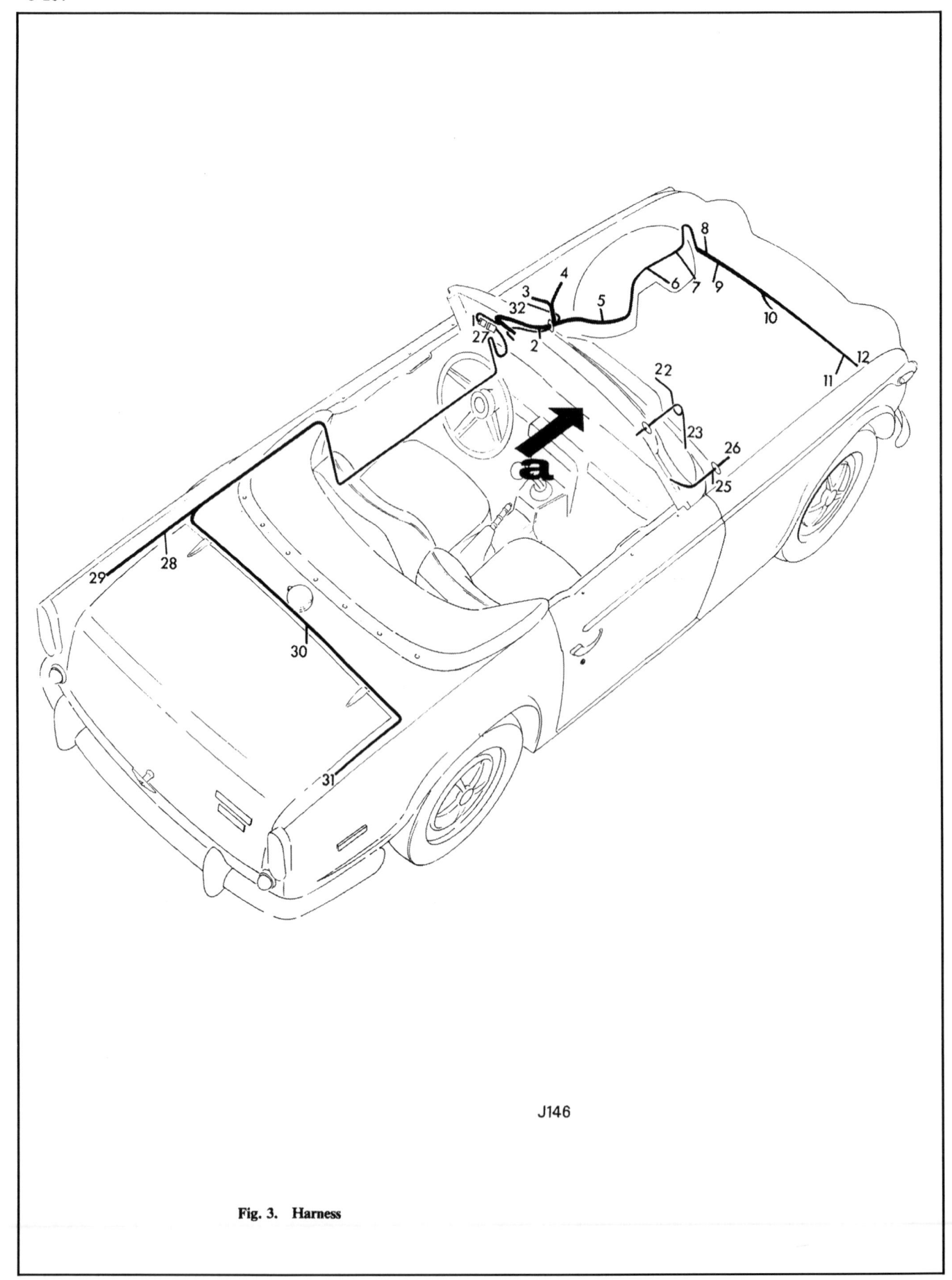

J146

Fig. 3. Harness

Harness details at bulkhead — view on arrow 'a'

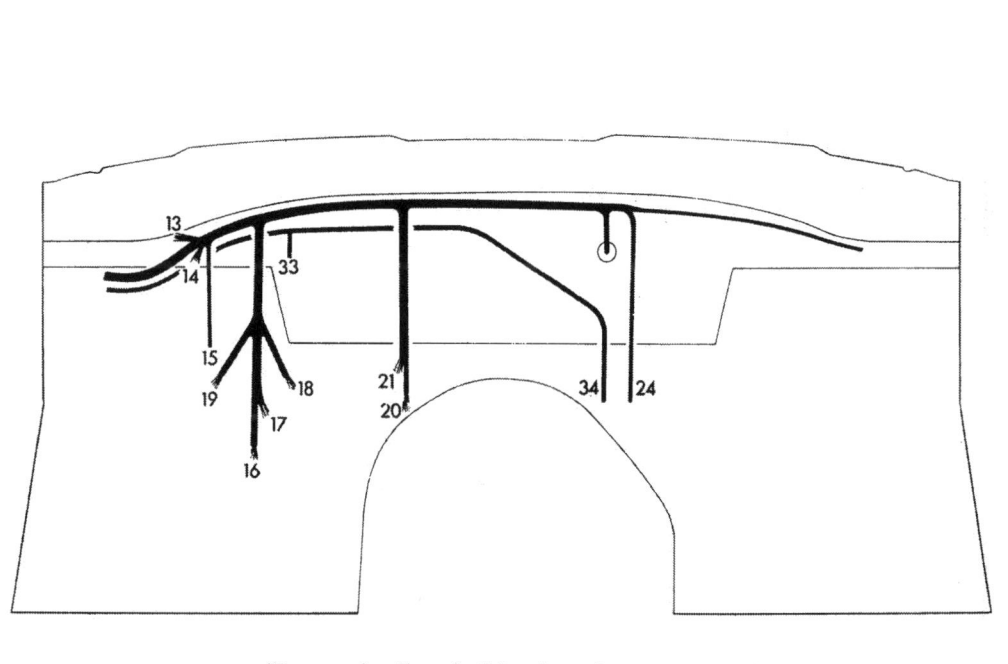

FACIA CONNECTIONS

KEY TO FACIA CONNECTIONS

Left hand steer shown — right hand steer similar

NO.	COLOUR	CONNECTION	COMPONENT
1	NW	Eyelet—2 wire	Ammeter
2	N	Eyelet	Ammeter
3	RW and B	Bulb holder	Ammeter
4	LG/G	Lucar	Fuel indicator
5	GB	Lucar	Fuel indicator
6	RW and B	Bulb holder	Fuel indicator
7	R	Lucar	Panel rheostat
8	RW	Lucar—2 wire	Panel rheostat
9	RW	Lucar—2 wire	Panel rheostat
10	RW and B	Bulb holder	Oil pressure indicator
11	LG/G	Lucar—2 wire	Temperature indicator
12	GU	Lucar	Temperature indicator
13	RW and B	Bulb holder	Temperature indicator
14	NW	Lucar	Ignition/starter switch
15	W	Lucar—2 wire	Ignition/starter switch
16	W	Lucar	Ignition/starter switch
17	WR	Lucar	Ignition/starter switch
18	G	Lucar	Heater switch
19	GN	Lucar	Heater switch
20	GY	Lucar	Heater switch
21	W and NY	Bulb holder	Tachometer — ignition warning light
22	WB and WN	Bulb holder	Tachometer — oil pressure warning light
23	RW	Bulb holder	Tachometer
24	RW	Bulb holder	Tachometer
25	B	Eyelet—2 wire	Tachometer
26	W and WB	Bulb holder	Brake line failure warning light
27	LG/P and B	Bulb holder	Hazard warning light
28	LG/N	Lucar	Hazard switch
29	LG/N	Lucar	Hazard switch
30	P	Lucar	Hazard switch
31	PR	Lucar	Hazard switch
32	NW with blue idents.	Double snap connector—2 wire	Column light switch
33	RG	Snap connector	Column light switch
34	U	Double snap connector	Column light switch
35	P with brown ident.	Snap connector	Column light switch
36	LG/N	Snap connector	Flasher switch
37	GR	Double snap connector—2 wire	Flasher switch
38	GW	Double snap connector—2 wire	Flasher switch
39	PB	Snap connector	Horn push
40	GR and GW	Bulb holder	Speedometer—flasher warning light
41	UW	Bulb holder	Speedometer — main beam warning light
42	RW	Bulb holder	Speedometer
43	RW	Bulb holder	Speedometer
44	B	Eyelet—3 wire	Speedometer
45	G	Lucar—2 wire	Voltage stabilizer
46	G	Lucar—2 wire	Voltage stabilizer
47	LG/G	Lucar blade	Voltage stabilizer
48	R/LG	Lucar	Windscreen wiper switch
49	N/LG	Lucar	Windscreen wiper switch
50	B	Lucar	Windscreen wiper switch
51	G	Lucar	Windscreen washer switch
52	LG/B	Lucar	Windscreen washer switch

a. GN and GY — to heater motor.   b. G and GP — to stop lamp switch.

6·109 ELECTRICAL

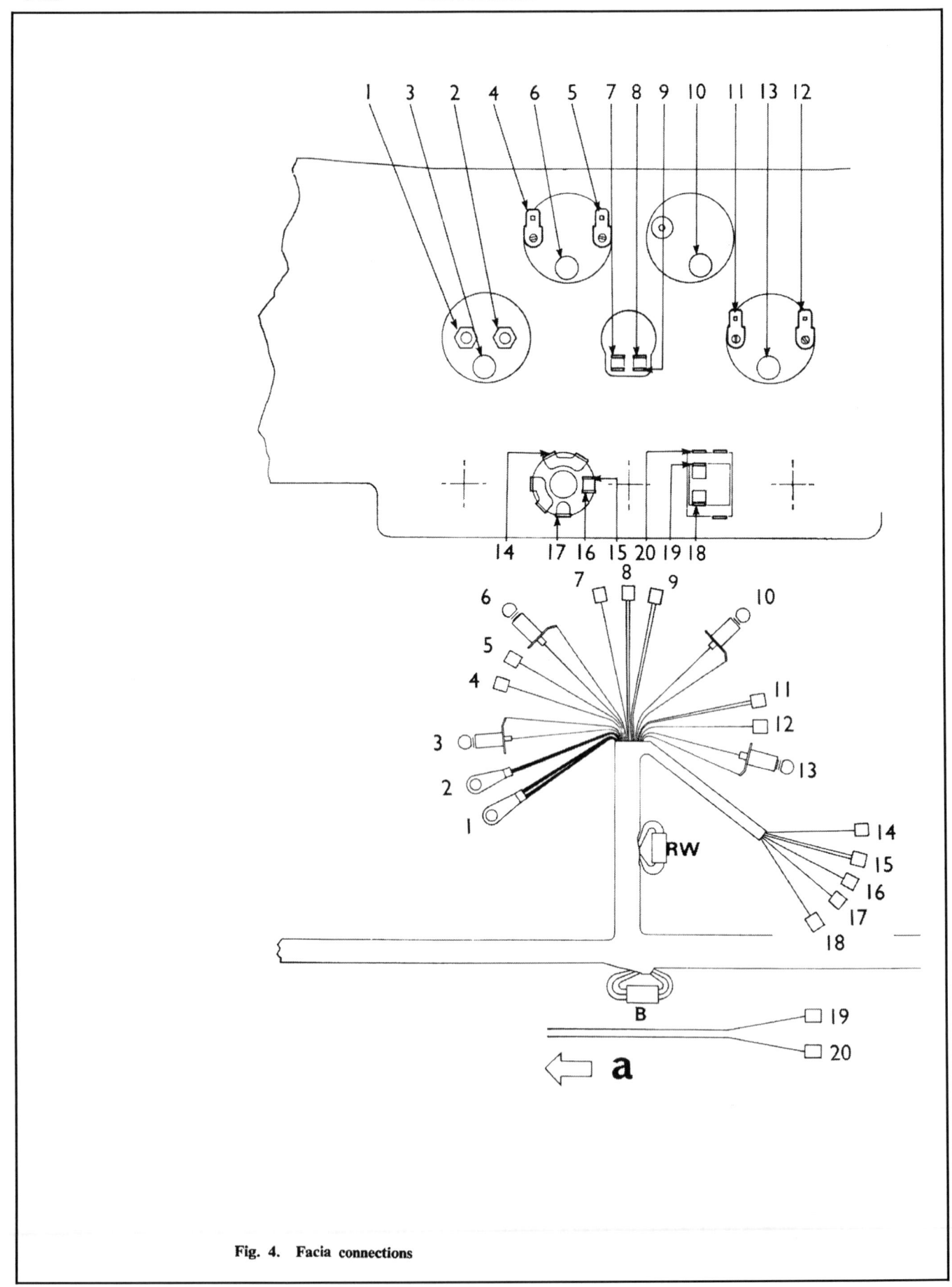

Fig. 4. Facia connections

H553

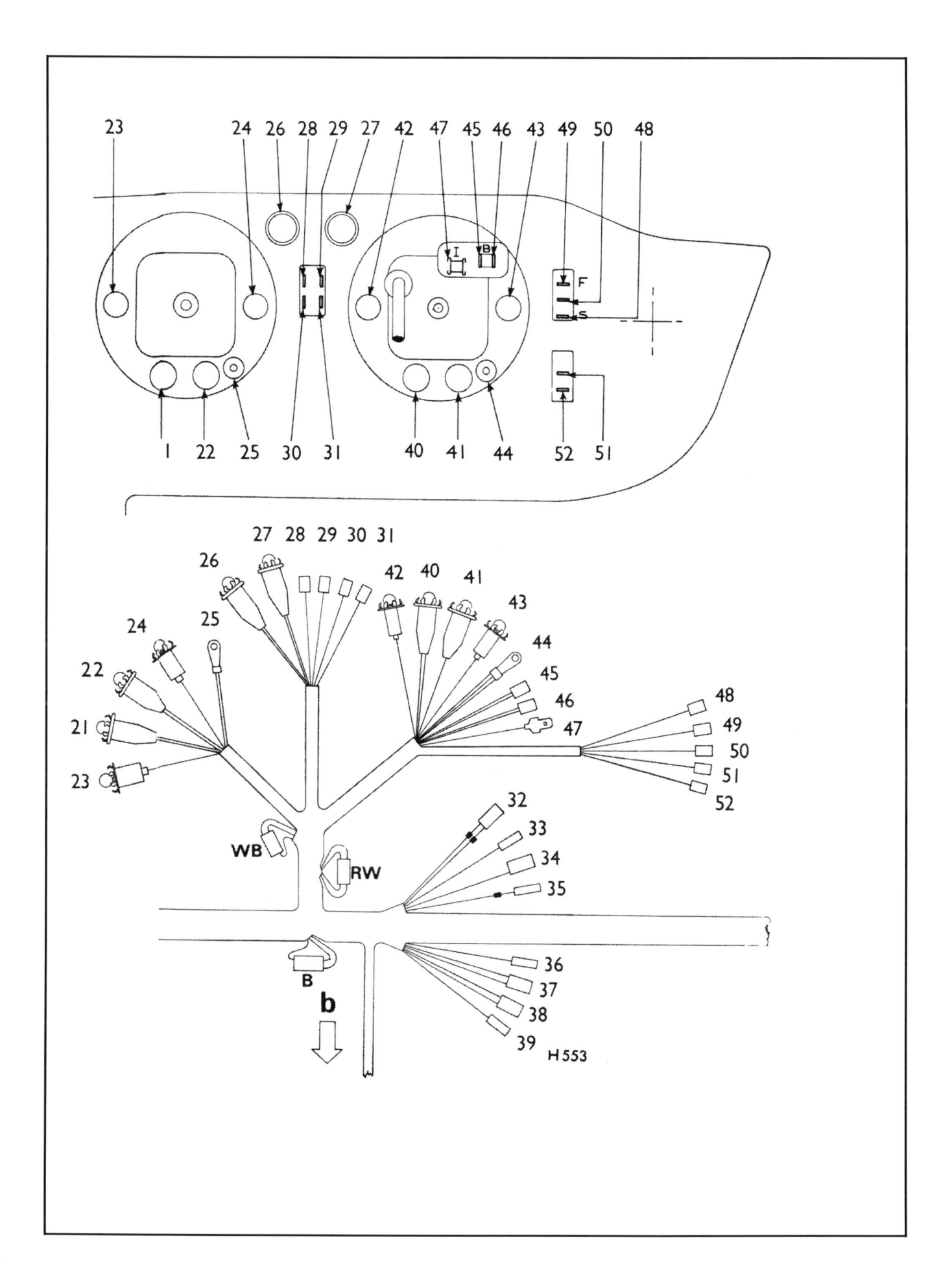

FUSE BOX

Data

Fuse

Manufacturer	Lucas
Rating	35 amp.
Lucas part No.	188218
Stanpart No.	58465
Lucas colour code	White
Current capacity	17·5 amp.
Fusing current — Prolonged	35 amp.
Instantaneous	40 amp.

Circuits

The top fuse is not used on a standard production vehicle. It may be employed in service to protect an accessory circuit.

The fuse fed by a white cable from the ignition/starter switch protects the following circuits:
- Turn signal flasher lamp circuit
- Stop lamp circuit
- Reverse lamp circuit
- Heater circuit
- Windscreen washer circuit
- Windscreen wiper circuit
- Fuel indication circuit
- Temperature indication circuit.

The fuse fed by a brown cable from the battery protects the following circuits:
- Headlamp flasher circuit
- Hazard warning circuit (L.H. Steer only)
- Horn circuit

The fuse fed by a red/green cable from the column light switch protects the following circuits:
- Front parking lamp circuit
- Rear marker lamp circuit
- Tail lamp circuit
- Plate illumination lamp circuit
- Instrument illumination circuit.

Description

The fuse box is mounted on the left hand side of the engine bay. The unit contains three operational fuses, one fuse available for use to protect an accessory circuit and has provision to house two spares. The fuses are protected by a pull off cover.

Failure of a particular fuse is indicated when all the circuits protected by it become inoperative. If a new fuse fails establish the cause and rectify the fault before fitting a second replacement.

Fig. 5. Fuse box installed

ELECTRICAL   6·111

ALTERNATOR

CAUTION: THE ALTERNATOR AND ALTERNATOR CONTROL UNIT CONTAIN POLARITY SENSITIVE COMPONENTS. REFER TO 'CAUTION' ON PAGE 6·103.

BATTERY LEADS MUST NOT BE DISCONNECTED WHILE THE ENGINE IS RUNNING OR DAMAGE TO COMPONENTS MAY OCCUR. IT IS ALSO ADVISABLE NOT TO BREAK OR MAKE ANY OTHER CONNECTIONS IN THE CHARGING CIRCUIT WHILE THE ENGINE IS RUNNING.

HIGH VOLTAGES MAY DAMAGE SEMICONDUCTOR DEVICES. REMOVE BOTH ALTERNATOR AND ALTERNATOR CONTROL UNIT MULTI-SOCKET CONNECTORS BEFORE BOOST CHARGING THE BATTERY OR PERFORMING ANY ELECTRIC ARC WELDING ON THE VEHICLE.

Data

Manufacturer	Lucas
Type	15AC
Lucas part No.	54021184
Stanpart No.	213051
Polarity	Negative earth only
Brush length — new	0·5 in.
— renew if less than	0·2 in. protrudes from brushbox when free
Brush spring pressure — face flush with brushbox	7 to 10 ozs.
Rectifier pack — output rectification	6 diodes (3 live side — 3 earth side)
— field winding supply rectification	3 diodes
Stator windings	Three phase — star connected
Field winding rotor — poles	12
— maximum permissible speed	12,500 r.p.m.
— shaft thread	$\frac{9}{16}$ in — 18 U.N.F. RH 2A
Field winding resistance	4·33 ± 5% ohm. at 20 deg. Centigrade
Output — hot at 6,000 alternator r.p.m. (2,870 engine r.p.m.) at 14 volts	28 amp.

Triumph — TR5:

Crankshaft pulley — effective diameter	5·75 in.
Alternator pulley — effective diameter	2·75 in.
Drive ratio — engine r.p.m. : alternator r.p.m.	11 : 23

Fig. 6. Alternator installed

ELECTRICAL

Fig. 7. Alternator details

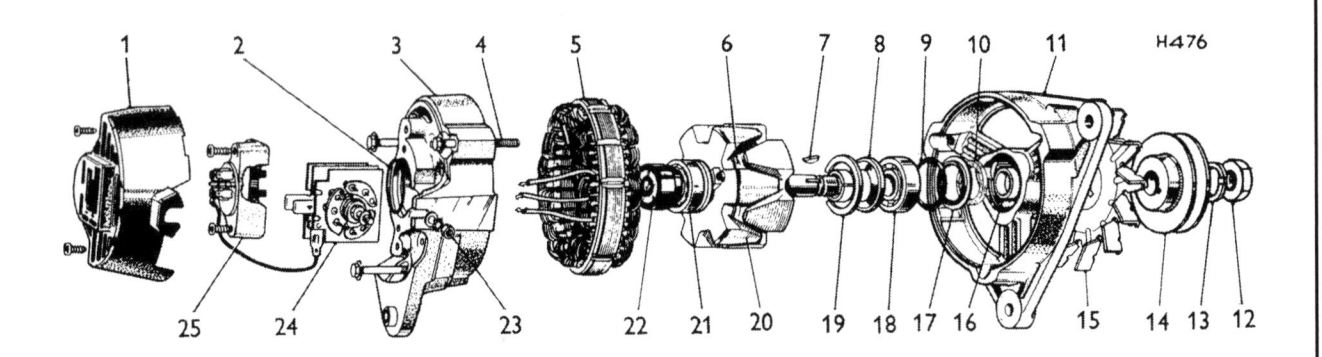

1. Moulded cover
2. Rubber 'O' ring
3. Slip ring end bracket
4. Through bolt
5. Stator windings
6. Field winding
7. Key
8. Bearing retaining plate
9. Pressure ring
10. Felt ring
11. Drive end bracket
12. Nut
13. Spring washer
14. Pulley
15. Fan
16. Spacer
17. Pressure ring and felt ring retaining plate
18. Drive end bearing
19. Circlip
20. Rotor
21. Slip ring end bearing
22. Slip ring moulding
23. Nut
24. Rectifier pack
25. Brushbox assembly

Description

The alternator is arranged to work in conjunction with an alternator control unit. A fan mounted at the drive end draws cooling air through the unit. The field winding rotor runs on two 'lubricated for life' ball bearings. (No routine lubrication is required.)

An alternating current is produced in the three phase-star connected static stator windings. This is partly rectified by six diodes—three on the live side and three on the earth side—to supply direct current to the vehicle electrical circuits and battery. Three additional diodes rectify part of the stator output to energise the field winding via a pair of brushes and slip rings. This circuit is controlled by the alternator control unit.

Ignition warning light—the three 'field winding supply' diodes enable a circuit similar to a conventional generator warning light circuit to be employed. When the ignition circuits are energised battery voltage is applied to the light. When the alternator is at rest an earth path exists through the alternator field winding and alternator control unit and the light illuminates. When the alternator commences to charge the voltage at terminal 'IND' approximately equals that at the battery and the light extinguishes. If the warning light remains illuminated during normal running a fault is indicated.

Constructional note

Some early vehicles are fitted with alternators that incorporate a rectifier pack of different design to that shown on Fig. 7—item 24. The early rectifier pack is a larger assembly screw mounted to both the slip ring end bracket and brushbox assembly.

Information contained in this section applies to both early and later alternators, with the exception of the following information, which applies fundamentally to early units and specifically to later units.

Fig. 7—items 23 and 24.
Disassemble alternator—operations 2 and 5.

Fig. 10
Assemble alternator—operations 8 and 10.

Fig. 12.
Diode check—operation 1.

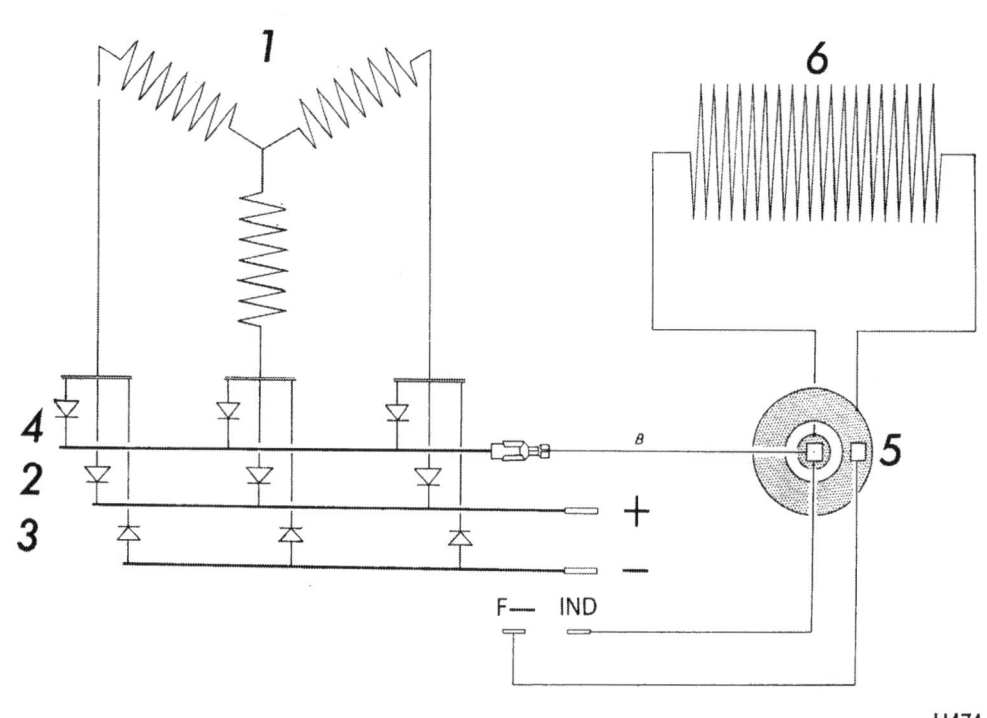

ELECTRICAL

6·113

1 Stator windings
2 Live side output diodes
3 Earth side output diodes
4 Field winding supply diodes
5 Brushes and slip rings
6 Field winding

Fig. 8. Component wiring diagram

Service

Ensure that the ventilation apertures in the moulded cover and slip ring end bracket remain clean.

Adjust tension of vee drive belt as detailed in Group 1.

CAUTION: WHEN TENSIONING BELT LEVER ON THE DRIVE END BRACKET ONLY USING A LEVER OF SOFT MATERIAL—PREFERABLY WOOD. DO NOT LEVER ON ANY OTHER PART OF THE ALTERNATOR OR BEARING DAMAGE MAY RESULT.

Defective charging system

In the event of a defective charging system check the alternator as follows:

Check multi-socket connector is correctly fitted.

Ensure that vee drive belt is not slipping on alternator pulley. If required adjust tension of vee drive belt as detailed in Group 1.

If required perform Alternator functional check as detailed below.

NOTE: If the ignition warning light indicates a fault, diode failure may be suspected. If equipment is not available to perform an Alternator functional check a Diode check as detailed below could be performed.

If alternator appears serviceable refer to Group 6—Alternator Control Unit—Defective charging system.

ELECTRICAL

Alternator functional check

The stated output may be exceeded slightly when the alternator is cold. To avoid misleading results the check should be performed with the unit as near to its normal operating temperature as possible.

1. Disconnect multi-socket connector.

2. Provide test circuit as shown on Fig. 9.

   CAUTION: THE ALTERNATOR CONTAINS POLARITY SENSITIVE COMPONENTS THAT MAY BE IRREPARABLY DAMAGED IF SUBJECTED TO INCORRECT POLARITY. OBSERVE POLARITY OF ALTERNATOR AND BATTERY TERMINALS.

   Do not connect variable resistor across battery for longer than is necessary to perform check.

3. Run engine gradually increasing speed.

   At 1500 alternator r.p.m. (720 engine r.p.m.) light should be extinguished.

   Hold speed at approximately 6000 alternator r.p.m. (2870 engine r.p.m.). Adjust variable resistor so voltmeter reads 14 volts. Ammeter reading should now be approximately 28 amps.

   If the ammeter reading is not approximately 28 amps. the indication is that the alternator requires overhaul or replacement.

   NOTE: If the indication is that the alternator requires overhaul or replacement, diode failure may be suspected. A Diode check as detailed below could be performed.

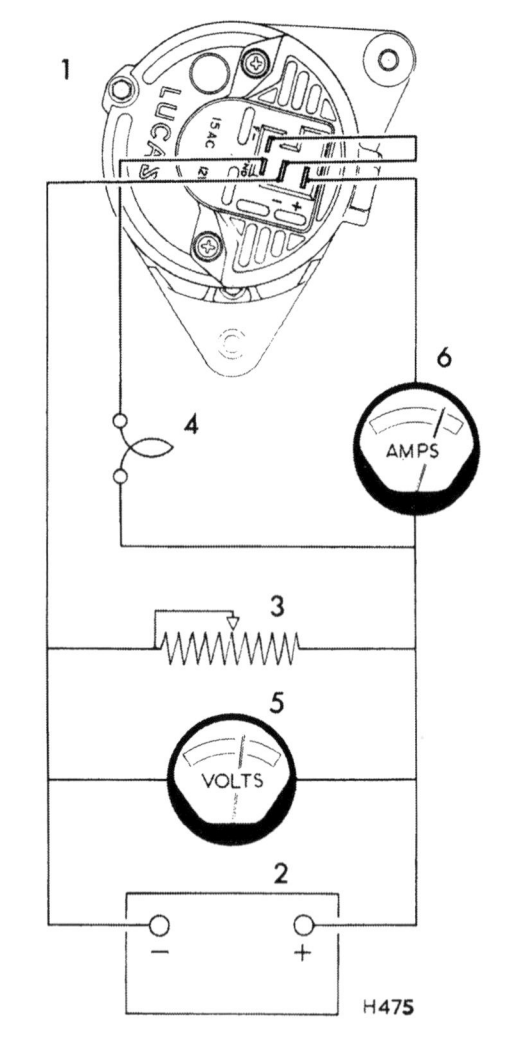

1	Alternator		
2	Battery	.. ..	12 volt
3	Variable resistor	..	0 - 15 ohm. - 35 amp.
4	Light	.. ..	12 volt - 2·2 watt
5	Voltmeter	.. ..	0 - 20 volt
6	Ammeter	.. ..	0 - 40 amp.

Fig. 9. Alternator functional check

Fig. 10. Soldering operation

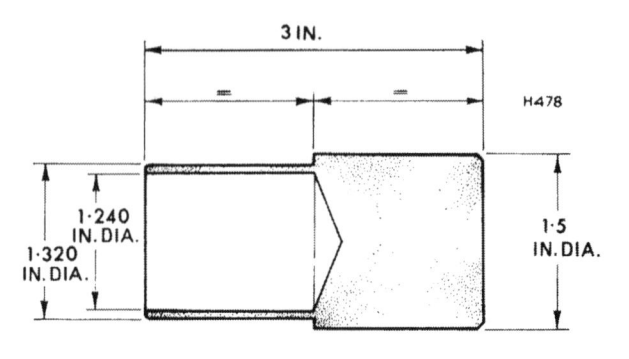

Fig. 11. Extractor tool

ELECTRICAL 6·115

Disassemble alternator

1. Remove moulded cover.

2. Remove brushbox by disconnecting 'Lucar type' connector from rectifier pack and unscrewing two screws.

    NOTE: To disconnect the connector it may be necessary to withdraw the cover and carefully manoeuvre the connector from the blade using long-nosed pliers.

3. Note position of three stator wires on rectifier pack.

4. Unsolder three stator wire connections.

    Take care not to overheat diodes or bend diode pins. Perform soldering operation as quickly as possible and provide a heat sink by lightly gripping diode pin with long-nosed pliers as shown on Fig. 10.

5. Slacken nut and withdraw rectifier pack.

6. Remove through bolts.

7. Provide extractor tool as detailed on Fig. 11.

    To remove slip ring end bracket position extractor tool to engage with outer journal of slip ring end bearing.

    NOTE: It may be necessary to carefully file away surplus solder from two field winding connections on slip ring moulding if extractor tool will not pass over moulding.

    Employ a second operator to support slip ring end bracket by hand. Carefully tap extractor tool to drive bearing from housing.

8. Rubber 'O' ring fitted in slip ring end bracket bearing housing may remain in situ unless replacement is contemplated.

9. Remove stator windings from drive end bracket.

10. Remove nut, spring washer, pulley and fan. If necessary use suitable extractor.

    NOTE: Prevent the shaft turning while removing the nut by wrapping a scrap fan belt round pulley and retaining by hand or vice.

11. Remove key.

12. Using suitable press, remove rotor from drive end bracket.

    CAUTION: DO NOT ATTEMPT TO REMOVE ROTOR BY APPLYING HAMMER BLOWS TO SHAFT END. SUCH ACTION MAY BURR OVER AND DAMAGE THREAD.

Assemble alternator

1. Using spacer (Fig. 7—item 16) and suitable tube fit rotor to drive end bracket by applying pressure to bearing inner journal.

    CAUTION: DO NOT USE DRIVE END BRACKET AS SUPPORT WHILE FITTING ROTOR.

    IF SPACER IS NOT EMPLOYED FELT RING MAY BE DAMAGED.

2. Fit key.

3. Fit fan, pulley, spring washer and nut. Torque load nut to 25 – 30 lb. ft.

    NOTE: Prevent the shaft turning while tightening the nut by wrapping a scrap fan belt round pulley and retaining by hand or vice.

4. Observe relationship of stator windings to drive end bracket determined by stator wire connections, rectifier pack position on slip ring end bracket, alignment of mounting lugs on end brackets and through bolt clearances on stator windings.

    Position stator windings to drive end bracket.

5. Ensure that rubber 'O' ring is fitted correctly in slip ring end bracket bearing housing.

6. Fit slip ring end bracket by carefully pushing bearing into housing.

7. Fit through bolts, tightening evenly.

8. Ensure that rubber locating piece is correctly fitted to rectifier pack. Position rectifier pack and secure with nut.

9. Position three stator wires on rectifier pack as noted at Disassemble alternator—operation 3 above.

    Solder three stator wire connections using only 'M' grade 45 – 55 tin lead solder.

    Take care not to overheat diodes or bend diode pins. Perform soldering operation as quickly as possible and provide a heat sink by lightly gripping diode pin with long-nosed pliers as shown on Fig. 10.

10. Ensure that brushes are entered correctly in brushbox. Fit brushbox by inserting two screws and connecting 'Lucar type' connector to rectifier pack.

11. Fit moulded cover.

ELECTRICAL

Brushes

Clean brushes with petrol moistened cloth. Ensure that the brushes move freely in the brushbox. If necessary lightly polish brush sides with a fine file.

Check brush length—renew brushbox assembly if less than 0·2 in. protrudes from brushbox when free.

Using a suitable push type spring scale check brush spring pressure. Pressure should be 7 – 10 ozs. with face flush with brushbox. If pressure is low renew brushbox assembly.

Slip rings

Clean slip rings with petrol moistened cloth. If there is evidence of burning use very fine glasspaper. The surfaces should be smooth and uncontaminated by oil or other foreign matter.

CAUTION: DO NOT USE EMERY CLOTH OR SIMILAR ABRASIVE.

DO NOT MACHINE SKIM — ANY ECCENTRICITY IN MACHINING WILL ADVERSELY AFFECT THE ALTERNATOR'S HIGH SPEED PERFORMANCE.

Diode check

If diode failure is suspected perform the following check on each of the nine diodes:

1. Remove moulded cover and brushbox and unsolder three stator wire connections as detailed in operations 1 – 4 of Disassemble alternator above.

2. Provide test circuit as shown on Fig. 12.

3. Place each diode in circuit with battery positive to diode pin. Repeat check with battery negative to diode pin.

   When placing each diode in circuit, wire 'A' must be connected to the heat sink plate to which the diode is associated.

   Light illumination—indicating current flow—should occur in one direction only.

   If light illuminates in both directions, or fails to illuminate in either, the diode is unserviceable and a new rectifier pack must be fitted.

Bearings

The field winding rotor runs on two 'lubricated for life' ball bearings. (No routine lubrication is required.)

The need for bearing replacement during the life of the alternator is extremely unlikely—provided the vee drive belt is correctly adjusted and the unit is mounted correctly.

Should bearing replacement be required proceed as follows:

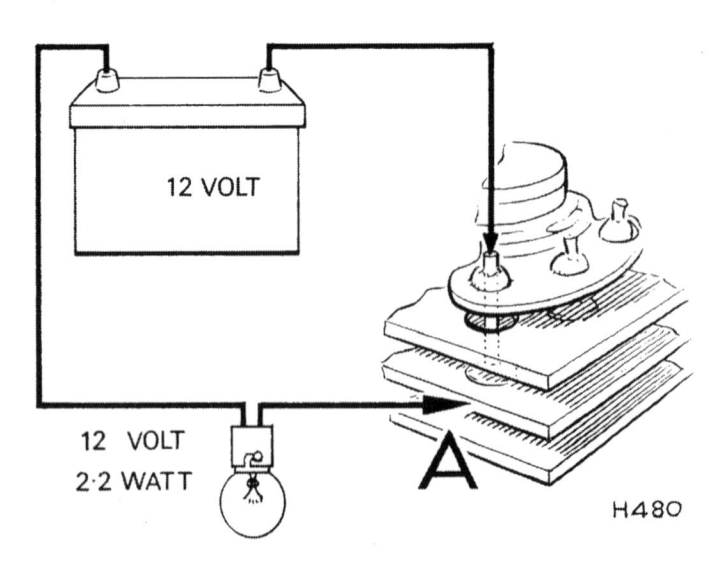

Fig. 12. Diode check

ELECTRICAL

Remove slip ring end bearing

1. Perform Disassemble alternator operations 1 – 9 as detailed above.

2. Unsolder two field winding connections to slip ring moulding.

3. Pull slip ring moulding from shaft.

4. Using suitable extractor, remove bearing.

Install slip ring end bearing

1. Ensure that bearing is correctly packed with lubricant 'Shell Alvania RA' grease or equivalent.

2. Using suitable tube, fit bearing to shaft by applying pressure to bearing inner journal. Ensure that shielded side faces slip ring moulding and bearing is positioned as far as it will go along shaft towards rotor.

3. Fit slip ring moulding to shaft. Ensure that projections engage correctly with shaft slot.

   NOTE: Slip ring moulding may be fitted either way round.

4. Solder two field winding connections to slip ring moulding using 'Frys H.T.3' solder.

Remove drive end bearing

1. Perform Disassemble alternator operations 1 – 12 as detailed above.

2. Insert large screwdriver in extractor notch and prise out circlip.

3. Remove bearing retaining plate.

4. Push out bearing and associated components.

Install drive end bearing

1. Ensure that bearing is correctly packed with lubricant 'Shell Alvania RA' grease or equivalent.

2. Assemble bearing, pressure ring, pressure ring and felt ring retaining plate, spacer and felt ring as detailed on Fig. 14. Fit assembly to drive end bracket.

3. Fit bearing retaining plate.

4. Fit circlip.

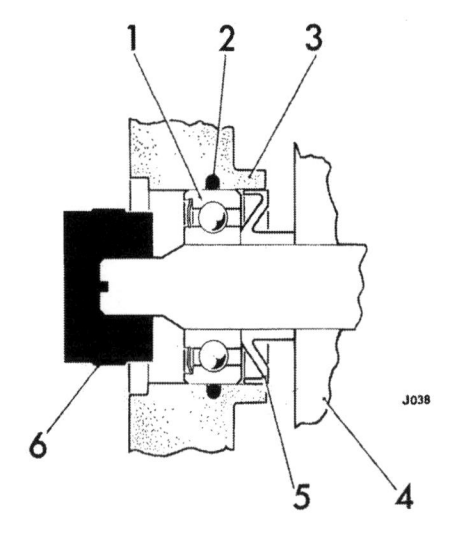

1 Bearing
2 Rubber 'O' ring
3 Slip ring end bracket
4 Rotor
5 Grease retainer
6 Slip ring moulding

Fig. 13. Slip ring end bearing

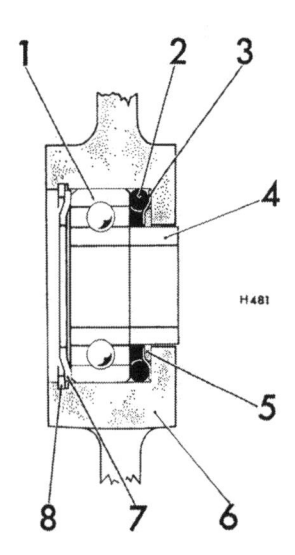

1 Bearing
2 Pressure ring
3 Pressure ring and felt ring retaining plate
4 Spacer
5 Felt ring
6 Drive end bracket
7 Bearing retaining plate
8 Circlip

Fig. 14. Drive end bearing and associated components

ELECTRICAL

ALTERNATOR CONTROL UNIT

CAUTION: THE ALTERNATOR AND ALTERNATOR CONTROL UNIT CONTAIN POLARITY SENSITIVE COMPONENTS. REFER TO 'CAUTION' ON PAGE 6·103.

BATTERY LEADS MUST NOT BE DISCONNECTED WHILE THE ENGINE IS RUNNING OR DAMAGE TO COMPONENTS MAY OCCUR. IT IS ALSO ADVISABLE NOT TO BREAK OR MAKE ANY OTHER CONNECTIONS IN THE CHARGING CIRCUIT WHILE THE ENGINE IS RUNNING.

HIGH VOLTAGES MAY DAMAGE SEMICONDUCTOR DEVICES. REMOVE BOTH ALTERNATOR AND ALTERNATOR CONTROL UNIT MULTI-SOCKET CONNECTORS BEFORE BOOST CHARGING THE BATTERY OR PERFORMING ANY ELECTRIC ARC WELDING ON THE VEHICLE.

Data

Manufacturer	Lucas
Type	4TR
Lucas part No.	37527
Stanpart No.	148416

Fig. 15. Alternator control unit installed

Description

The alternator control unit adjusts the current flow through the alternator field winding to control the alternator output to suit the electrical requirements of the vehicle and the state of charge of the battery. Control is achieved by a voltage sensitive electronic circuit.

(No current regulator is required as the inherent self regulating properties of the alternator limit the output current. No cut out is required since the diodes incorporated in the alternator prevent reverse currents from flowing.)

Service

The only maintenance required is to ensure that the moulded cover, connector blades and multi-socket connector remain clean and dry.

ELECTRICAL

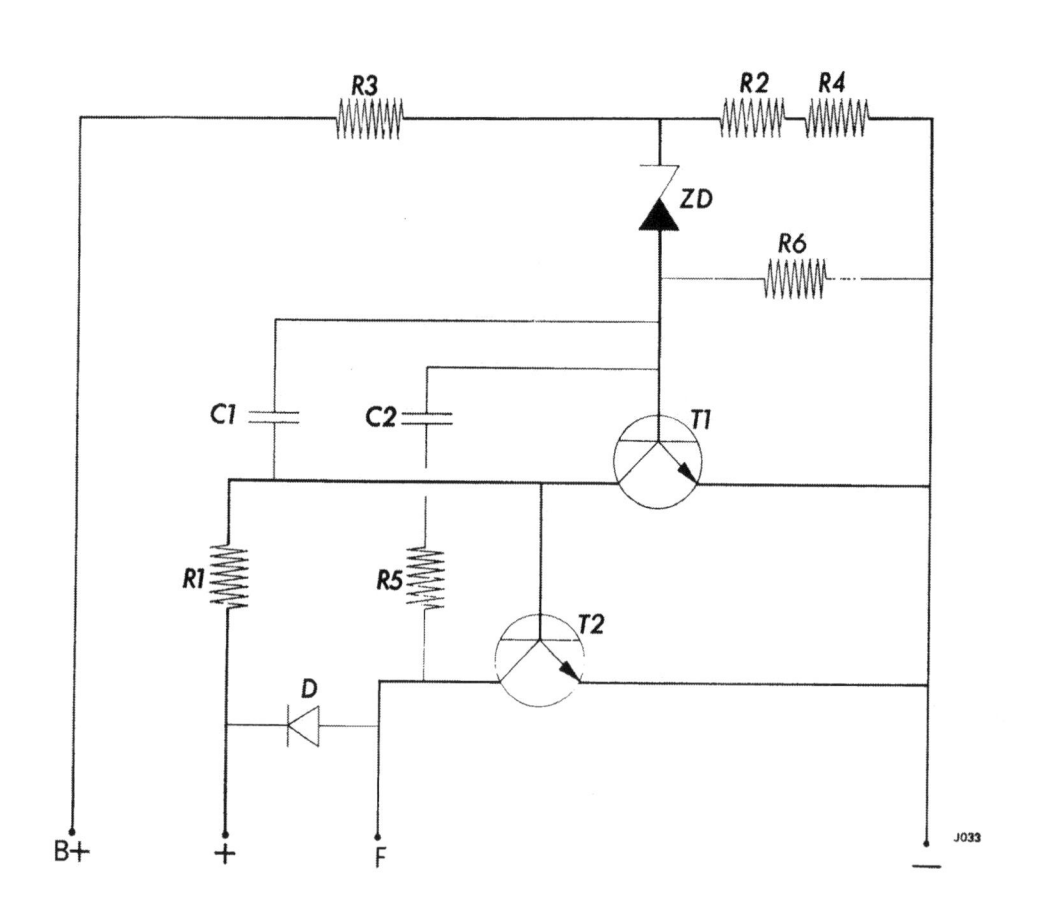

R1	Resistor	Restricts T2 base current supplied from alternator 'field winding supply' diodes
T2	Power transistor	Controls alternator field winding earth return circuit
R3	Resistor	Potential divider — sensing battery reference voltage
R2	Resistor	
R4	Resistor	
ZD	Zener diode	Voltage sensitive component. Opposes passage of current until breakdown voltage — approximately 10 volts — is reached. Controls T1 base current
T1	Driver transistor	Controls T2 base current by diverting current to earth when ZD is conducting
C2	Capacitor	Prevents T2 overheating by providing positive feed back circuit to ensure quick switching
R5	Resistor	of T2 from 'fully on' to 'fully off'
R6	Resistor	Path for small leakage current which may pass through ZD at high temperatures
D	Surge quench diode	Connected across alternator field winding. Protects T2 from field winding high induced voltage surge and smooths field winding current
C1	Condenser	Radio interference suppression

Fig. 16. Component wiring diagram

ELECTRICAL

Defective charging system

In the event of a defective charging system check the following items:

Check the alternator. Refer to Group 6—Alternator—Defective charging system.

Inspect charging system wiring. Perform continuity checks between alternator, alternator control unit, ignition warning light and battery. With alternator running at 6000 r.p.m. (2870 engine r.p.m.), and headlamps switched on voltage drop between alternator '+' connector blade and battery positive terminal should not exceed 0·2 volt. Similarly with the same running conditions voltage drop between alternator '−' connector blade and battery negative terminal should not exceed 0·2 volt.

Check multi-socket connector and single Lucar connector are correctly fitted to alternator control unit.

Check alternator control unit earthing. Inspect earth connection on unit and harness earth connection below fuse box. Resistance between alternator control unit '−' connector blade and good earth should not exceed 0·04 ohm.

Check attachment of battery leads to ensure good electrical contact.

Check the battery is in a serviceable condition. Perform a Specific gravity check and a Heavy discharge check.

If required perform Alternator control unit functional check as detailed below.

Alternator control unit functional check

1. Ensure that the vehicle battery is in a well charged condition.

   If this cannot be assured the battery must be temporarily replaced by a well charged nine plate battery for the duration of the check.

   CAUTION: THE ALTERNATOR AND ALTERNATOR CONTROL UNIT — AND POSSIBLY SOME ACCESSORIES — CONTAIN POLARITY SENSITIVE COMPONENTS THAT MAY BE IRREPARABLY DAMAGED IF SUBJECTED TO INCORRECT POLARITY. OBSERVE POLARITY OF BATTERY TERMINALS.

2. At battery unscrew positive lead bolt assembly. Disconnect heavy brown wire. Replace bolt assembly and tighten.

   Connect ammeter suitable for 0 – 40 amp. range between battery positive terminal and removed heavy brown wire battery lug as shown on Fig. 17.

3. Connect voltmeter suitable for battery voltage and with accuracy of 1 per cent or better between battery terminals as shown on Fig. 17.

   NOTE: A voltmeter of the suppressed-zero type with 12 – 15 volt range is ideal.

4. Run engine at approximately 5000 alternator r.p.m. (2400 engine r.p.m.). Allow approximately one minute for the system to stabilize. Apply—or remove—electrical load on battery to achieve a condition at which ammeter reads a current flow towards battery of approximately 5 amps.

   Voltmeter reading should then be 14·3 – 14·7 volts.

   If the voltmeter reading is not steady or is outside the limits the indication is that the alternator control unit requires replacement.

   NOTE: If the ammeter reading remains considerably above 5 amps. the indication is that the battery is not in a well charged condition. Refer to operation 1 above.

Repair — Repair is by replacement.

ELECTRICAL

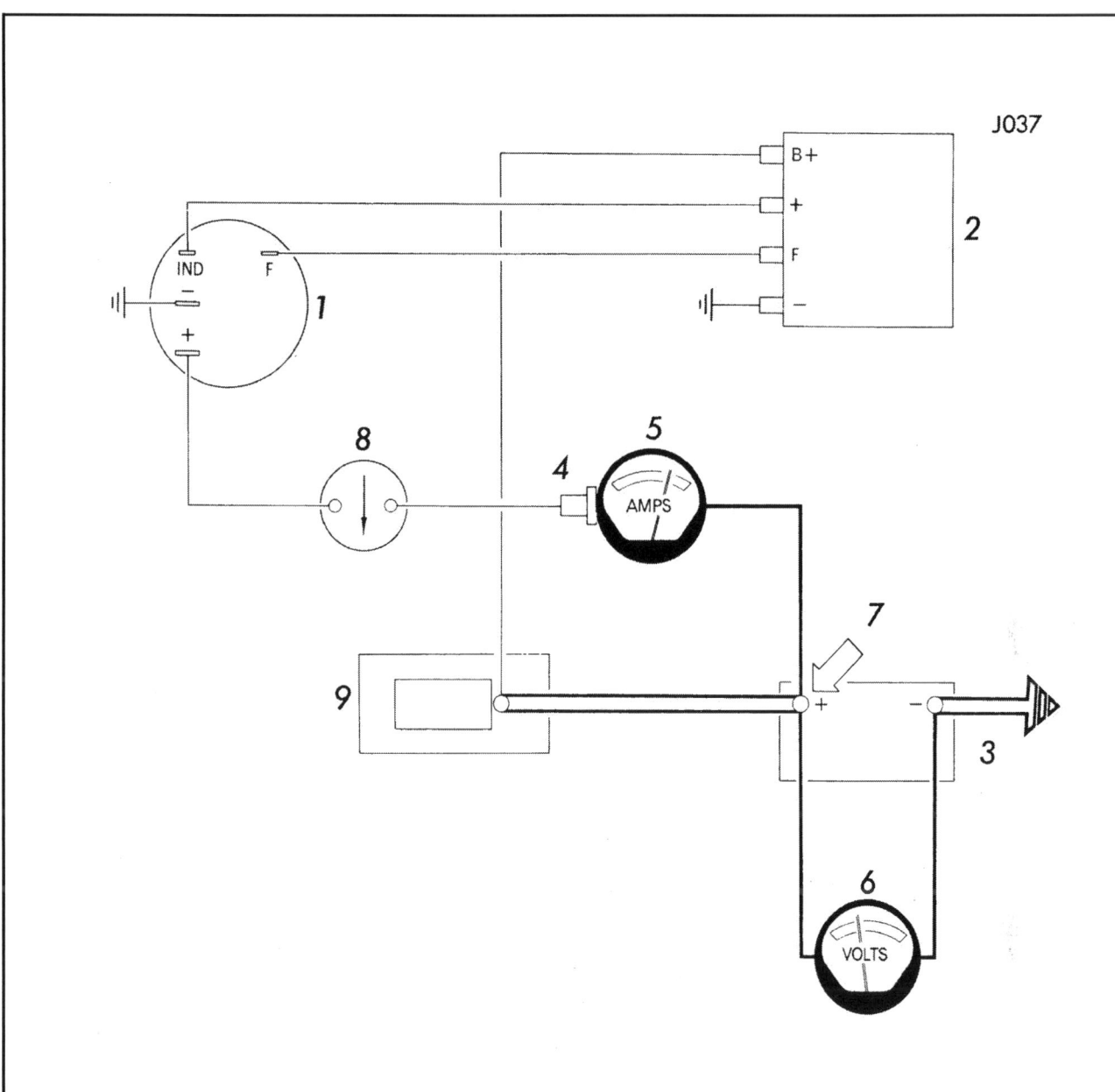

1. Alternator
2. Alternator control unit
3. Battery
4. Heavy brown wire
5. Ammeter (test circuit unit)
6. Voltmeter
7. Apply - or remove - electrical load here
8. Ammeter (vehicle unit on facia panel)
9. Starter motor

Fig. 17. Alternator control unit functional check

ELECTRICAL

PETROL PUMP

CAUTION: THE PETROL PUMP MOTOR IS POLARITY SENSITIVE. REFER TO 'CAUTION' ON PAGE 6·103.

OBSERVE POLARITY WHEN CONNECTING WIRE SNAP CONNECTORS ADJACENT TO THE PETROL PUMP OR PERFORMING ANY TESTING OF THE UNIT.

THE PETROL PUMP IS CONTROLLED DIRECTLY BY THE IGNITION/STARTER SWITCH. IT SHOULD BE APPRECIATED THAT THE MOTOR WILL NORMALLY RUN CONTINUALLY WHILE THE IGNITION CIRCUITS ARE ENERGISED. IF DURING SERVICING THE IGNITION EVER HAS TO REMAIN ON FOR A LONG PERIOD WITH THE ENGINE NOT RUNNING DISCONNECT THE WIRE SNAP CONNECTORS ADJACENT TO THE UNIT.

BEFORE DISMANTLING ANY PART OF THE HIGH PRESSURE FUEL LINE, DISCONNECT THE WIRE SNAP CONNECTORS ADJACENT TO THE UNIT. THIS ACTION WILL ENSURE THAT THE PETROL PUMP IS NEVER INADVERTENTLY STARTED WITH THE FUEL LINE DISCONNECTED.

Data

Manufacturer	Lucas
Lucas part No.	54073012
Stanpart No.	214347
Running current	4 amps. approximately
Light running current at 2,200 r.p.m. at 13·5 volts	1·4 amps.
Armature winding resistance—adjacent commutator bars	0·16 to 0·24 ohms. at 15 degrees Centigrade
Armature end float	0·004 to 0·010 in.
Brush length — new	$\frac{3}{8}$ in.
renew if less than	$\frac{3}{16}$ in.
Brush spring pressure—when compressed to 0·158 in (4 mm.)	5 to 7 ozs.
Maximum delivery	16 gallons per hour
Delivery pressure—controlled by pressure relief valve unit	100 p.s.i. approximately

Description

The petrol pump is a component of the 'Petrol injection system' detailed in Group 1.

It is located at the forward end of the luggage boot on the left-hand side behind the trim panel. To obtain access to the unit remove two screws and turn back the trim panel.

The unit consists of a composite permanent magnet field motor driving a gear pump. The drive is transmitted by a drive coupling which has a spiral formed on its upper surface to throw fuel up to lubricate the shaft seal. Failure of the shaft seal would be indicated by fuel leakage from the 'tell tail' pipe projecting from the base casting.

Fig. 18. Petrol pump installed

The motor and gear pump may be considered as two units. Replacement of either may be undertaken.

CAUTION: SOME EARLY GEAR PUMPS HAVE A NARROW TOP PLATE—SEE FIG. 19. TO PREVENT TOP PLATE DISTORTION CAUSING GEAR BINDING, THE TOP PLATES WERE MATCHED TO THE MOTOR BASE CASTINGS DURING PRODUCTION.

A 'NARROW TOP PLATE' GEAR PUMP SHOULD NOT BE FITTED WITH A REPLACEMENT MOTOR. A NEW MOTOR SHOULD ONLY BE OBTAINED BY REPLACING THE COMPLETE PETROL PUMP UNIT.

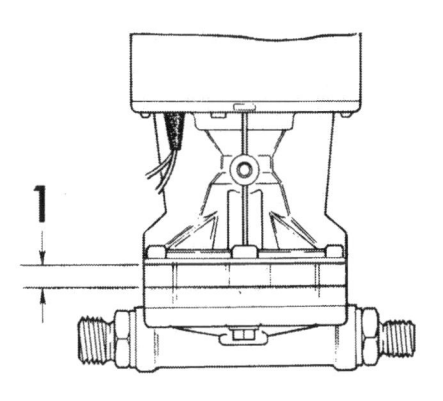

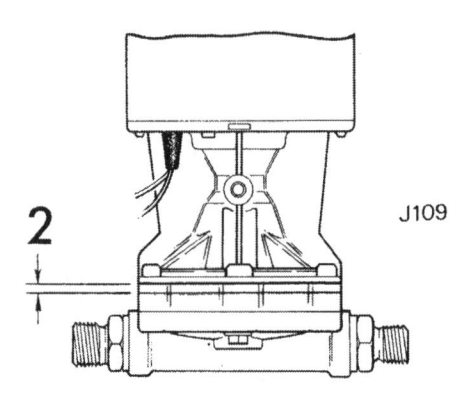

1 Normal top plate

2 Narrow top plate

Fig. 19. 'Narrow top plate' gear pump identification

Service

No regular maintenance is required.

If, after extensive service, the petrol pump becomes noisy, adjust armature end float.

Adjust armature end float

With petrol pump assembled hold unit vertical with adjuster uppermost. Slacken lock nut. Screw adjuster in until resistance is felt. Screw adjuster out quarter of a turn—maintain in this position and tighten lock nut.

Defective 'Petrol injection system'

Comprehensive 'Fault finding' for the complete system are detailed in Group 1.

To ensure that the petrol pump is running, switch on ignition, open luggage boot lid and check audibly. If this does not provide a positive result obtain access to the unit by removing two screws and turning back trim panel. Check petrol pump is running by touch. If petrol pump operation is suspect check the following:

Electrical supply of 12 volts on positive wire.

Wire snap connections adjacent to petrol pump are connected positive to positive and earth to earth. If connections are not correct motor will run in reverse direction.

Connect ammeter into supply circuit. Switch on ignition. Ammeter reading should be approximately 4 amps. If the ammeter reading is not approximately 4 amps. the indication is that the petrol pump requires overhaul or replacement.

NOTE: No reading indicates a defective brush assembly or open circuit armature winding.

High reading indicates a tight pump, stalled motor or short circuit armature winding.

Pump output and operation of pressure relief valve unit may be checked employing a pressure gauge with 'T' piece as detailed in Group 1.

ELECTRICAL

1 Armature end float adjuster
2 Cover
3 Commutator
4 Brushplate assembly
5 Base casting
6 Bearing
7 Aligning marks
8 Rubber 'O' ring
9 Top plate
10 Rubber 'O' ring
11 Gear pump
12 Outlet connection
13 Inlet connection
14 Strainer
15 Drive coupling
16 Shaft seal
17 'Tell tail' pipe
18 Thrust washer
19 Circlip
20 Armature
21 Permanent magnet
22 Bearing
23 Through bolt

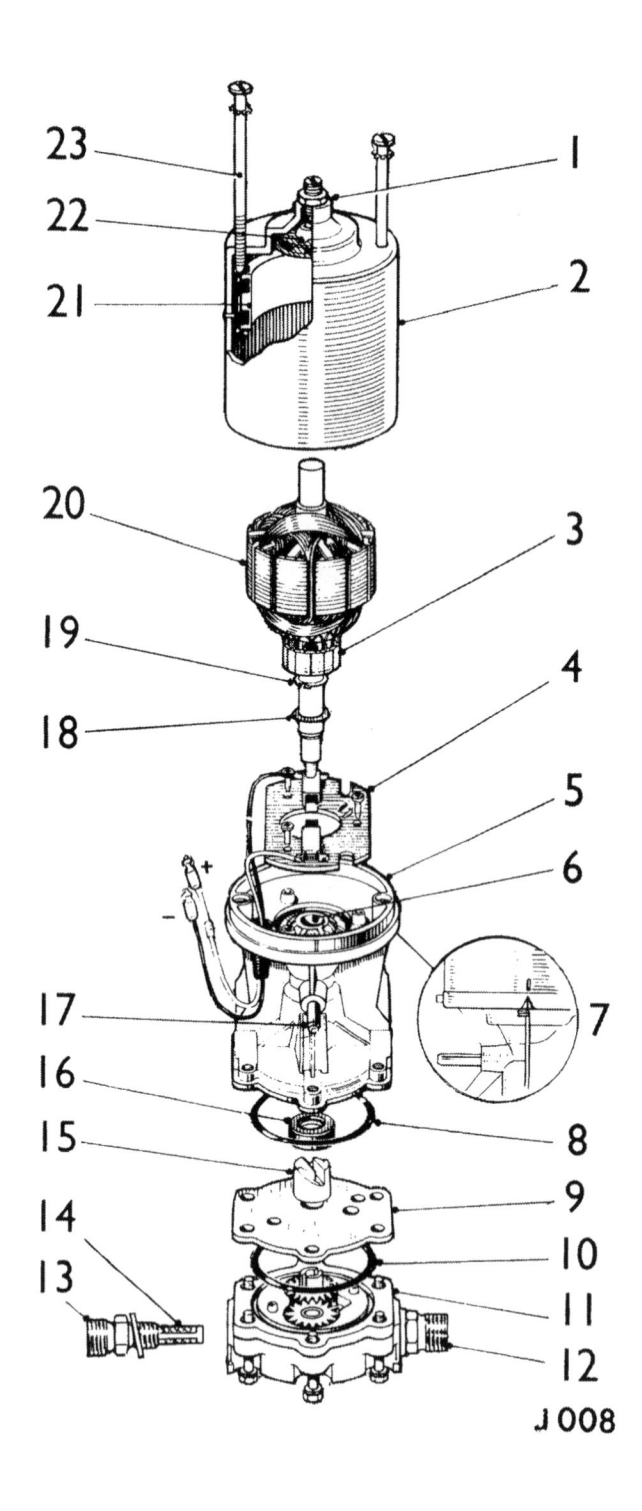

Fig. 20. Petrol pump details

ELECTRICAL 6·125

Disassemble petrol pump

1. Remove inlet connection and outlet connection. Withdraw strainer from inlet connection.

2. Slacken six bolts equally and remove gear pump assembly.

3. Remove drive coupling.

4. Remove through bolts.

5. Carefully withdraw cover and armature about 0·5 in. Brushes will drop clear of commutator. Push each brush back to clear circlip and thrust washer. Complete withdrawal of cover and armature.

   CAUTION: TO PREVENT DAMAGE TO THE BRUSH ASSEMBLY OR THRUST WASHER, SPECIAL CARE SHOULD BE TAKEN TO OBSERVE THIS INSTRUCTION.

6. Remove thrust washer.

7. Pull armature from cover against action of permanent magnet.

8. If necessary remove circlip.

9. Remove brush assembly. Release wires by carefully manoeuvring rubber grommet upwards through hole.

10. If necessary, force shaft seal from base casting.

    CAUTION: DO NOT PERFORM THIS REMOVAL UNLESS A NEW SHAFT SEAL IS AVAILABLE.

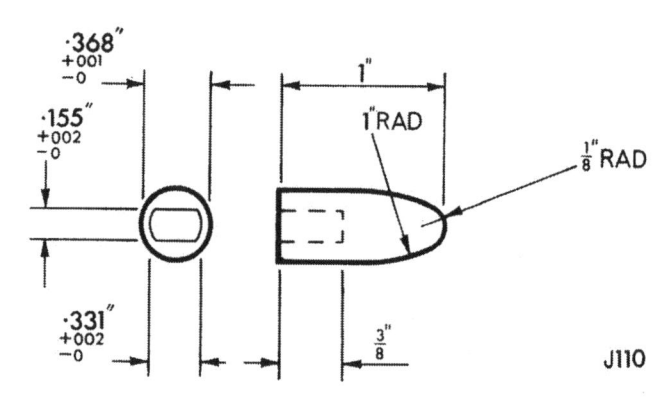

Fig. 21. Protective bullet

Assemble petrol pump

1. Fit brush assembly.

2. If necessary fit circlip.

3. Position armature to cover against action of permanent magnet.

4. Fit thrust washer.

5. If shaft seal is in situ only —

   Provide protective bullet as detailed on Fig. 21.

   Position protective bullet over shaft key. Lightly grease bullet. Carefully insert armature shaft through base casting. Align bullet to shaft seal. Push each brush back to clear thrust washer, circlip and commutator.

6. If shaft seal is not fitted only —

   Carefully insert armature shaft through base casting. Push each brush back to clear thrust washer, circlip and commutator.

7. Seat cover against base casting flange. Turn cover to align marks shown on Fig. 20. Fit through bolts.

   CAUTION: IF MARKS ARE NOT ALIGNED MOTOR WILL RUN IN REVERSE DIRECTION.

8. If shaft seal is not fitted only—

   Provide protective bullet as detailed on Fig. 21.

   Position protective bullet over shaft key. Lightly grease bullet. Carefully insert shaft seal into base casting.

9. Position drive coupling to motor.

10. Renew all disturbed rubber 'O' rings. Fit gear pump assembly. Tighten six bolts equally.

    CAUTION: EFFECTIVE SEALS CANNOT BE ASSURED IF NEW RUBBER 'O' RINGS ARE NOT FITTED TO DISTURBED JOINTS.

11. Insert strainer through inlet connection. Fit inlet connection and outlet connection.

12. Adjust armature end float as detailed above.

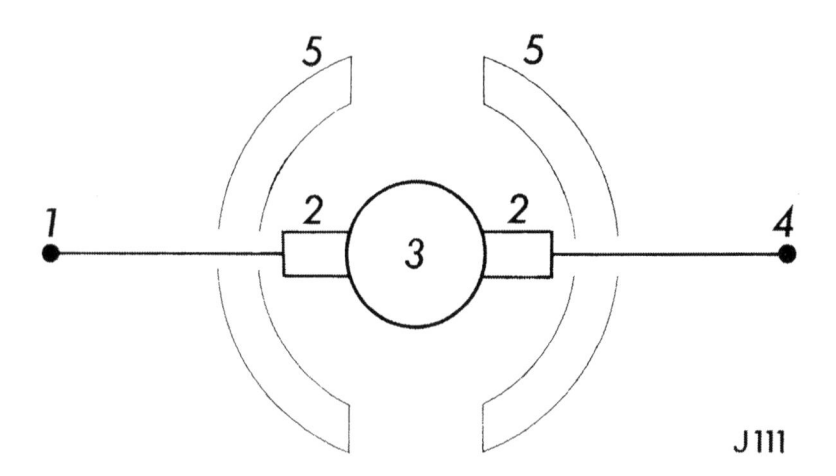

1 Supply connection
2 Brushes
3 Commutator
4 Earth connection
5 Permanent magnets

Fig. 22. Component wiring diagram

Strainer

Remove inlet connection. Withdraw strainer from connection. Inspect and wash in clean petrol.

Gear pump

If necessary an indication of the gear pump condition may be obtained by performing a flow test. With a motor terminal voltage of 13·5 volts approximately one gallon should be delivered in 3¾ minutes at 100 p.s.i.

Examine the interior of the gear pump. If there are indications of wear or damage replace the gear pump assembly.

Do not replace gears or housing individually. The components are mated and replacement must be by a complete gear pump assembly only.

Commutator

Clean commutator with petrol-moistened cloth. If the unit is in good condition it will be smooth and free from pits or burned spots. If necessary polish with fine glass paper. If excessively worn replace armature.

Brushes

Clean brushes with petrol-moistened cloth. Ensure that the brushes move freely in the brushplate.

Check brush length—renew brushplate assembly if less than 3/16 in.

Using a suitable push type spring scale, check brush spring pressure. Pressure should be 5 to 7 ozs. when compressed to 0·158 in. (4 mm.). If pressure is low renew brushplate assembly.

Shaft seal

Failure of the shaft seal would be indicated by fuel leakage from the 'tell tail' pipe projecting from the base casting.

If necessary an indication of the seal condition may be obtained by performing a bubble test. Connect a short pipe to the inlet connection and a short pipe to the outlet connection. Position the petrol pump above an open tank of paraffin. Immerse the free end of each pipe in the paraffin. Run petrol pump. A continuous flow of bubbles from the outlet pipe indicates a defective seal.

If seal failure is suspected petrol may have contaminated the motor. The unit should therefore be disassembled as detailed above and all components inspected before a new shaft seal is fitted.

Bearings

The two self-aligning motor bearings are not replaceable.

ELECTRICAL 6·127

STARTER MOTOR

Data

Manufacturer	Lucas
Type	M418G
Lucas part No.	25626
Stanpart No.	214914

Motor

Yoke diameter	4·187 to 4·218 in.
Light running current at 5,500 to 8,000 r.p.m.	80 amp.
Torque at 1,000 r.p.m. with 280 amp. at 9·0 volts	7 lb. ft.
Lock torque with 465 amp. at 7·0 volts	15 lb. ft.
Skim commutator—minimum skimming diameter	1 17/32 in.
Brush length—renew if less than	5/16 in.
Brush spring tension	36 ozs.

Solenoid

Pull in winding resistance—measured between unmarked 'WR wire' connector and 'STA' terminal with motor lead disconnected	0·13 to 0·15 ohm.
Hold in winding resistance—measured between unmarked 'WR wire' connector and unit body	0·63 to 0·73 ohm.

Description

The pre-engage starter motor consists of a solenoid unit, engaging lever, starter drive and motor unit.

The solenoid unit is mounted 'pick-a-back' fashion on the yoke. It contains a heavy pull in winding, a light hold in winding, a plunger and a contact assembly. Applying battery voltage to the unmarked 'WR wire' connector energises both windings. The combined action of the two windings pulls in the plunger to cause initially, engagement of the pinion and, secondly, contact of the solenoid battery terminal with the 'STA' terminal. The pull in winding is shorted out by the contact of the terminals, leaving the hold in winding to maintain the plunger position.

Movement of the plunger actuates the engaging lever. Pressure is applied to the drive operating plate and the starter drive is pushed along the shaft.

The starter drive consists basically of two sections. The drive operating plate and distance piece mounted on the internally splined drive sleeve rotate with the armature. The pinion and pinion bearing may—subject to roller clutch action—rotate about the shaft.

After the pinion is engaged with the engine flywheel ring gear contact of the terminals occurs. The motor is energised and the engine is cranked.

Fig. 23. Starter motor

ELECTRICAL

When the engine has started the roller clutch action prevents the armature being driven by the engine at high speed. Termination of battery voltage to the unmarked 'WR wire' connector allows the plunger to move out under the action of the contact assembly spring and the return spring. As the combined action of these two springs is stronger than the lost motion spring—and a certain amount of 'lost motion' is designed into the linkage—the contact of the terminals is broken and the motor current terminated before the pinion retracts.

Tooth-to-tooth abutment — if pinion engagement is stopped by direct abutment of the pinion teeth with the engine flywheel ring gear teeth, the engaging springs are compressed. This allows the plunger movement to continue to cause contact of the terminals. The abutment is cleared by rotation of the armature. The pinion is moved into full engagement by the action of the engaging springs and the push screw action of the shaft/drive sleeve helix.

Service

The only maintenance required is to ensure that the terminals and connectors remain clean and dry.

Disassemble starter motor

1. Remove starter motor from vehicle.
2. Disconnect motor lead from 'STA' terminal.
3. Remove two nuts and withdraw solenoid leaving plunger attached to engaging lever.
4. Remove return spring.
5. Remove plunger from engaging lever.
6. Slacken locknut. Unscrew and withdraw eccentric pin.
7. Remove cover band.
8. Withdraw brushes from holders.
9. Remove through bolts.
10. Carefully tap fixing bracket mounting lugs to separate yoke from fixing bracket.
11. Separate commutator end bracket from yoke.
12. Remove steel thrust washer and fabric thrust washer.
13. Remove rubber moulding.
14. Withdraw armature and starter drive assembly. Remove engaging lever.
15. Remove thrust washer.

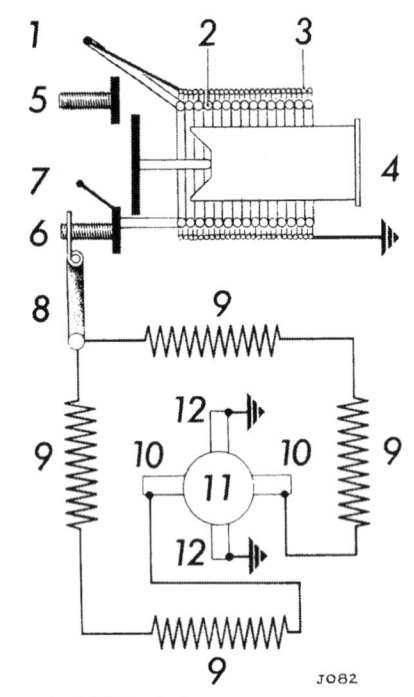

1 Unmarked 'WR wire' connector
2 Pull in winding
3 Hold in winding
4 Plunger
5 Solenoid battery terminal
6 'STA' terminal
7 'IGN' connector
   Not used on Triumph - TR5. This connector is only used on a vehicle fitted with a 'ballast ignition system'. Full system voltage is available at the connector when the solenoid is energised.
8 Motor lead
9 Field windings
10 Field winding brushes
11 Commutator
12 Earth brushes

Fig. 24. Terminals and connectors
and
Fig. 25. Component wiring diagram

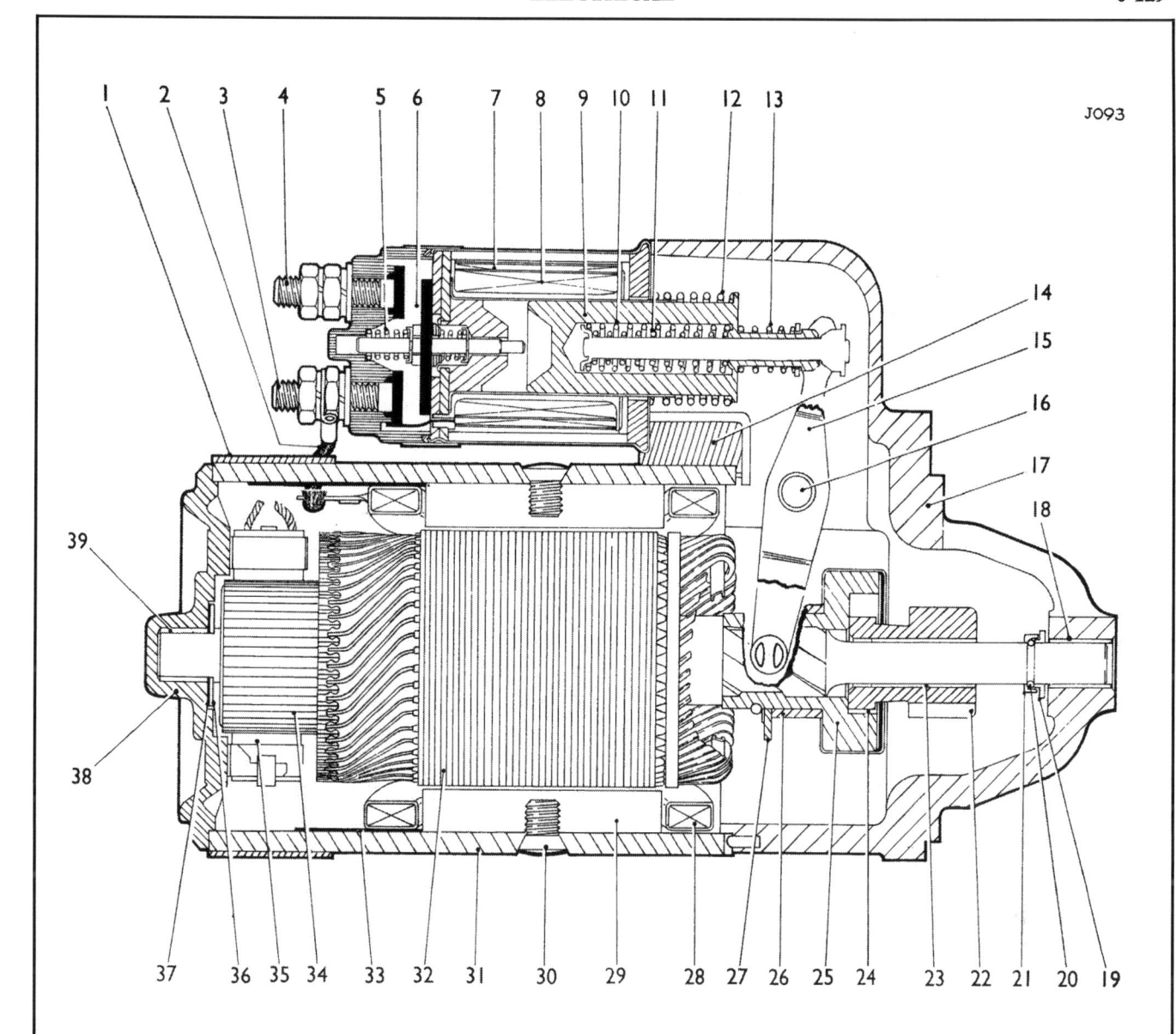

ELECTRICAL 6·129

1	Cover band	15	Engaging lever	28	Field winding
2	Motor lead	16	Eccentric pin	29	Pole shoe
3	'STA' terminal	17	Fixing bracket	30	Pole shoe screw
4	Solenoid battery terminal	18	Fixing bracket bearing bush	31	Yoke
5	Contact assembly spring	19	Thrust washer	32	Armature
6	Contact assembly	20	Jump ring	33	Insulation strip
7	Hold in winding	21	Thrust collar	34	Commutator
8	Pull in winding		Starter drive—	35	Brush
9	Plunger	22	Pinion	36	Steel thrust washer
10	Outer engaging spring	23	Pinion bearing	37	Fabric thrust washer
11	Inner engaging spring	24	Roller clutch action	38	Commutator end bracket
12	Return spring	25	Drive sleeve	39	Commutator end bracket bearing bush
13	Lost motion spring	26	Distance piece		
14	Rubber moulding	27	Drive operating plate		

Fig. 26. Starter motor — section view

Assemble starter motor

1. Fit thrust washer to shaft with lip facing starter drive as shown on Fig. 26.
2. Position engaging lever to drive operating plate.

    NOTE: Engaging lever may be fitted either way round.

    Lightly lubricate fixing bracket bearing bush with engine oil. Insert armature and starter drive assembly with engaging lever into fixing bracket.

3. Position rubber moulding.
4. Position yoke to fixing bracket.
5. Fit steel thrust washer and fabric thrust washer to shaft as shown on Fig. 26.
6. Lightly lubricate commutator end bracket bearing bush with engine oil. Ensure no brushes are inserted in holders. Position commutator end bracket.
7. Fit through bolts. Tighten bolts equally and torque load to 8·0 lb. ft.
8. Insert brushes into holders.
9. Fit cover band.
10. Lightly grease eccentric pin bearing surface. Insert eccentric pin. Ensure to align through engaging lever. Screw in to maintain position only.
11. Position plunger to engaging lever.
12. Position return spring to solenoid inner tube.
13. Insert solenoid so 'STA' terminal is positioned adjacent to yoke. Fit two nuts and torque load to 4·5 lb. ft.
14. Adjust pinion movement as detailed below.
15. Connect motor lead to 'STA' terminal. Torque load nut to only 2·2 lb. ft.

Remove starter drive

1. Provide tube with internal diameter of $\frac{5}{8}$ in.

    Place tube over shaft end and force thrust collar from jump ring towards starter drive.

2. Prise jump ring from shaft groove.
3. Remove thrust collar.
4. Remove starter drive.

Install starter drive

1. Lubricate drive sleeve splines and pinion bearing with 'Shell Retinax A' grease or equivalent. Fit starter drive.

2. Fit thrust collar to shaft with open side facing shaft end as shown on Fig. 26.
3. Prise jump ring into shaft groove.
4. Force thrust collar over jump ring.

Remove bearing bushes

1. Disassemble starter motor as detailed above.
2. Fixing bracket bearing bush only —

    Remove bearing bush. This operation can be performed by pressing out using suitable bar.

3. Commutator end bracket bearing bush only —

    Remove bearing bush. This operation can be performed using suitable extractor or by screwing a $\frac{5}{8}$ in. tap squarely into bush and withdrawing.

Install bearing bushes

1. Prepare porous bronze bearing bushes by immersing in thin engine oil for 24 hours.

    If required this period may be reduced by immersing in thin engine oil heated to 100 degrees centigrade for two hours. Allow oil to cool before removing bushes.

2. Fixing bracket bearing bush only —

    Using highly polished shouldered mandrel of 0.4729 ± 0.0005 in. diameter and suitable press fit bush.

    Do not ream bush after fitting or porosity may be impaired.

3. Commutator end bracket bearing bush only —

    Using highly polished shouldered mandrel of 0.5000 ± 0.0005 in. diameter and suitable press fit bush.

    Do not ream bush after fitting or porosity may be impaired.

Remove field winding brushes

1. Disassemble starter motor as detailed above.
2. Unsolder flexibles from field windings.

Install field winding brushes

NOTE: New brushes are pre-formed. Bedding of brushes to commutator is not required.

1. Position ends of new flexibles. Squeeze up and solder.

ELECTRICAL

Remove earth brushes

1. Disassemble starter motor as detailed above.
2. Unsolder flexibles from clips on commutator end bracket.

Install earth brushes

NOTE: New brushes are pre-formed. Bedding of brushes to commutator is not required.

1. Open clips and position ends of new flexibles. Squeeze up and solder.

Remove field windings

1. Disassemble starter motor as detailed above.
2. Mark pole shoes and yoke so original positions are known.
3. Using suitable wheel operated screwdriver, remove four pole shoe screws.
4. Remove insulation strip.
5. Withdraw assembly from yoke.
6. Remove pole shoes from field windings.

Install field windings

1. Observe relationship of field windings to yoke determined by motor lead grommet recess on yoke. Fit pole shoes to field windings so original positions in yoke are maintained.
2. Insert assembly into yoke. Ensure that taping of field windings is not damaged. Fit four pole shoe screws finger tight.
3. Fit insulation strip.
4. Using suitable wheel operated screwdriver, tighten four pole shoe screws.

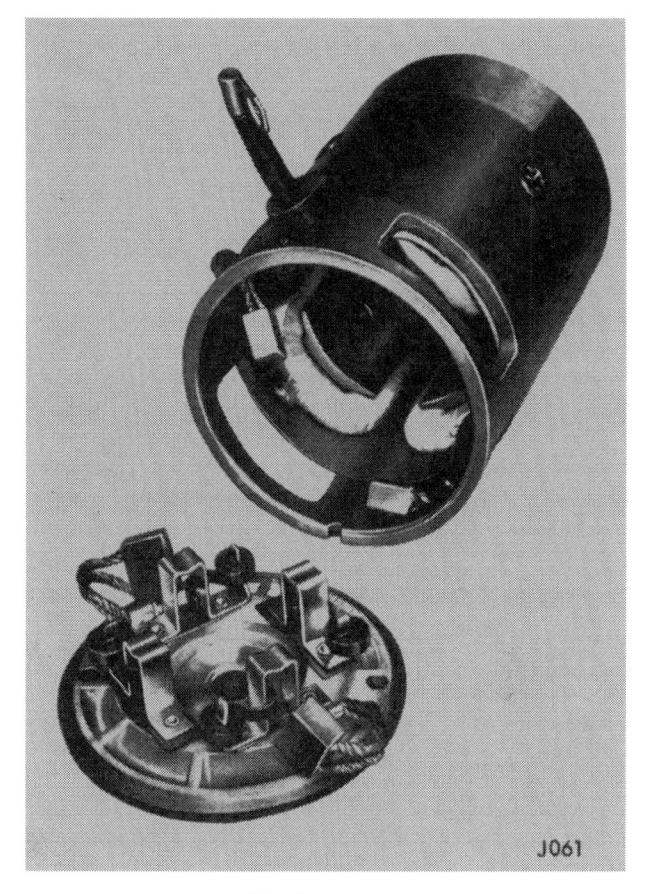

Fig. 27. Brushes

Adjust pinion movement

After assembly of the starter motor the pinion movement must be adjusted as follows:

1. Disconnect motor lead from 'STA' terminal
2. Provide six volt test circuit as shown on Fig. 29.
3. Slacken locknut. Screw eccentric pin fully in.
4. Note arc of adjustment is 180 degrees. After adjustment arrow on eccentric pin must be pointing towards arc indicated by two arrows on fixing bracket.
5. Energise both pull in winding and hold in winding to move starter drive to the engage position.
6. Position a feeler gauge between pinion and thrust collar as shown on Fig. 29. Press pinion lightly towards motor to take up any 'lost motion' in linkage. Rotate eccentric pin to adjust gap to 0·005 - 0·015 in. Tighten locknut.
7. Check correct gap has been maintained.

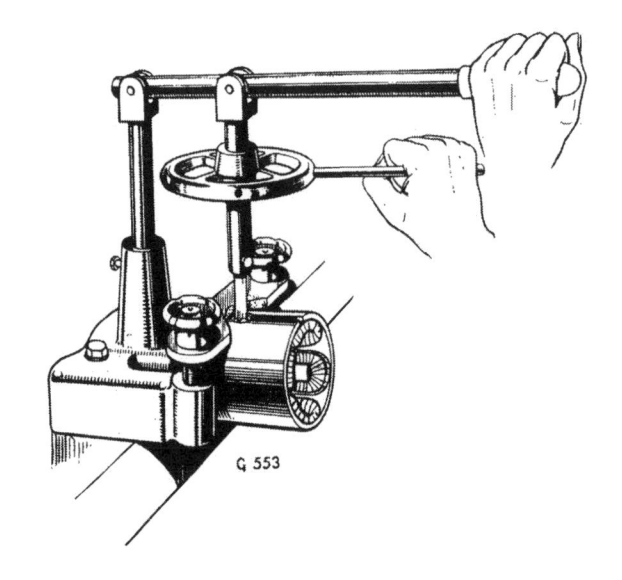

Fig. 28. Wheel operated screwdriver

ELECTRICAL

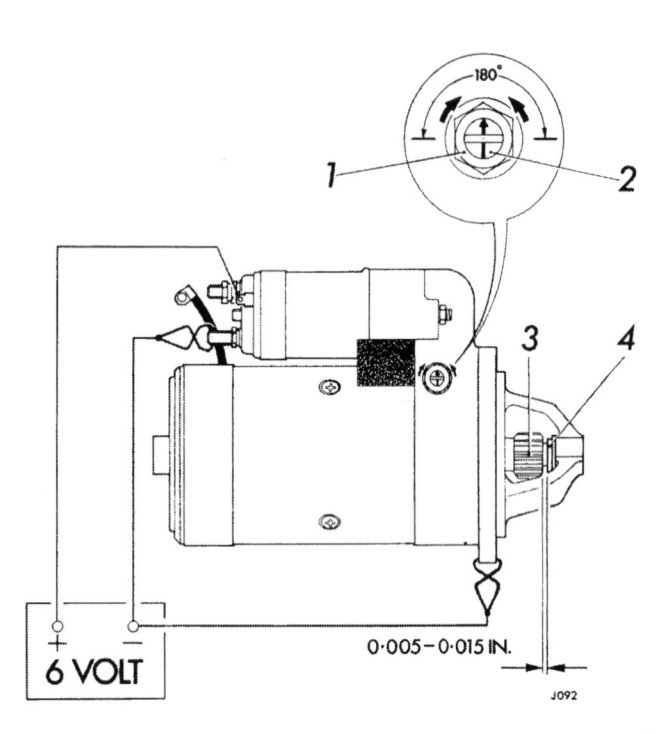

1 Locknut
2 Eccentric pin
3 Pinion
4 Thrust collar

Fig. 29. Adjust pinion movement

Light running current

1. Secure starter motor in suitable vice.

2. Provide suitable test circuit. Connect battery positive terminal via switch and ammeter to solenoid battery terminal. From solenoid battery terminal provide wire to unmarked 'WR wire' connector. Connect battery negative terminal to yoke. Switch and ammeter must be capable of carrying 600 amp. Use leads similar to those in vehicle starter motor circuit.

3. Provide tachometer to indicate starter motor speed.

4. Perform test. Ammeter reading should be 80 amp. with speed 5,500 to 8,000 r.p.m.

5. During test check brushes and commutator for excessive sparking or brush movement.

Lock torque

1. Secure starter motor in suitable vice.

2. Provide suitable test circuit. Connect battery positive terminal via switch and ammeter to solenoid battery terminal. From solenoid battery terminal provide wire to unmarked 'WR wire' connector. Connect battery negative terminal to yoke. Switch and ammeter must be capable of carrying 600 amp. Use leads similar to those in vehicle starter motor circuit.

3. Provide voltmeter across battery terminals.

4. Provide suitable equipment to measure lock torque. See Fig. 30.

5. Perform test. Lock torque should be 15 lb. ft. with ammeter reading of 465 amp. and voltmeter reading of 7·0 volts.

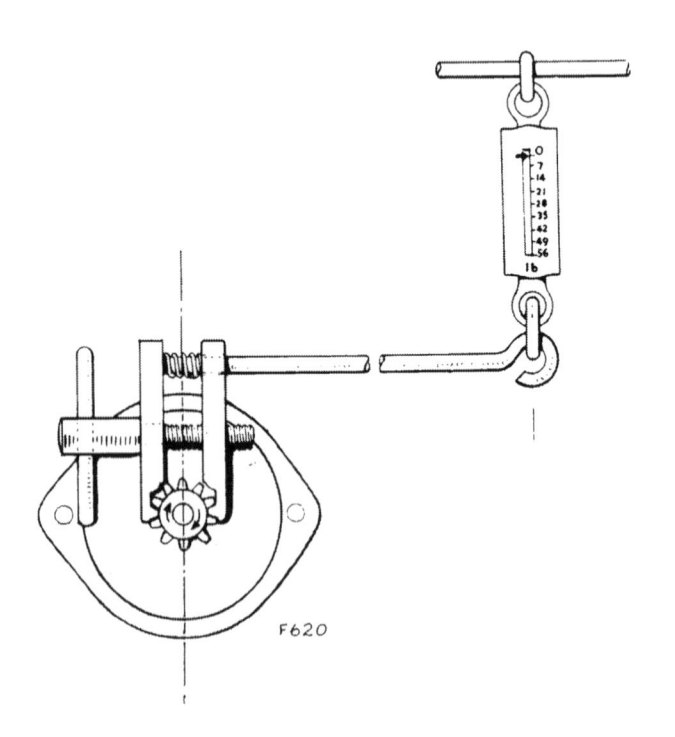

Fig. 30. Measuring lock torque

ELECTRICAL

Solenoid

It is not advisable to attempt to service the solenoid contact assembly. If the solenoid operation is suspect repair by unit replacement.

It is possible to disassemble the contact assembly. However, as assembly involves soldering and sealing complications, this procedure should not normally be required.

To disassemble contact assembly remove adhesive tape wrapped around body. Remove all nuts from 'STA' terminal. Remove two screws. Apply hot soldering iron to unmarked 'WR wire' connector. When solder has melted to release winding wires carefully withdraw contact assembly.

Brushes

Clean brushes and holders with petrol-moistened cloth. Ensure that the brushes move freely in the holders. If necessary lightly polish holder sides with a fine file.

Check brush length—renew if less than $\frac{5}{16}$ in.

Using a suitable spring scale check brush spring tension as shown on Fig. 31. Tension should be 36 ozs. If tension is low renew brush springs.

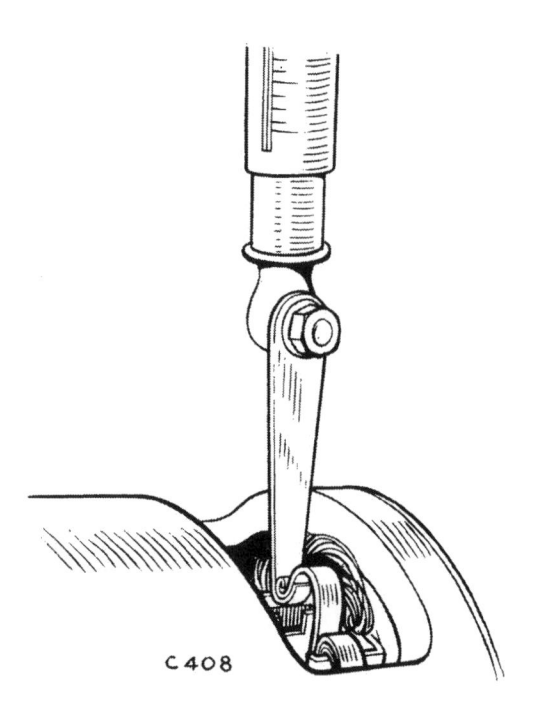

Fig. 31. Checking brush spring tension

Armature

Inspect for lifted armature conductors from commutator risers. This defect may result if the armature is over-revved by defective roller clutch action. Refer to Roller clutch below.

Ensure the shaft is not bent. Score marks on the laminations may indicate a bent shaft, worn bearing bushes or a loose pole shoe on the yoke.

Do not attempt to rectify a defective armature. Repair is by replacement.

Commutator

Clean commutator with petrol-moistened cloth. If the unit is in good condition it will be smooth and free from pits or burned spots. If necessary polish with fine glass paper. If excessively worn skim commutator.

Skim commutator

1. Remove starter drive as detailed above.

2. Mount armature in lathe.

3. Rotate at high speed. Using a very sharp tool take a light cut. Do not remove more metal than necessary. Do not cut below minimum skimming diameter, $1\frac{17}{32}$ in.

4. Polish with fine glass paper.

   CAUTION: THE INSULATORS BETWEEN THE SEGMENTS MUST NOT BE UNDERCUT.

Starter drive

Clean starter drive by wiping carefully with petrol-moistened cloth.

CAUTION: DO NOT WASH STARTER DRIVE IN PETROL OR PARAFFIN. SUCH ACTION WOULD REMOVE LUBRICANT FROM SEALED ROLLER CLUTCH.

Roller clutch

The roller clutch is sealed by a rolled-over steel outer cover. Do not attempt to service the unit. If the roller clutch action is suspect repair by unit replacement.

IGNITION DISTRIBUTOR

Data

Manufacturer	Lucas
Type	22D6
Lucas part No.	41219
Stanpart No.	214459
Contact gap	0·014 to 0·016 in.
Rotation—viewed on rotor	Anticlockwise
Firing angles	60 ± 1 degrees
Dwell angle	35 ± 3 degrees
Open angle	25 ± 3 degrees
Moving contact spring tension	18 to 24 ozs.
Capacitor capacity	0·20 mfd.
Engine firing order	1 - 5 - 3 - 6 - 2 - 4

Centrifugal advance — early units only

Check at decelerating speeds

Distributor r.p.m.	Degrees distributor advance Minimum	Degrees distributor advance Maximum	Crankshaft r.p.m.	Degrees crankshaft advance Minimum	Degrees crankshaft advance Maximum
Below 250	No advance to occur		Below 500	No advance to occur	
400	0	2	800	0	4
850	2	4	1700	4	8
1300	4	6	2600	8	12
2000	4	6	4000	8	12

Centrifugal advance — later units with suffix B added to Lucas part No.

Check at decelerating speeds

Distributor r.p.m.	Degrees distributor advance Minimum	Degrees distributor advance Maximum	Crankshaft r.p.m.	Degrees crankshaft advance Minimum	Degrees crankshaft advance Maximum
Below 175	No advance to occur		Below 350	No advance to occur	
450	0	2·0	900	0	4
800	2·5	4·5	1600	5	9
1300	6·0	8·0	2600	12	16
2000	6·0	8·0	4000	12	16

ELECTRICAL

6·135

Description

The distributor shaft rotates at half crankshaft speed driven from the engine camshaft via a drive gear.

The shaft and action plate rotate in two bearing bushes contained in the body.

The centrifugal timing control advances the spark under increasing engine speed. This is achieved by two weights extending outwards about the cam spindle weight pillars. The resulting cam action about the action plate cam surfaces causes the cam spindle to rotate slightly anticlockwise relative to the shaft.

When the contacts close a circuit is completed via the low tension wire, moving contact, fixed contact, moving plate and moving plate earth lead to earth. When the contacts open the low tension circuit is broken causing a collapse of the magnetic field in the ignition coil.

The moving contact, fixed contact and capacitor are located on the moving plate. This assembly can be rotated through a limited angle by the micrometer adjustment control. Ignition timing can be adjusted by rotating the micrometer adjustment nut which positions the moving plate assembly relative to the body.

The capacitor is connected between the moving contact spring and moving plate—that is parallel with the contacts—and functions to produce the desirable quick collapse of the magnetic field in the ignition coil. Capacitor action also prevents arcing across the contacts.

High tension surges initiated in the ignition coil are distributed in the correct sequence to the sparking plugs by the high tension carbon brush, rotor, cover electrodes and high tension leads.

The high tension carbon brush is of composite construction. The centre portion is of resistive compound which gives a measure of radio interference suppression. The ends are of softer carbon.

A drive gear contained within the body provides a drive for the tachometer.

Fig. 32. Centrifugal timing control

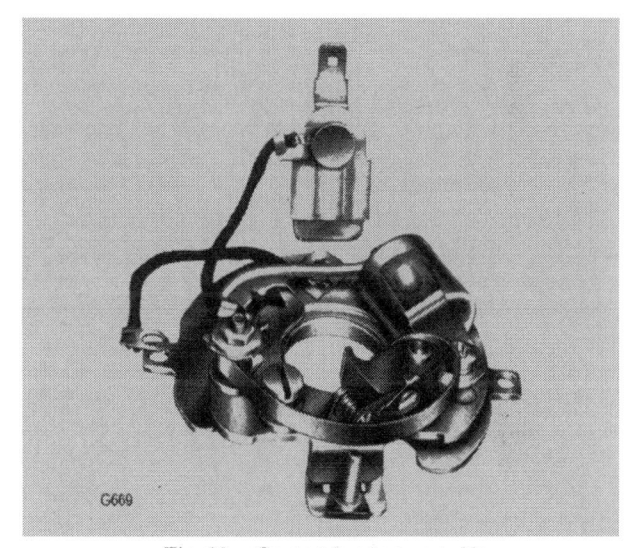

Fig. 33. Contact breaker assembly

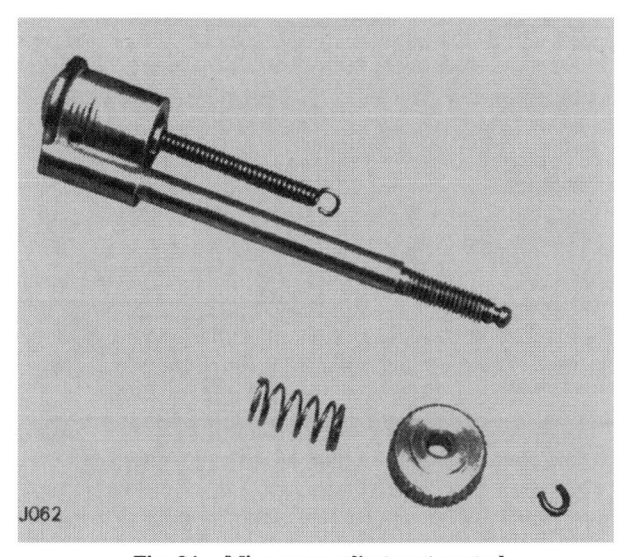

Fig. 34. Micrometer adjustment control

Fig. 35

Lubrication

Remove cover and rotor.

1. Few drops of engine oil to cavity to lubricate cam spindle bearing.
2. One drop of engine oil to lubricate moving contact pivot.
3. Few drops of engine oil through aperture at edge of contact breaker assembly to lubricate centrifugal timing control.
4. Lightly grease with Mobilgrease No. 2 or equivalent to lubricate cam.

Wipe away any surplus oil. Ensure contacts are oil free. Any oil on contacts may result in burning.

Contacts

The contact surfaces should be oil free. If the surfaces are burned or blackened clean as detailed below. If excessively worn or pitted renew contact set.

Clean contacts—use fine carborundum stone or emery cloth followed by a petrol-moistened cloth.

Contact gap—it is important that the correct gap be maintained. Contacts set too closely may tend to burn rapidly. Contacts set too wide may tend to cause a weak spark at high speed.

Adjust contact gap

1. Remove cover and rotor.
2. Rotate cam so moving contact is positioned on a cam peak.
   NOTE: When distributor is in situ rotate cam by turning crankshaft mounted cooling fan.
3. Slacken lock screw (5).
4. Position a 0·014 to 0·016 in. feeler gauge between contacts. Move fixed contact (6) about moving contact pivot (2) to adjust gap. Tighten lock screw.
   NOTE: This operation may be facilitated by inserting a screwdriver in slots (7) and twisting to move fixed contact.
5. Check 0·014 to 0·016 in. gap has been maintained.

Ignition timing control action

Centrifugal timing control action—this can be checked by removing cover and turning rotor anti-clockwise against control springs. Rotation through a small angle should be possible and rotor should return to its original position when released.

Ignition timing control operation

Centrifugal timing control operation—this can only be checked by employing an electronic engine tester or timing light.

Ignition timing

Refer to Group 1.

ELECTRICAL

6·137

Remove ignition distributor

NOTE: To facilitate re-timing do not slacken clamp bolt.

1. Remove cover.
2. Disconnect low tension connector from distributor.
3. Remove tachometer drive.
4. Remove side attachment bolt.
5. Withdraw distributor from pedestal. A sharp upward pull may be required.

Install ignition distributor

NOTE: To facilitate re-timing do not slacken clamp bolt.

1. Insert distributor into pedestal. Ensure driving dog tongue locates correctly in offset slot.
2. Fit side attachment bolt.
3. Fit tachometer drive by inserting cable and securing with knurled connector.
4. Check ignition timing as detailed in Group 1.
5. Connect low tension connector to distributor.
6. Fit cover.

Fig. 36. Remove/install ignition distributor

Remove contacts

1. Remove cover and rotor.
2. Remove nut, insulation piece, low tension wire eyelet and capacitor wire eyelet.
3. Withdraw moving contact.
4. Remove large insulation washer and small insulation washer.
5. Remove lock screw.
6. Withdraw fixed contact.

Install contacts

1. Ensure contacts are clean. If a new contact set is being fitted ensure preservative is removed from contact faces.
2. Position fixed contact.
3. Fit lock screw.
4. Fit large insulation washer and small insulation washer.
5. Position moving contact.
6. Fit capacitor wire eyelet, low tension wire eyelet, insulation piece and nut.
7. Adjust contact gap as detailed above.

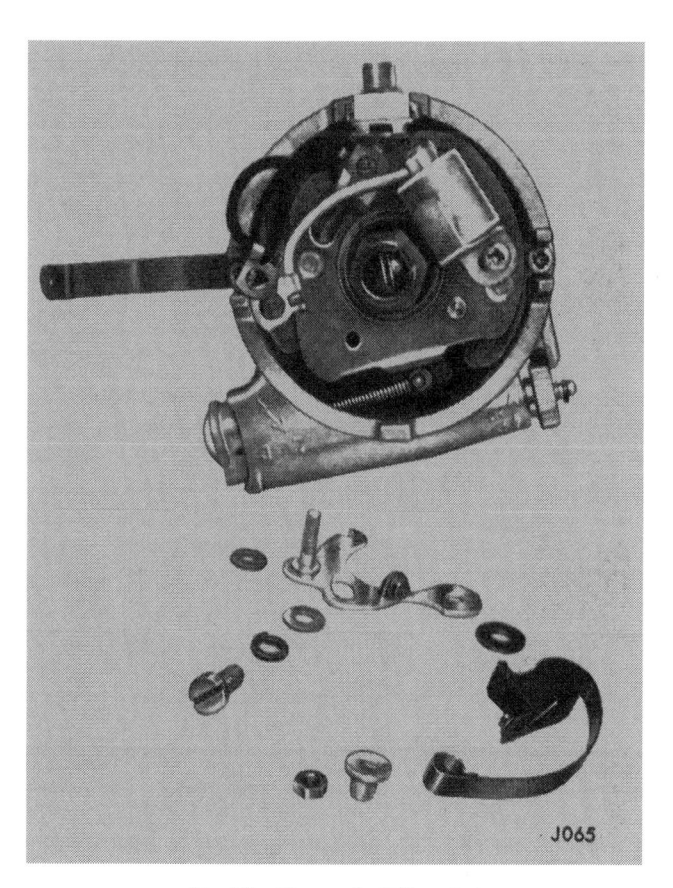

Fig. 37. Remove/install contacts

ELECTRICAL

1 Rotor
2 Terminal block
3 Capacitor
4 High tension carbon brush
5 Cover
6 Side screw
7 Cam spindle screw
8 Cam
9 Cam spindle
10 Control spring
11 Weight
12 Distance collar
13 Shaft and action plate
14 Body
15 Tachometer drive gear
16 Gasket
17 Cover
18 Circlip
19 Micrometer adjustment nut
20 Spring
21 Ratchet spring
22 Driving dog pin
23 Driving dog
24 Thrust washer
25 Rubber "O" ring
26 Link carrier
27 Moving plate
28 Moving plate earth lead
29 Fixed contact
30 Large insulation washer
31 Lock screw
32 Small insulation washer
33 Moving contact
34 Insulation piece
35 Nut

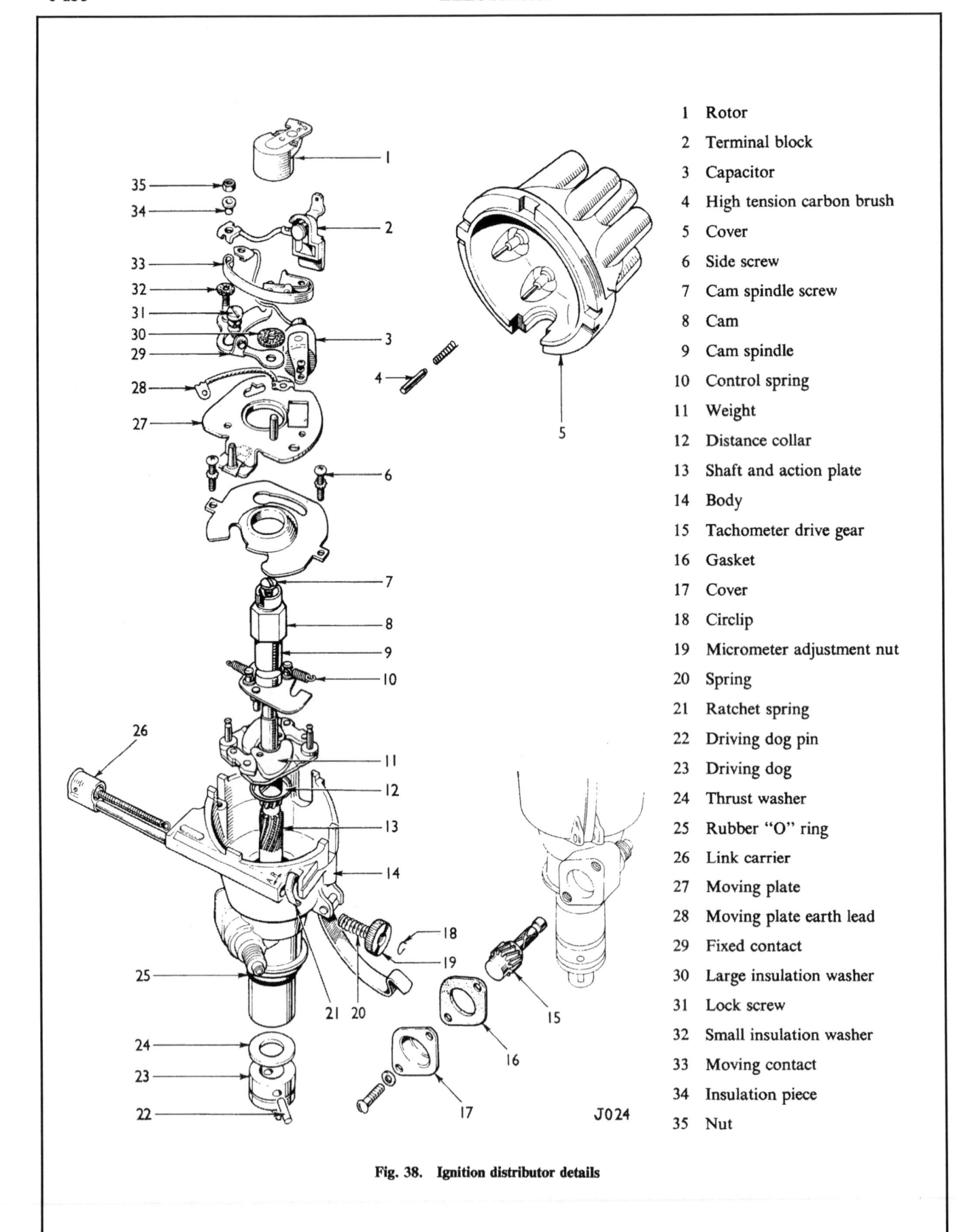

Fig. 38. Ignition distributor details

ELECTRICAL

Disassemble ignition distributor

1. Remove ignition distributor as detailed above.
2. Remove rotor.
3. Remove two side screws. Withdraw terminal block. Lift off micrometer adjustment control link. Withdraw contact breaker assembly.
4. Prise off circlip. Unscrew micrometer adjustment nut and remove spring. Withdraw link carrier. If required push off ratchet spring.
5. Remove cover, gasket and tachometer drive gear.
6. **CAUTION: ENSURE TACHOMETER DRIVE GEAR HAS BEEN REMOVED.**

   Tap out driving dog pin. Remove driving dog and thrust washer. Ensure shaft is burr free and withdraw. Remove distance collar.
7. Remove control springs exercising care not to distort springs.
8. Remove cam spindle screw. Withdraw cam spindle.
9. Remove weights.

Assemble ignition distributor

1. Lubricate action plate sliding surfaces and cam surfaces with engine oil. Position weights on action plate.
2. Lubricate cam spindle bearing and cam spindle weight pillars with engine oil. Fit cam spindle ensuring that it is the correct way round so that relationship of driving dog offset tongue to rotor will be as shown on Fig. 39. Fit cam spindle screw.
3. Fit control springs exercising care not to distort springs.
4. **CAUTION: ENSURE TACHOMETER DRIVE GEAR IS NOT FITTED.**

   Fit distance collar. Lubricate shaft with engine oil and insert into body. Fit thrust washer and driving dog. Secure with driving dog pin.
5. Lubricate tachometer drive gear with engine oil. Fit tachometer drive gear, gasket and cover.
6. If required push on ratchet spring. Insert link carrier. Fit spring and screw on micrometer adjustment nut. Prise on circlip.
7. Insert contact breaker assembly. Lift on micrometer adjustment control link. Insert terminal block. Fit two side screws—include moving plate earth lead tag in appropriate screw assembly.
8. Apply one drop of engine oil to moving contact pivot and lightly grease cam with Mobilgrease No. 2 or equivalent.
9. Fit rotor.
10. Install ignition distributor as detailed above.

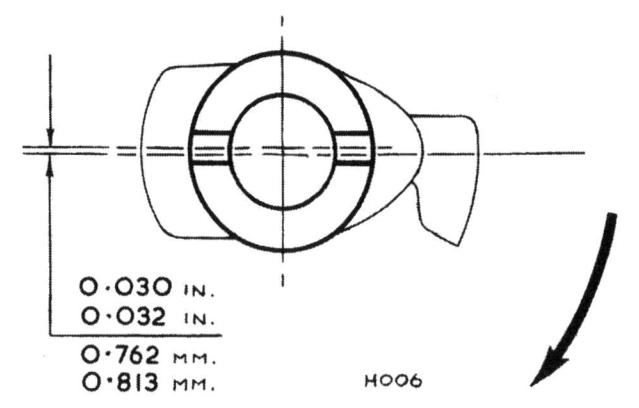

0·030 IN.
0·032 IN.
0·762 MM.
0·813 MM.

Fig. 39. Relationship of driving dog offset tongue to rotor—view on driving dog

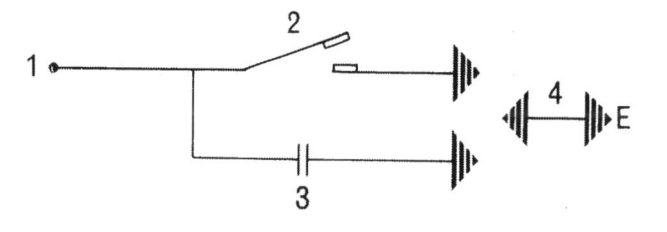

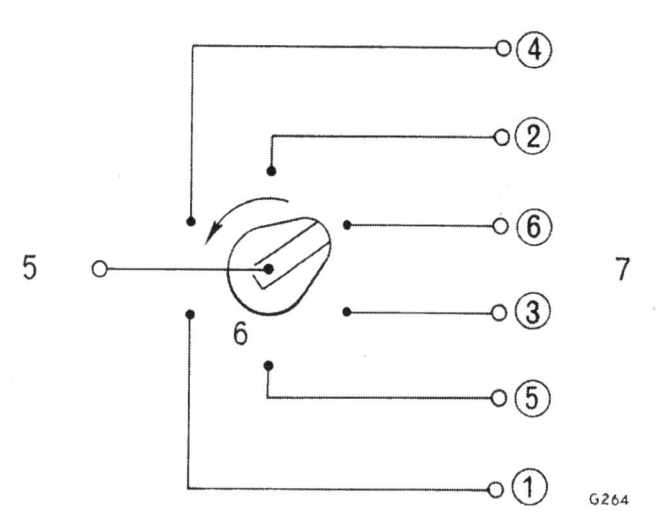

1 Low tension connector
2 Contacts
3 Capacitor
4 Moving plate earth lead
5 High tension input from ignition coil
6 High tension distribution
7 High tension output to sparking plugs

Fig. 40. Component wiring diagram

ELECTRICAL

BULB CHART

Lamp	Watts	Lucas Part No.	Stanpart No.	
Headlamps —				
L.H. Dip	60/45	54521872	512231	*
R.H. Dip — Normal	45/40	410	510218	
France	45/40	411	510219	
U.S.A.	50/40	54522231	—	*
Front flasher lamps — Normal (Not Switzerland)	21	382	502379	
Front parking and flasher lamps — Switzerland	6/21	380	502287	
Front parking lamps	6	989	59467	
Flasher repeater lamps	5	501	514797	
Rear marker lamps	5	501	514797	
Rear flasher lamps	21	382	502379	
Tail/stop lamps	6/21	380	502287	
Reverse lamps	21	382	502379	
Plate illumination lamps	6	207	511029	
Instrument illumination	2·2	987	59492	
Warning lights	2·2	987	59492	

* Sealed beam light unit

ELECTRICAL

6·141

TURN SIGNAL FLASHER UNIT

Data

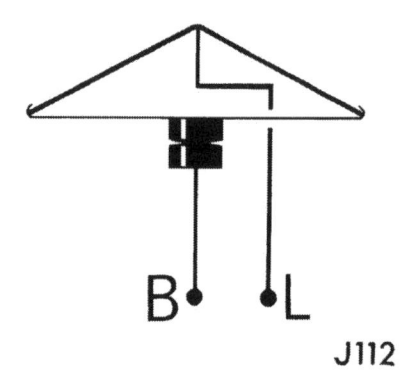

Manufacturer	Lucas
Type	8FL 4·1A
Lucas part No.	35049
Stanpart No.	148645
Nominal voltage	12 volts
Flashes per minute	60 to 120
Percentage on time—flasher lamps are on for this percentage of each flash cycle	30 to 75%
Total bulb load	49·2 watts
Rating	4·1 amp.

Description

The turn signal flasher unit consists of a moulded base carrying a snap action metal vane held in tension by a metal ribbon. A set of normally closed contacts are positioned on the base and ribbon. A pressed cover is gimped to the base.

Current supplied to terminal B flows immediately across the contacts, through the ribbon and vane to terminal L. From terminal L it flows to the selected lamps giving immediate indication of the driver's selection.

The current heats the ribbon causing expansion which finally allows the vane to relax and the contacts to open.

The current flow is terminated, the lamps extinguish and the ribbon cools and contracts. The vane is re-tensioned until the contacts close and a second cycle commences.

Service—No maintenance is required.

Remove turn signal flasher unit

Locate unit attached to clip secured to bulkhead end panel adjacent to passenger's feet. Pull turn signal flasher unit from clip. Disconnect electrical connectors.

Install turn signal flasher unit

Connect electrical connectors. Insert turn signal flasher unit into clip.

Repair—Repair of the unit is by replacement.

CAUTION: TO ENSURE THE CORRECT OPERATION OF THE FLASHER SYSTEM WITHIN LEGAL LIMITS, IT IS IMPORTANT THAT A NEW UNIT SHOULD BE OF THE CORRECT TYPE WITH A RATING OF 4·1A.

Fig. 41. Turn signal flasher unit installed

B Supply
L Output terminal to lamps

Fig. 42. Component wiring diagram

BRAKE LINE FAILURE INDICATION — LEFT HAND STEER ONLY

Data

Brake line failure switch —

Stanpart No. — early unit with single pin	148809
later unit with twin pins	149971
Pressure differential required to actuate switch	150 to 200 PSI
Plunger load — with plunger contact surface 0·522 in. below seat flange	5·1 to 6·6 lb.
Thread	⅜ in. 24 UNF 2A
Torque load — fitting switch to pressure differential warning actuator body	1·00 to 1·25 lb. ft.

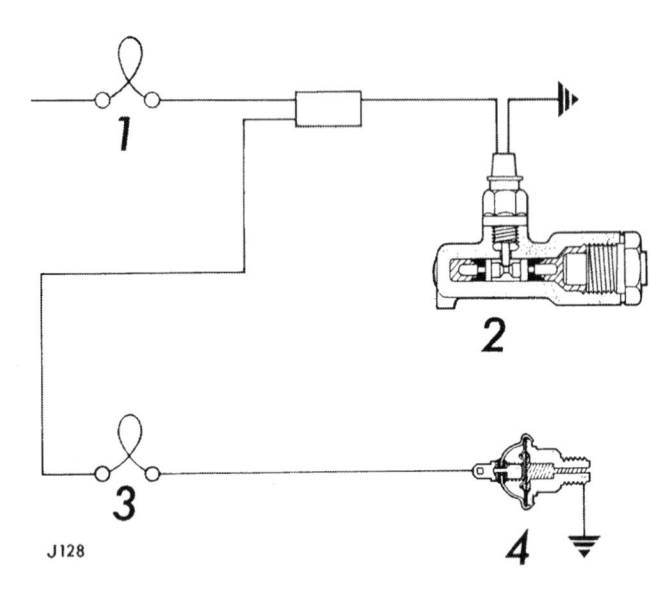

1 Brake line failure warning light
2 Brake line failure switch
3 Oil pressure warning light
4 Oil pressure switch

Fig. 43. System wiring diagram

Description

The system consists of a brake line failure warning light mounted on the facia panel and a brake line failure switch which is a component part of the pressure differential warning actuator detailed in Group 3.

The system circuit is amalgamated with the oil pressure indication circuit so that when the ignition circuits are energised both warning lights will illuminate faintly to indicate no bulb filament failure.

When the engine is started the oil pressure will raise causing the oil pressure switch to break the earth contact. Both warning lights will extinguish.

Should pressure loss occur in either front or rear brake lines the brake line failure switch will actuate as detailed in Group 3. The "BRAKE" warning light will illuminate brightly.

Should the oil pressure fall below the safe operating pressure while the engine is running the oil pressure switch will actuate. Both the "OIL" and the "BRAKE" warning lights will illuminate faintly.

Service—No maintenance is required.

Repair

Repair of both the warning light and the switch is by replacement.

Brake and oil warning light summary

Condition	"BRAKE" warning light	"OIL" warning light
Ignition on—Engine not running	ON FAINT	ON FAINT
Engine running	OFF	OFF
Engine running—Brake line pressure low	ON BRIGHT	OFF
Engine running—Oil pressure low	ON FAINT	ON FAINT

ELECTRICAL

HAZARD WARNING SYSTEM — LEFT HAND STEER ONLY

Data

Hazard flasher unit —

Manufacturer	Signal-stat (made in Brooklyn, New York, U.S.A.—available through Lucas dealers)
Type	180
Lucas part No.	54362147
Stanpart No.	148576
Nominal voltage	12 volts
Flashes per minute	60 to 120
Percentage on time — flasher lamps are on for this percentage of each flash cycle	30 to 75 %
Total bulb load	96·2 watts

Hazard relay —

Manufacturer	Lucas
Type	6RA
Lucas part No.	33231
Stanpart No.	148643
Winding connectors	W1 and W2
Contact connectors	C1, C2 and C4
Contacts	Double pole—normally open—with common moving contact C2 which makes simultaneously with C1 and C4
Contact pull in voltage	6 to 9 volts
Contact release voltage	2 volts minimum

Description

Operating the hazard switch on the facia panel isolates the turn signal flasher lamp circuit and applies battery voltage to the hazard flasher unit and hazard relay W1 connector.

The relay winding positioned across connectors W1 and W2 is energised to make the contacts C1, C2 and C4 common. A circuit now exists through the hazard flasher unit to both the left hand and right hand flasher lamps. A hazard warning light mounted on the facia panel flashes in unison with the lamps.

In the event of minor crash damage the system may safely be selected. If one or more lamps are inoperative the remaining lamps may continue to flash at the correct speed. If the circuit has become earthed the selection will 'blow' a fuse and the system will then be inoperative. Fire or a harness 'burn out' should not result from system selection.

Service—No maintenance is required.

Repair

Repair of the hazard switch, hazard flasher unit, hazard relay and hazard warning light are by replacement.

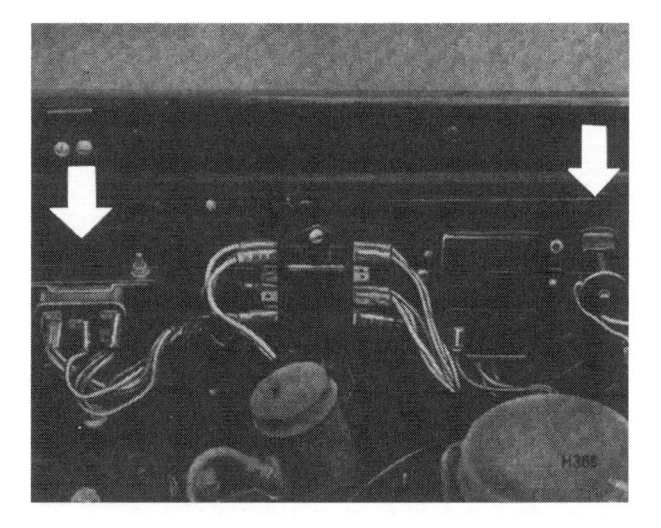

Fig. 44. Hazard flasher unit and hazard relay installed

ELECTRICAL

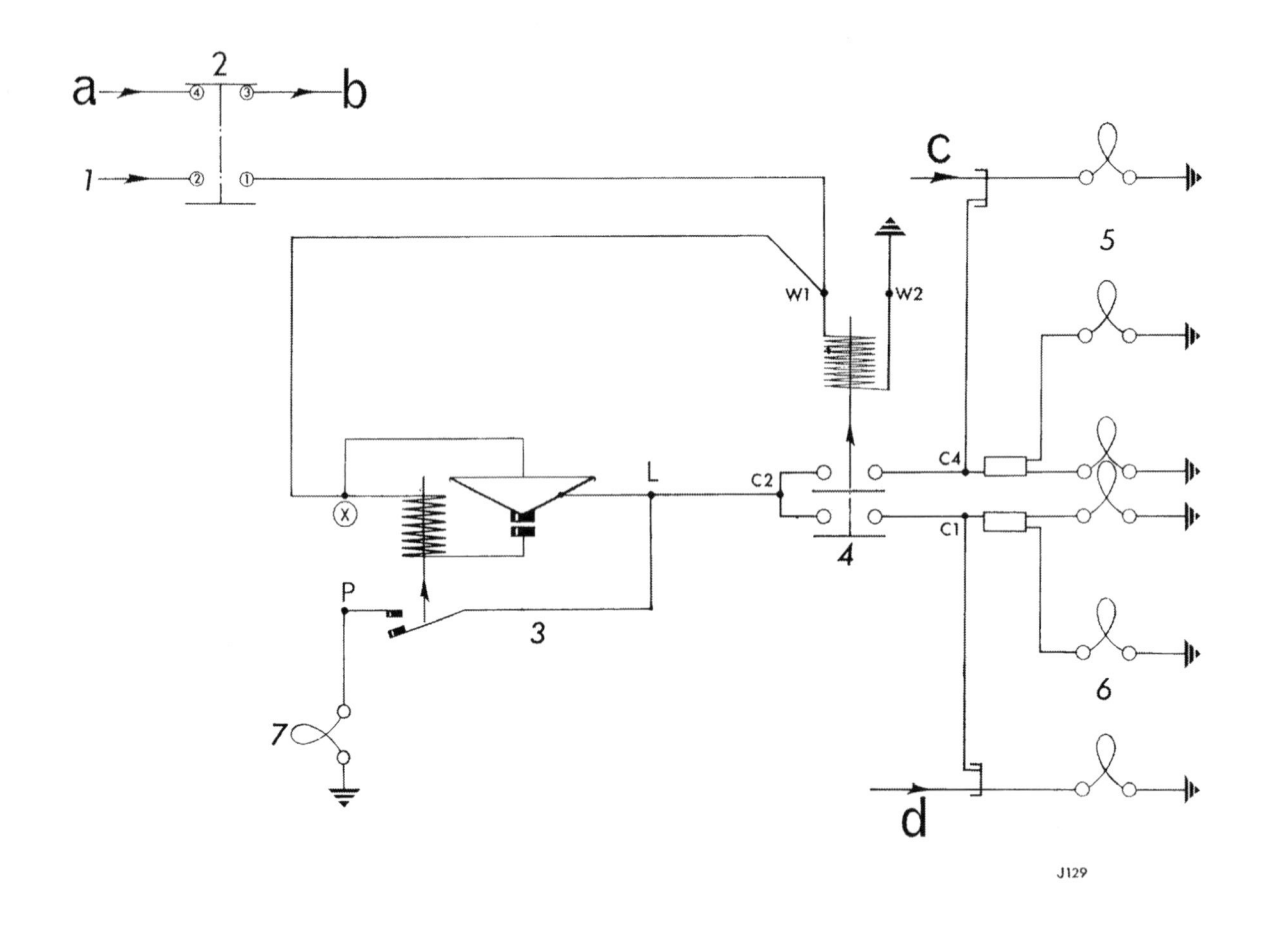

a From turn signal flasher unit
b To turn signal flasher switch

1 From fuse box
2 Hazard switch
3 Hazard flasher unit
4 Hazard relay
5 L.H. Flasher lamps
6 R.H. Flasher lamps
7 Hazard warning light

c From turn signal flasher switch
d From turn signal flasher switch

Fig. 45. System wiring diagram

WINDSCREEN WASHER PUMP

CAUTION: THE WINDSCREEN WASHER PUMP MOTOR IS POLARITY SENSITIVE. REFER TO 'CAUTION' ON PAGE 6.103.

OBSERVE POLARITY WHEN CONNECTING ELECTRICAL CONNECTORS TO THE UNIT OR PERFORMING ANY TESTING OF THE UNIT.

Data

Manufacturer	Lucas
Type	Screenjet 5SJ
Lucas part No.	54071460
Stanpart No.	211710
Maximum running current	2 amps.
Armature winding resistance—adjacent commutator segments	2·8 — 3·1 ohms.
Brush length—renew if less than	$\frac{1}{16}$ in.
Minimum delivery	3·5 cc. per second
Minimum delivery pressure	4·5 PSI
Container capacity	1·1 litres
Container usable capacity	1·0 litre
For use with nozzle orifice diameter	0·025—0·028 in. dia.

Description

The windscreen washer pump consists of a plastic fluid container fitted with a removable pump assembly. The two parts are retained together by a bayonet fitting.

The pump assembly consists of a small externally mounted permanent magnet field motor driving a submerged centrifugal pump. The drive is transmitted by a drive coupling and shaft.

Service

Replenish the fluid container to the base of the filler neck.

Use clean water and to obtain improved vision the use of 'Lucas crystal clear' or an equivalent additive is recommended.

Under freezing conditions ice and snow on the windscreen may be combated by replenishing the container with a mixture of one part methylated spirits to two parts water.

Do not allow sediment to accumulate in the container. When required clean the container and pump inlet gauze filter. Also maintain the associated nozzle orifices in a clean condition.

Fig. 46. Windscreen washer pump

Disassemble windscreen washer pump

1. Ensure that output tube and electrical connectors are disconnected.
2. Rotate cover anticlockwise to release bayonet fitting. Remove pump assembly from container.
3. Remove motor retaining screw. Remove motor unit.
4. Remove intermediate coupling.
5. Using long nosed pliers to secure shaft use a second pair of pliers to withdraw armature coupling.
6. Remove two screws. Remove bearing plate and rubber gasket.

NOTE: Hold clamping member in position during operations 7, 8 and 9.

7. Remove bearing washer.
8. Remove terminal screws, connector blades and nuts.
9. Using long nosed pliers carefully lift out brushes.
10. Lift out clamping member.
11. Remove armature and permanent magnet. Separate two components against action of permanent magnet.

Assemble windscreen washer pump

1. Lubricate motor casing bearing by filling recess with 'Rocol molypad molybdenised' grease. Wipe excess grease from boss.
2. Position permanent magnet with narrower pole adjacent to terminal position. Ensure poles locate correctly around circular spigot.

   CAUTION: IF NARROWER POLE IS NOT ADJACENT TO TERMINAL POSITION MOTOR WILL RUN IN REVERSE DIRECTION.

3. Position clamping member.

NOTE: Hold clamping member in position during operations 4, 5, 6 and 7.

4. Position armature to motor casing bearing against action of permanent magnet.
5. Using long nosed pliers carefully position brushes. Ensure that arm ends are inserted in slits provided in casing.

   CAUTION: TO ACHIEVE THE ABOVE CONDITION THE BRUSH POSITIONS MUST NOT BE INTERCHANGED.

6. Fit nuts, connector blades and terminal screws.
7. Fit bearing washer.
8. Position rubber gasket and bearing plate. Secure with two screws.
9. Push armature coupling fully onto shaft.
10. Position intermediate coupling to pump shaft.
11. Position motor unit. Secure with motor retaining screw.
12. Fit pump assembly to container.

Brushes

Clean brushes with petrol moistened cloth.

Check brush length — renew brushes if less than $\frac{1}{16}$ in.

Check brushes bear firmly against commutator. If pressure is low renew brushes.

Commutator

Clean commutator with petrol moistened cloth. If the unit is in good condition it will be smooth and free from pits or burned spots. If necessary polish with fine glass paper. If excessively worn replace armature.

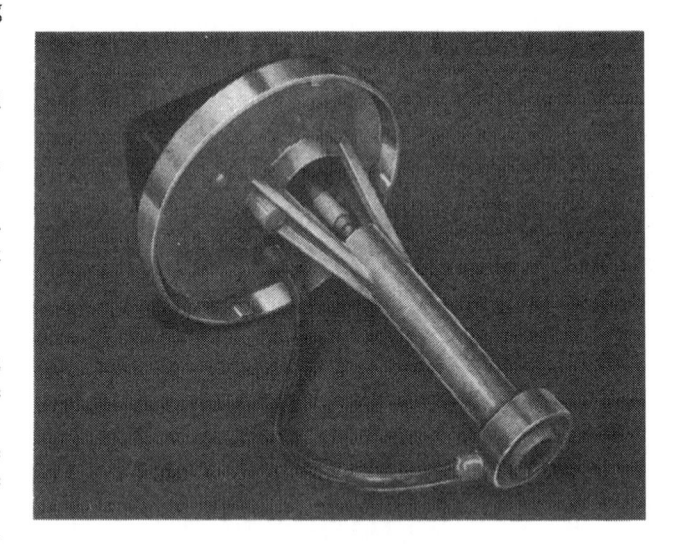

Fig. 47. Pump assembly

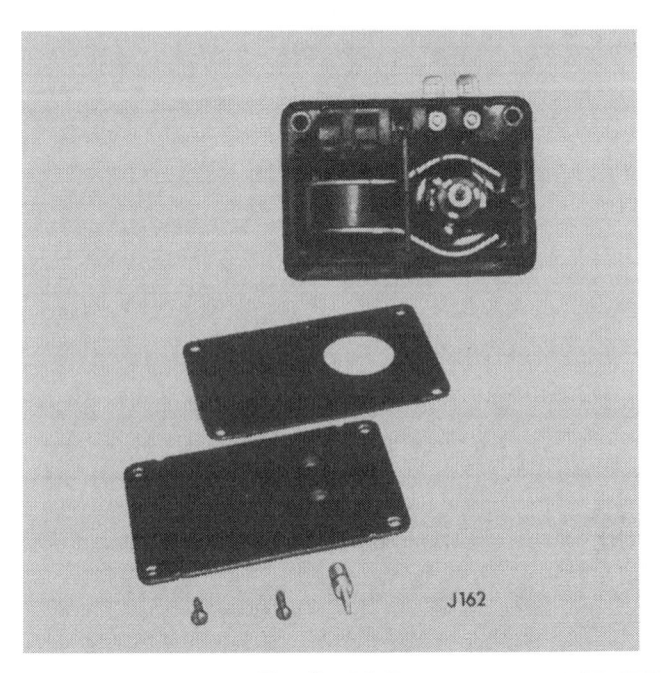

Fig. 48. Motor

TRIUMPH

OFFICIAL TECHNICAL BOOKS

Brooklands Technical Books has been formed to supply owners, restorers and professional repairers with official factory literature.

Workshop Manuals

Title	Ref	ISBN
TR2 & TR3	502602	9780948207693
TR4 & TR4A	510322	9780948207952
TR5, TR250 & TR6 (Glove Box Autobooks Man.)		9781855201835
TR5-PI Supplement	545053	9781869826024
TR250 Supplement	545047	9781783181759
TR6 inc. TC & PI	545277/E2	9781869826130
TR7	AKM3079B	9781855202726
TR7	Autobooks Manual	9781783181506
TR8	AKM3981A	9781783180615
Spitfire Mk 1, 2 & 3 & Herald 1200, 12/50, 13/60 & Vitesse 6	511243	9780946489992
Herald 948, 1200, 12/50, 13/60 Autobooks Man.		9781783181513
Spitfire Mk 4	545254H	9781869826758
Spitfire 1500	AKM4329	9781869826666
Spitfire Mk 3, 4, 1500 (Glove Box Autobooks Man.)		9781855201248
2000 & 2500	AKM3974	9781869826086
GT6 Mk 1, 2, 3 & Vitesse 2 Litre	512947	9780907073901
GT6 Mk 2, GT6+ & Mk 3 & Vitesse 2 Litre - Mk 2 1969-1973	Autobooks Manual	9781783181322
Stag	AKM3966	9781855200135
Stag	Autobooks Manual	9781783181490
Dolomite Sprint	AKM3629	9781855202825

Parts Catalogues

Title	Ref	ISBN
TR2 & TR3	501653	9780907073994
TR4	510978	9780907073949
TR4A	514837	9780907073956
TR250 US	516914	9781869826819
TR6 Sports Car 1969-1973	517785A	9780948207426
TR6 1974-1976	RTC9093A	9780907073932
TR7 (1975-1978)	RTC9814CA	9781855207943
TR7 1979+	RTC9828CC	9781870642231
TR7 & TR8	RTC9020B	9781870642651
Herald 13/60	517056	9781869826154
Vitesse 2 Litre Mk 2	517786	9781869826147
Stag	519579	9781870642996
GT6 Mk 1 and Mk 2 /GT6+	515754/2	9781783180448
GT6 Mk 3	520949/A	9780948207938
Spitfire Mk 3	516282	9781870642873
Spitfire Mk 4 & Spitfire 1500 1973-1974	RTC 9008A	9781869826659
Spitfire 1500 1975-1980	RTC9819CB	9781870642187
Dolomite Range 1976 on	RTC9822CB	9781855202764

Owners Handbooks

Title	Ref	ISBN
Triumph Competition Preparation Manual TR250, TR5 and TR6		9781783180011
TR4	510326	9780948207662
TR4A	512916	9780948207679
TR5 PI	545034/2	9781855208544
TR250 (US)	545033	9780948207273
TR6	545078/1	9780948207402
TR6-PI	545078/2	9781855201750
TR6 (US 73)	545111/73	9781855204348
TR6 (US 75)	545111/75	9780948207150
TR7	AKM4332	9781870642736
TR8 (US)	AKM4779	9781855202832
Stag	545105	9781855206830
Spitfire Mk 3	545017	9780948207181
Spitfire Mk 4	545220	9781870642439
Spitfire Mk 4 (US)	545189	9781855207967
Spitfire 1500	RTC9221	9781870642453
Spitfire Competition Preparation Manual		9781870642606
GT6	512944	9781855201583
GT6 Mk 2 & GT6+	545057	9781855201422
GT6 Mk 3	545186	9780946489848
GT6, GT6+ & 2000 Competition Preparation Manual		9781855200678
2000, 2500 TC and 2500S	AKM3617/2	9781855202788
Herald 1200 12/50	512893/6	9781855200616
Herald 13/60	545037	9781855201415
Vitesse 2 Litre	545006	9781855200746
Vitesse Mk 2	545070/2	9781855200418
Vitesse 6	511236/5	9781855207974

Carburetters

Title	ISBN
SU Carburetters Tuning Tips & Techniques	9781855202559
Solex Carburetters Tuning Tips & Techniques	9781855209770
Weber Carburettors Tuning Tips and Techniques	9781855207592

Truimph - Road Test Books

Title	ISBN
Triumph Herald 1959-1971	9781855200517
Triumph Vitesse 1962-1971	9781855200500
Triumph 2000 / 2.5 / 2500 1963-1977	9780946489237
Triumph GT6 Gold Portfolio 1966-1974	9781855202443
Triumph TR6 Road Test Portfolio	9781855209268
Triumph Spitfire Road Test Portfolio	9781855209534
Triumph Stag Road Test Portfolio	9781855208933

From Triumph specialists, Amazon or all good motoring bookshops.

Brooklands Books Ltd., P.O. Box 146, Cobham, Surrey, KT11 1LG, England, UK
Phone: +44 (0) 1932 865051   info@brooklands-books.com
www.brooklands-books.com

www.brooklandsbooks.com

Printed in Great Britain
by Amazon